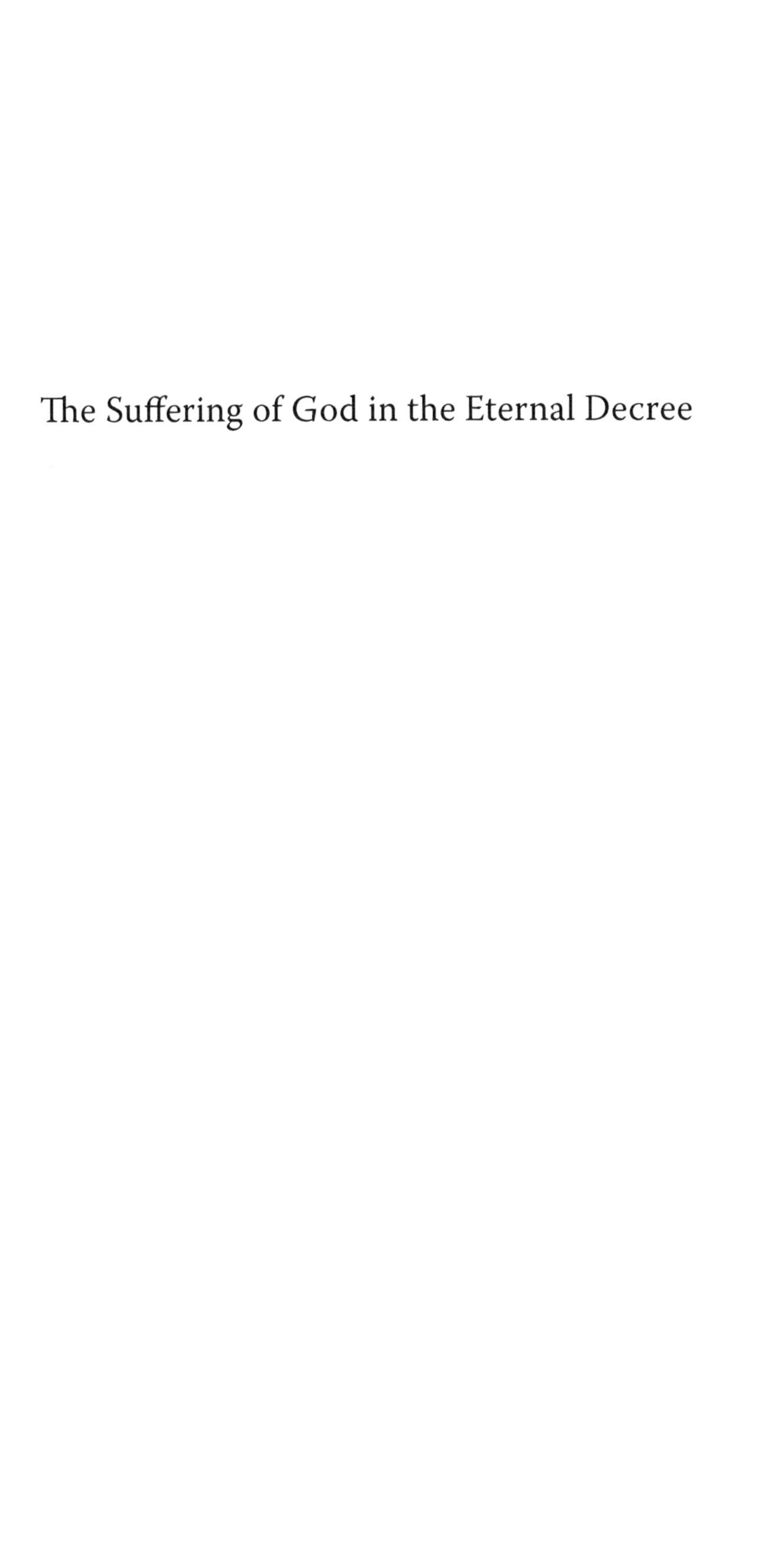

The Suffering of God in the Eternal Decree

The Suffering of God in the Eternal Decree

A Critical Study of Karl Barth on Election

Nixon de Vera

PICKWICK *Publications* • Eugene, Oregon

THE SUFFERING OF GOD IN THE ETERNAL DECREE
A Critical Study of Karl Barth on Election

Pickwick Publications
An Imprint of Wipf and Stock Publishers
199 W. 8th Ave., Suite 3
Eugene, OR 97401

www.wipfandstock.com

PAPERBACK ISBN: 978-1-7252-6415-1
HARDCOVER ISBN: 978-1-7252-6416-8
EBOOK ISBN: 978-1-7252-6417-5

Cataloguing-in-Publication data:

Names: de Vera, Nixon, author.

Title: The suffering of God in the eternal decree : a critical study of Karl Barth on election / by Nixon de Vera.

Description: Eugene, OR: Pickwick Publications, 2020 | Includes bibliographical references.

Identifiers: ISBN 978-1-7252-6415-1 (paperback) | ISBN 978-1-7252-6416-8 (hardcover) | ISBN 978-1-7252-6417-5 (ebook)

Subjects: LCSH: Barth, Karl, 1886–1968 | Election (Theology) | Election (Theology)—History of doctrines | Suffering of God | Suffering of God—History of doctrines

Classification: BT810.2 D484 2020 (print) | BT810.2 (ebook)

I dedicate this book to Methyl—my lifelong conversation partner.

Contents

Acknowledgments | ix

Introduction | 1

Chapter I: Election and Divine (Im)passibility in the Early Barth | 16
1. 1922 Lectures on John Calvin | 16
2. 1924 *The Göttingen Dogmatics* | 30
3. 1936 Pierre Maury's Lecture in Geneva | 40

Chapter II: Election and Divine (Im)passibility in Barth's Theology Between 1938 and 1942 | 60
1. Barth's Treatment of Impassibility | 61
2. Election and Divine Suffering | 76
3. God's Sovereignty in Sacrifice | 91

Chapter III: Election and Divine (Im)passibility in Barth's Theology Between 1951 and 1955 | 112
1. The Relation of God to Outside Events and Actions | 113
2. The Relation of God's Suffering to Jesus Christ's Condescension | 115
3. The Relation of Jesus Christ's Suffering to the God-self | 128

Chapter IV: Implications for the Doctrine of God Proper: Impassibility, Election, and Trinity | 169
1. The Faithfulness of the Suffering God | 170
2. God's Perfection in Suffering | 181
3. The Eternality of Divine Suffering | 206

Conclusion | 223

Bibliography | 231

Acknowledgments

Thanks to God who has given me wisdom without finding fault on my part. Thanks to my wife Methyl for her untiring support in all aspects through the intense years of my research and writing. Thanks to my daughters Zenji and Yuji for their extraordinary understanding to bear with my busy schedule. Thanks to my supervisors Revd Prof. Mark Lindsay and Revd Dr Jason Goroncy for their solid commitment to bring out the best in me as a scholar especially in Barth studies. Thanks to Revd Dr Christopher Holmes, Dr Scott Kirkland, and Prof. John McDowell for their critical encouragement by approving my candidature. Thanks to Revd Dr John Capper, Revd Dr Charles Sherlock, and Revd Dr Michael O'Neil for their rich input to make my points clearer. And, thanks to Revd Dr Robin Parry for his editorial talent in publishing this book; also to the production team at Wipf and Stock.

Introduction

Interest in the Topic

In February 2018, a Filipino woman, an overseas worker, was found dead inside a freezer in an apartment in the Middle East. The parents could hardly believe that her beaten body had been hidden there for over a year. I am lost for words whenever I contemplate that this tragic incident mirrors the suffering of countless household helpers worldwide from abusive employers. The horrific domestic and international violence makes the question of God's participation in suffering as vital as it was when Jürgen Moltmann first wrote *The Crucified God* wherein he argued that God's suffering in Jesus Christ is fundamental to our understanding of the image of God in us.[1]

The more I contemplate God's reflected image, the more I think about how God relates with us, and, how God interacts in this world.[2] God's relation and interaction have always been a source of fascination and serious inquiry because of the good and bad things that happen day by day. But I am convinced that God's will is for the welfare of humanity.[3] With attention to God's love, I have concentrated on what God has done for all in Jesus Christ—the Subject in God's ultimate manifestation of love. That is why I wanted to study in depth about God's will and whether such translates to having affinity with human suffering. So, I envisioned to write on this topic.

When I enrolled for a PhD at the University of Divinity in Melbourne, Australia, Revd Prof. Mark Lindsay (at the time, the University's Director of Research) introduced me to Karl Barth's doctrine of election—a worthy starting point for my research interest. In preparation for engaging with Barth's complex thought due to his dialectical theology, I had to consider first, and also substantially, John Calvin's teaching on predestination. It is

1. Moltmann, *The Crucified God*, 227.

2. de Vera, "The Crack in the Rock," 12.

3. Ps 138:8.

due to the fact that Barth developed his doctrine of election by conversing with Calvin.[4] Upon my exploration of Calvin and the Calvinist theology on predestination, I can say that although Calvin succeeds in helping us understand God's judicial character clearly, he fails in explicitly showing us Jesus Christ's unconditional commitment for humankind.[5] It seems that I have been back to where I began—being uncertain of whether or not God is a suffering God. Then I had acquainted myself with Barth's thought on this matter.

Karl Barth (1886–1968), author of the monumental thirteen-volume work *Church Dogmatics* (*CD*), is one of the giants of twentieth-century theology and arguably the most influential yet controversial theologian of his era. One of the main reasons for his prominence is his reconception of the notion of election.[6] Despite the vast array of attention on Barth's work, there has been little substantial work undertaken on his understanding of divine (im)passibility.[7] This project will investigate Barth's doctrine of election from the angle of impassibility in order to offer fresh perspective on this matter, and to defend an argument which furthers conversation. I will argue that God is *both* impassible *and* passible in Barth's mature doctrine of election.

Definition of Terms

In studying Barth, Thomas Weinandy's perspective on impassibility is helpful in understanding and categorizing how Barth conceives of divine suffering.[8] Here God is conceived in terms of: (1) external impassibility, or the immunity to be acted upon from without; (2) internal impassibility, or the inherent incapacity for changing the emotions from within; and (3) sensational impassibility, or the liability to feelings of pleasure and pain caused

4. My essay is entitled: "The Controversy of a Calvinist Theology on Election." Barth's dialectical theology here is defined as a middle ground to positive and negative expressions of a certain theological thought or doctrine. In this book, it is Barth's middle or balanced position in reaction to the doctrine of divine impassibility that will be critically explored.

5. McCormack, *Karl Barth's Critically Realistically Dialectical Theology*, 35.

6. McGrath, *The Christian Theology Reader*, 76. Gockel, "How to Read Karl Barth with Charity," 259.

7. Whenever the term (im)passibility is used, it refers to the impassibility *and* passibility of God.

8. This is because Weinandy converses with Barth on impassibility from a traditional Roman Catholic perspective—a source of inspiration for the Reformed treatment of impassibility. See Weinandy, *Does God Suffer?*

by the action of another being.[9] This work will focus on the first category because in *CD* II/1–2 and IV/1–2, Barth engages with the doctrine of divine impassibility on the ground that God is immune from external actions and events. A passible God, then, would mean that God "is capable of being acted upon from without."[10] The ideas conveyed by the words "capacity" and "capability" however are deficient in speaking of God in Barth's theology; thus the terms "decision" and "choice" in relation to being acted upon are the right fit for this enterprise.[11]

When the words "capacity" and "capability" are used to refer to God being affected, it denotes a potentiality in God to be affected by outside factors. These could be events and actions in time, or any element that is not from God.[12] In this sense, God is somewhat dependent *ad extra*, which, as I shall argue, is not the case in Barth's treatment of impassibility. Conversely, when passibility is seen as contingent upon *God's decision or choice*, then the idea of God merely allowing himself to be affected by outside factors becomes plausible, but, inconclusive. It is plausible insofar as God's self-election is concerned; whereas it is inconclusive insofar as other essentialities in God are yet to be explored. In other words, passibility becomes God's essential quality viewed against the notion of potentiality. As Barth puts it:

> But the personal God has a heart. He can feel, and be affected. *He is not impassible.* He cannot be moved from outside by an extraneous power. But this does not mean that He is not capable of moving Himself. No, God is moved and stirred, yet not like ourselves in powerlessness, but in His own free power.[13]

For Barth, passibility is affiliated with God's sole willing (God's "own free power"); while impassibility is associated with something inherent in God vis-à-vis aseity. God is sovereign over what is not God or against God. No outside events and actions in eternity can affect God simply because these have no potentiality to cause him to change.

But before we proceed too far, it is important to be cognizant of how Barth conceives of time in connection with God's being. For Barth, God's

9. Livingstone, *The Oxford Dictionary of the Christian Church*, 823.

10. Weinandy, *Does God Suffer?* 39.

11. Weinandy, *Does God Suffer?* 39. For an alternative position on divine decision and capability; cf. Yewangoe, *Theologia Crucis in Asia*, 147n195.

12. For clarity, this book uses the word "time" to refer to the created time and whenever God is considered in his being the word "eternity" is used.

13. Barth, *Church Dogmatics* II/1, 370; *Die Kirchliche Dogmatik* IV/1, 416. Italics mine. Hereafter, *Church Dogmatics* will be abbreviated *CD* and *KD* for *Die Kirchliche Dogmatik*.

being in time is key in understanding why God can be seen to have suffered in a sovereign manner. In Barth's framework of time, God is the source of time; hence time is non-existent without God.[14] In God's creation, time exists; and, more importantly, God chooses to reveal himself in time. God in time does not necessarily mean that he is contingent upon time because while being in it—God is said to be "supremely temporal." God is so by being in time but not subjugated by it.[15] It is in time however, as Barth sees it, where God limits himself.

Concerning divine history, it is inherent in Barth's theology that God's history includes, but is not confined to, human history. In other words, God's history is eternity, which embraces time. Whenever Barth refers to divine suffering, it is always within divine history (eternity). Hence that history can be referred to as a history of suffering. Also, divine history in connection with time is also taken to mean revelational history—a history determined by God to reveal himself in and as Jesus Christ. When God is revealed as Jesus Christ, God is said to have been affected. Prior to being incarnated, however, God is understood to be immutable, by virtue of his being transcendent. Impassibility then, as Barth approaches it, only proceeds from immutability. So, in this circumstance, it is impossible for God to be moved, unless by God's own initiative. This is Barth's perspective on what it means for God to be affected.

As Barth's impulse on election progresses, it also tends to express God's will to be vulnerable, i.e., to be acted upon externally.[16] God is seen as a fellowship-initiating-God who determines himself to be this God. The self-electing God is far from the Stoic view of God being "unreceptive of anything bad."[17] Barth's God is otherwise. Although, according to Barth, God is indeed self-sufficient, such sufficiency combined with God's aseity does not make him exclusive but rather inclusive.[18] God in this way decides of his own accord to include *humanness* (human essence) in God's very life.[19]

14. Read §47 of *CD* on "Man in His Time."

15. *CD* I/2, 50; III/2, 437.

16. For another perspective on God's vulnerability; cf. Moltmann, *The Crucified God*, 193.

17. Laertius, *Lives of Eminent Philosophers*, 7.147.

18. This formulation could have arisen from Barth's opposition to Nazified deity and religion. See Peterson, *The Early Karl Barth*, 3–5, 169–70. Hunsinger, *Karl Barth and Radical Politics*, 186.

19. In Barth's thinking, the humanness of a being contradicts God and self. *CD* II/2, 163–64.

God, according to Barth, has feelings because God wills it so.[20] With respect to divine will, feelings are always associated with what is outside of God; in particular, feelings toward humankind. It is not because divine emotions are reliant to creaturely existence, but rather God chooses to respond to what affects humanity. In fact, Barth posits that in the divine intimacy, God also adopts what befalls humans by becoming one of them. In so arguing, Barth is also cautious to note that divine feelings before and after the incarnation are fundamentally the same in intent, i.e., having humankind as the object.

Divine feelings toward the plight of humankind, says Barth, are appropriate for God rather than a liability. God moves out of compassion and empathy for what humans have to go through after "the fall." God's emotions are not emotions bound to human fate, but are simultaneously over and above conditions that govern creaturely beings. Divine feelings of mercy and sympathy are feelings of amity. When God feels for humans, he is in union with them. Such feelings imply positive outcome—humans will eventually be out of their predicament due to God's unity with them. Correspondingly, Barth formulates the divine suffering in this way: God suffers in eternity so that humans do not have to suffer eternally. The suffering of God however is not never-ending because God is determined to triumph over suffering itself.

Theoretical Framework

As pointed out by J. K. Mozley and Paul Tillich, the significance of the question on (im)passibility cannot be underestimated. In fact, it still resonates today.[21] It is due to the challenge posed by the previous revisit of the doctrine of God vis-à-vis the sovereignty of God over creaturely reality. As I mentioned earlier, what has been undertaken in Barth studies on the topic of impassibility remains quite inadequate. It is inadequate in a sense that the focus is either on the exegesis of biblical texts about the alleged suffering of God, or, on the topic of theodicy.

20. *CD* II/1, 370; II/2, 167.

21. Lee, *God Suffers for Us*, 1.

In fifty relevant materials written by forty scholars,[22] only Bruce McCormack discusses impassibility via substantial engagement with Barth.[23] Less than half of these studies are impassibilist in their theology. They assert (with nuances) that God is impassible because of God's self-continuity over creation. Their commitment to preserve the integrity of God's inner life, even in God's intervention in time and in the world makes them avoid any Patripassianist or Nestorian tendencies.[24] They also argue that despite Barth's actualization and historicization of God's suffering, Barth maintains a broadly traditional view of God (as advanced by the Church Fathers and medieval theologians), i.e., the suffering God remains unconstrained by creation.[25] This is due to the preconception of God being always non-contingent *ad extra*. The majority of scholars have a passibilist mindset.[26] They

22. E.g., Molnar, *Divine Freedom and the Doctrine of the Immanent Trinity*, 58–62; Kirkland, *Into the Far Country*, xxiii–xxiv; Hunsinger, *Reading Barth with Charity*, 122–41; Johnson, *God's Being in Reconciliation*, 99–102; Mozley, *The Impassibility of God*, 170–78; Webster, *The Domain of the Word*, 111–19; Harasta and Brock, *Evoking Lament*, 90–95; Marshall, "The Dereliction of Christ and the Impassibility of God," 246–98; Holmes, *Revisiting the Doctrine of the Divine Attributes*, 221–24; Klooster, *The Significance of Barth's Theology*, 24–30; Langdon, *God the Eternal Contemporary*, 60–62; Hart, "No Shadow of Turning: On Divine Impassibility," 184–206; Torrance, *The Christian Doctrine of God*, 88–98; McDowell, *Hope in Barth's Eschatology*, 5–20; Hoogsteen, "Vere Deus, Vere Homo," 79–91.

23. McCormack, "Divine Impassibility or Simply Divine Constancy?" 150–86. Most center their discussion on immutability in dialogue with the Church Fathers. McCormack's article appears to be the last published material that directly matches this book.

24. Patripassianism teaches that the Father himself suffers with the Son, whereas Nestorianism teaches that only the human Jesus suffers because divinity and humanity cannot be in union.

25. For instance, Paul Molnar argues that for Barth, "there remains a clear distinction between the Father and the Son and between the Father's suffering as a mystery grounded in the immanent Trinity and the creature's suffering which, while not part of God's nature, is experienced by God for the salvation of creatures." Molnar, *Divine Freedom and the Doctrine of the Immanent Trinity*, 414. In addition, Adam Johnson reasons that Barth's dialectic God speaks of Trinitarian appropriations in which the distinction between the Father and the Son is clear "such that only the Son is incarnate and suffers death and abandonment of the Father." Johnson, *God's Being in Reconciliation*, 82.

26. Nimmo, "The Compassion of Jesus Christ," 67–79; Jones, "The Riddle of Gethsemane," 124–54; Migliore, "The Journey of God's Son," 80–105; McCormack, "The Passion of God Himself," 155–72; Asbill, *The Freedom of God for Us*, 183–202; Moltmann, *The Crucified God*, 147–265; Jüngel, *God as the Mystery of the World*, 178–212; Lindsay, *Reading Auschwitz with Barth*, 141–69; Sumner, *Karl Barth and the Incarnation*, 130–220; Thompson, *Christ in Perspective*, 55–60; Mikkelsen, *Reconciled Humanity*, 198–221; Hector, "God's Triunity and Self-Determination," 246–61; Jenson, *God after God*, 66–156; Leftow, "God's Impassibility, Immutability, and Eternality," 173–86; Bauckham, "God's Self-Identification with the Godforsaken in the Gospel of Mark," 254–68; Kitamori, *Theology of the Pain of God*, 39–70; Fiddes, *The Creative Suffering*

advocate a passible God with their emphasis on theopaschism, but reject theopaschitism itself.[27] Paramount in their discussion is the significance of Jesus Christ in conceiving God in light of God's essential attributes. They also claim (with nuances) that in Barth, the suffering of the Son is the suffering of the Father also.[28] A third group of scholars argue for an (im)passibilist position, informed by Barth's conception of God's unity, freedom, love and openness.[29] They argue for an immutable suffering God with caution against Monarchianism and Monophysitism.[30] In other words, they appear to argue that God can be viewed to be impassible and passible.[31]

The striking difference in the above assertions is chiefly christological—the relation of Jesus Christ's divinity and humanity to God's eternal being. While all agree in upholding the unity-in-diversity between the two natures, the impassibilists insist that the being of Jesus Christ is eternally and rigidly consistent with God's ontology. In contrast, the passibilists stress that the incarnation of Christ speaks of the eternal God. Those in the middle, the (im)passibilists, employ both strategies at different times.

Such work is suggestive of a rekindling of interest in Barth's thought on divine suffering during the last decade.[32] But what is insufficiently achieved is to offer a fresh insight to the conflicting views mentioned. For example, to

---

of God, 54–72; Goetz, "The Suffering God, 385–89; Pannenberg, *Jesus—God and Man*, 196–202; Braaten, "A Trinitarian Theology of the Cross," 113–21; Lee, *God Suffers for Us*, 2–28.

27. Theopaschism teaches that God truly suffers, while theopaschitism teaches that since Jesus Christ has only one nature, the divine, his divine nature suffers.

28. For example, Paul Nimmo asserts that in Barth's thinking, God's association with humankind is said to have penetrated "every moment of the essence of God. Nimmo, "The Compassion of Jesus Christ," 79. Also Paul Daffyd Jones cites Barth in explaining that "He [Jesus Christ] commits to fulfilling 'voluntarily that which is resolved concerning Him' (IV/2, 259), and thereby supplies the temporal counterpoint to an eternal divine decision—for what is now rejected is not just an *impossible*-possibility for the divine life, but the impossible-*possibility* that has overtaken and corrupted human life. Jones, "The Riddle of Gethsemane," 148. For Barth, the Father's suffering is unique because such suffering is not in flesh, but *in union* with the Son. Read *CD* IV/1, 43–44.

29. They posit that God is both impassible and passible.

30. Monarchianism teaches that God, being one person, suffers whereas Monophysitism teaches that Jesus Christ is only divine, and what is divine cannot suffer.

31. See Komline, "Friendship and Being," 1–17; Graham, *Representation and Substitution in the Atonement Theologies of Dorothee Sölle, John Macquarrie, and Karl Barth*, 340–55; Pinnock, *Most Moved Mover*, 70–88; Shippey, "The Suffering of God in Karl Barth's Doctrines of Election and Reconciliation," 150–87; Loewe, "Two Theologians of the Cross," 510–39.

32. The most recent example is Daniel Migliore's edited book *Reading the Gospels with Barth* published in the latter part of 2017.

challenge McCormack's comment that Barth totally abandons any doctrine of impassibility in his late Christology.[33]

Background

Early in his academic career, Barth retained a Reformed orthodox view of impassibility. His 1924 lectures on various Reformed confessions betray no sign of deviation from his predecessors on this subject. Even in his lectures on the Heidelberg Catechism, delivered between 1940 and 1942, in which some development of thought can be seen, can be read as being consistent with general Reformed doctrine.[34] For example, he writes:

> In the recognition and confession of the mercy of God, what we are accustomed to take so seriously as the tragedy of human existence is dissolved. There is something far more serious and tragic, viz., the fact that our distress—the anguish of our sin and guilt—is freely accepted by God, and that in Him, and only in Him, it becomes real agony.[35]

It is God's will to act according to his mercy towards creatures. It emerges here that, for Barth, the suffering in Jesus Christ is ascribed to God's self. Such will and act is the foundation upon which Barth relates suffering with God.

But we will see in this study that immutability and impassibility are not dependent on one another, as in the Reformed orthodox sense.[36] Barth redefines impassibility in a way that it is closely related to God's constancy with his decree, rather than it being relegated to metaphysical injunctions. God's essential nature coincides with God's self-determination. Barth even posits that divine movability is within the divine plan. The fact that God is self-moved means that such movement then proves the consistency of God in himself, and, in God's will for humanity; not otherwise.

Barth is wary of any Nestorian tendencies, and of the subtle influences of Monophysitism and Monarchianism. For instance, the suggestion that Christ's divinity and humanity cannot be in union leads to the isolation of suffering to his humanity only; or the suggestion that since God can only be divine, so Jesus Christ being divine cannot be said to have truly suffered. These formulations presuppose a suffering-free God; a God who is understood in close proximity to the Trinity. For Barth, God can be said to have

33. McCormack, "Divine Impassibility or Simply Divine Constancy," 183.

34. Lindsay, *Reading Auschwitz with Barth*, 149–51.

35. *CD* II/1, 374.

36. *CD* II/1, 302–6; 493–95. Cf. Dolezal, *God without Parts: Divine*, 84–88.

truly suffered in Jesus Christ. The suffering of Jesus Christ can be articulated in a way that will not compromise the triunity.

Barth then navigates his way through the christological terrain without detriment to the essence of the Trinity. In reconfiguring the underlying significance of Jesus Christ to the being of God, Barth inevitably has to reconsider his previous vista of the triune life in relation to the decree.[37] The relevance of time in God's history of suffering becomes pivotal in formulating an ontological statement on the Trinity. We will see in this study that Barth has no intention to construe a triune God apart from the decree. The election of the suffering of God is a triune decision. Here Barth finds a way to safeguard the Godhead from any trinitarian misappropriation, i.e., the distinctiveness of the three Persons in suffering.[38]

It is true that a "passible" deity could be reduced to a mere ontic reality. Nonetheless, I will argue that this is not true in Barth's view. God's ontic reality *ad extra* does not undermine God's will and act for humanity.[39] Indeed, Calvin saw as much.[40] God is free to be in whatever state he desires, i.e., to be capable or incapable of suffering. This freedom is not self-centred, but rather, others-centered.

Jürgen Moltmann's reading of Barth shows a similar concept about divine selflessness because God is seen to have willed his freedom to be a suffering freedom in order to manifest God's boundless love for humanity.[41] This selfless God, according to Robert Jenson, suffers *in eternity*; an interpretation of Barth's treatment of the history of suffering.[42] Yet God's suffering in eternity, Mark Lindsay alludes, is conceivable in the Son's suffering especially at Calvary.[43] It is within this line of thinking that Bruce McCormack develops what he regards to be the inescapable logic of Barth's mature doctrine of election, i.e., Barth's Christology necessitates a total abandonment of any doctrine of divine impassibility.[44] Such a position however does not sit well with George Hunsinger's analysis of Barth's understanding of God.[45]

37. Refer to *CD* III/1, 15.

38. Gavrilyuk, *The Suffering of the Impassible God*, 173.

39. Keating and White, *Divine Impassibility and the Mystery of Human Suffering*, 11–12.

40. See Calvin, *Institutes of the Christian Religion*, 3.22.4

41. Moltmann, *Crucified God*, 129–30.

42. Jenson, *God after God*, 68–69.

43. Lindsay, *Reading Auschwitz*, 160–61.

44. McCormack. "Divine Impassibility or Simply Constancy," 184.

45. Hunsinger, *Reading Barth with Charity*, 167–68.

Significance of the Study

The issues inherent in this research intersect with some current and heated debates, among some Barth scholars.[46] More particularly, it illustrates the claim that although there are considerable agreements between them concerning Barth's rendition of divine suffering, "there is no shortage of disagreement" when it comes Barth's later accommodation or rejection of impassibility.[47]

Barth's reconception of divine suffering in the *Church Dogmatics* is crucial in investigating his engagement with impassibility, and also, for evaluating the extent and outcome of such engagement. If it is true that the Reformed orthodox notion of impassibility is sustained in Barth's reconception of election, then a more rigorous argument for this position must be provided. This is to address the concern of those who argue that Barth has deviated from the Reformed teaching of impassibility. However, if Barth's doctrine of election does not retain a traditional Reformed understanding of impassibility, then an intensive counter argument is also required. This is to address the concern of those who argue for Barth's consistency with the Reformed teaching of impassibility. But if Barth accounts God as both impassible and passible, then this position needs to be thoroughly supported to answer the objections of those who argue otherwise—a challenge I take in this project.[48]

Potential Contribution to Scholarship

Evidently, this work is unique because there are no in-depth studies on Barth's doctrine of election that singularly address the issue of impassibility. In this

46. McCormack and Hunsinger part ways in conceiving the Godhead's prior reality in relation to the decree: 1) For McCormack, the election constitutes the Trinity; in contrast, for Hunsinger the Trinity constitutes the election; 2) They differ also in their treatment of ontology. For McCormack, it is a system in understanding God's actions; whereas for Hunsinger, ontology is a distraction in understanding God's actuality; 3) They deviate over the issue of historicization of divine being in view of God's dynamic being-in-act. For McCormack, God's being is actualized in common history; but for Hunsinger, it is already established pre-temporally, hence it is only revealed temporally. On the one hand, McCormack's Barth can speak of God in a passibilist manner; on the other hand, Hunsinger's Barth can speak of God with an impassibilist tone. See McCormack, "Divine Impassibility," 154–82; Hunsinger, *Reading Barth*, 8–10, 116–33, 166–67.

47. Keating, *Divine Impassibility*, 26.

48. Although McCormack concludes in his article in 2009 that Barth is said to be "neither an impassibilist nor a passibilist," he however favors a passibilist Barth in considering the *Church Dogmatics*. "Divine Impassibility or Simply Divine Constancy," 186. Cf. "The Doctrine of the Trinity," 115–16; "The Passion of God Himself," 160–62.

study, I hope to (1) provide a critical account of divine suffering in strict conjunction with impassibility as expressed in Barth's developing and mature doctrine of election; and (2) critically converse with Barth on God's decision to suffer as "the One who loves in freedom."[49] I shall argue that in being so, God can be said to be simultaneously impassible and passible.

Facility in a Methodology Appropriate to the Project

In order to examine Barth's discussion of (im)passibility within his doctrine of election, I aim to: (1) examine the ontological considerations of impassibility as regards the decree; and (2) investigate Barth's actualization of the suffering of God in history. It is not my intention to cover the biblical, medieval, and contemporary formulations on the epistemology of Jesus Christ as it relates to the Trinity; or the ontic emphasis of the divine nature based on classical metaphysics; or the ethical repercussions arising from questions of theodicy or of God's involvement or non-involvement in human suffering. Notwithstanding the importance of such matters, these remain beyond the purview of this particular project.

What I envision to specifically answer are the following questions: (1) Why did Karl Barth's conceptions of impassibility and the suffering of God change between 1924 and the early 1940s, and then again by the time of writing of the fourth volume of *Church Dogmatics*?; (2) Is there a relationship here between this development in Barth's thinking and that regarding his doctrine of election? And if so, what precisely is the nature and content of that relationship?; (3) Does Barth's understanding of impassibility as a critique of Chalcedonian Christology shed further light on the relationship to (2) above? And, if so, what precisely is that light? In order to attend to these matters, Barth's theology will be considered in light of the patristic and Reformed traditions, analyzing the implications of his thought for the doctrine of (im)passibility.

Chapter Synopsis

Chapter 1

This chapter concerns itself with whether the young Barth had a doctrine of impassibility or passibility, or both. It will try to find out as to what length

49. *CD* II/1, 491–92; IV/1, 187.

his work was influenced by the Western tradition in viewing election with impassibility. It will also ask whether or not Barth departed from Reformed orthodoxy in this matter and, if so, examine the reason for his departure or deviation from the tradition. It will be shown how early in his academic career—namely, in his lectures on John Calvin (1922), and on those given at Göttingen (1924–26) and in Geneva (1936)—Barth retains a relatively Reformed and orthodox stance on impassibility. This is so because he upholds God's eternal immovability (which is the prevalent view) and Calvin's understanding of God's absolute freedom.

Up until 1942, the evidence suggests that Barth's position on divine impassibility is largely consistent with the general Reformed doctrine. That said, it is clear that between the 1920s and the early 40s, Barth is rethinking the doctrine of election in light of his developing Christology, with some implications for the idea of divine suffering. For example, Barth endeavors to conceive God to have elected the Son as a propitiation for the sins of humanity. When he starts to seriously study Calvin's teaching on predestination in 1922, he is at the same time learning about the Reformed tradition. This systematic exploration leads to considerable agreement *and* disagreement with Calvin, and, by extension, with the Reformed thought on predestination more generally. When Barth considers predestination under the doctrine of God, it paves the way for the revision of some aspects in Calvin's teachings vis-à-vis the fixed number of the elect and the actuality of election. This development is crudely evident in 1924, and in more considered form in the *Göttingen Dogmatics*, first published posthumously.

Barth devotes the late 1920s to develop his own dogmatics as he reconfigures his Christology. The impressive articulation of God's revelation-in-concealment in Jesus Christ truly advances Barth's Christology. This specifically exposits the incarnate Logos in relation to the decree. The treatment of the Logos becomes inseparable from Jesus Christ, i.e., the being of the Logos is the being of this human, and vice-versa. It makes the discussion on (im)passibility relevant in Barth's progressive theology, especially when he situates the doctrine of election at the end of the doctrine of God. In 1936, Barth develops Pierre Maury's lecture on election claiming Jesus Christ as both the Subject and Object of God's election. This is the consequence of Barth's, and of Maury's, quest to accurately conceive this doctrine to be the election of grace. It is only by being rigorously christocentric in approach that Barth can finally reach a more satisfactory proposal regarding the *doubleness* of predestination.

Chapter 2

The interest here centers on investigating the reason for Barth's discussion of impassibility in view of election in *CD* II/1–2. The investigation will include the specifics of the decree in order to know what Barth means by saying God is self-determined to be a suffering God in unity with human beings. The impact of such a formulation will be considered in understanding Barth's reinterpretation of divine suffering.

In *CD* II/1–2, the notion of God's absolute freedom impacts Barth's view of impassibility. In his modified doctrine of election, the divine full autonomy is demonstrated by self-sacrifice. Barth's attention to the subject is mostly by way of passing references, but consistently serves his more basic concern to rethink the doctrine of election, and so the doctrine of God. The quality of God as revealed in Jesus Christ is pivotal in knowing Barth's position on whether or not God is essentially impassible. The potential of the being of Jesus Christ in explicating God's nature and will is also considered.

In Barth's theology, God's being in and of himself is for the benefit of humans; God elects for our sake. This act is central to the decree, and also, in knowing the God behind the decree. Here, the reality of God is best understood in the way in which God elects himself as the Son of God *and* the Son of Man. Such christocentric formulation informs Barth's consequential argument on impassibility as well as his proposal of a suffering God in eternity. When God decides to suffer in the Son, it shows God's undeniable identification with humanity.

In this chapter, Barth's understanding of the perfections of God is also correlated with freedom and love. The eternal attributes of God are accounted in his free love.[50] I will argue that Barth builds an argument on divine suffering by pointing out that in Jesus Christ, God is indeed constantly involved in exercising sovereignty with compassion.[51] In other words, when Barth says God is true to God's works, it is conveyed in the context of God being himself as illustrated in the themes of divine perfection.

Chapter 3

The interest in Barth's treatment of impassibility finds satisfaction in this chapter, and its focus on *CD* IV/1–2. Barth, at this point, directly confronts

50. *CD* II/1, 351–438. The perfections of God is key to Barth's conception of the reality of God. For Barth, the perfection of God is not undermined by the suffering of God.

51. *CD* II/1, 440–608. Although Barth begins his articulation of the being of God in §28 of *CD*, it is only from §30 onwards that the suffering of God is dealt with intensity.

the issue of impassibility by discussing it in light of God's will. (Im)passibility is viewed in a unique category—in God's decree, specifically in the *Logos incarnandus*. This chapter will then examine the rationale for Barth's proposition that God is not only capable of suffering, but, crucially, that God wills to suffer in eternity. Here the arising concern will be: What is the implication of such will on God's sovereignty?

In *CD* IV/1–2, we begin to see an indication of the fuller impact of God's self-sacrifice on Barth's conception of (im)passibility. Consequently, his early view of impassibility is no longer relatively orthodox, i.e., inclined to the Western tradition, but has become *dialectically orthodox*.[52] It is orthodox insofar as God is seen as ontologically impassible. It is also unorthodox insofar as the will to be passible in Jesus Christ is maintained. Here, the Formula of Chalcedon will be critically analyzed with Barth's reconfigured Christology. The inseparability of the Logos and Jesus Christ plays a major role in allowing an (im)passible God in election. Nonetheless, God remains immutable, in the sense that God is seen as unchangeable in his autonomous commitment. In being so, God is said to have willed to suffer. This formulation results from Barth's doctrine of reconciliation—the consummation of his doctrine of election.

By examining the relationship of God to external actions and events, God's self-humility is said to significantly influence Barth's view of divine suffering. It overhauls his understanding of who the eternal God is in relation to humanity. Moreover, Barth's rendition of the atonement fortifies a God of suffering. This results in a re-evaluation of Barth's soteriology.

The chapter ends with a critical concern which resonates with the first lines of the introduction, i.e., God's will is undeniably for the good of humanity. In Barth's theology, the reconciling God is also the redeeming God.

Chapter 4

Congruent with previous considerations, the final chapter seeks to unpack some implications of divine suffering on the doctrine of the Trinity. To that end, it will critically inspect Barth's handling of divine suffering in the context of God's "constancy."[53] In such "constancy," the triune life will be explored in

52. This means that Barth's position on divine impassibility can be seen as radical yet still in proximity with the teachings of the Roman Catholics, Reformed and the Lutherans.

53. The discussion will also attend to the reason for Barth's preference of the word "constancy" over "immutability."

conjunction with Christ's two natures. This chapter also looks at the effect of Barth's later Christology on his perception of Chalcedon.

I will argue that in Barth's view, the suffering of God is not confined to the Son, but may also be attributed to the Godhead. The anticipated flesh of the Logos is seen as an eternal reality in God. This formulation has serious implications for how we think of the essential nature of the triune God. Since Jesus Christ is both the electing God and the elected Man, so the logical consequence is that the Father and Spirit in the triune paradigm also share in suffering. The notion of a suffering Trinity shows Barth's openness to see the incarnation as the undivided outworking of divine sacrifice. This however is not cemented due to his dialectical conception of God as both impassible and passible. Such tension will be addressed by engaging with Barth's treatment of divine perfection as he appropriates (im)passibility. The self-contained view of triunity will be challenged here against the idea of God's everlasting selflessness as it relates to God's vulnerability to change.

In my conclusion, I shall reflect on divine suffering, as it is unfolded within Barth's basic argument: God is in what he does; and what God does, strictly speaking, is for the good of humanity.

Chapter I

Election and Divine (Im)passibility in the Early Barth

THIS CHAPTER EXPLORES THE history of the evolution of Karl Barth's doctrine of election and how such theological development impacted (or not) his view of divine impassibility. I shall argue that Barth reconceives the God of election as the One who is self-determined for humanity. To support this, I will begin with a study of passages in which the concepts of election and impassibility appear in Barth's early lectures on John Calvin, in the *Göttingen Dogmatics* and in Pierre Maury's paper in Geneva.

Principally, this chapter is concerned with the following question: does Barth have a doctrine of (im)passibility? Also, to what extent is Barth's work in the early 1920s can be taken as a continuation of the Western traditional articulation of the doctrines of election and impassibility; and to what degree might it represent a deviation, or at least the beginnings of a departure from that tradition? In order to answer these questions, I will examine Barth's reconstruction of the Reformed notion of dual predestination. I will investigate how he relates predestination to the doctrine of God. And lastly, I will analyze why Barth's flourishing Christology could potentially trigger a reconsideration of impassibility.

We will now inspect Barth's early thoughts on election and impassibility (or immutability) as he considers Calvin's theology.

1. 1922 Lectures on John Calvin

In 1918 after the Great War, very early on in Barth's career, he yearned for a deity who is sovereign over the affairs of this world.[1] He struggled to see God in full control amidst the chaos and devastation caused by the previous world

1. Busch, *Karl Barth*, 81–82.

war.[2] Such theological yearning might have been stimulated by the Blumhardts since Barth at this period is attracted to their catch-cry: "Thy kingdom come!" which centers on the eschatological hope only God can give.[3] This is due to Barth's dissatisfaction with what modern theology offers which is geared more on what humans can do, instead of what God can do for humanity. Barth wishes to tackle the social trouble of his time by addressing what he perceives to be the root cause of it, namely, the world's disinterest in God, also, people's ingratitude for the grace of God.[4] In other words, Barth occupies himself with scrutinizing the fundamental crisis in Christian theology.[5]

Barth was transformed from being a staunch supporter of liberal theology, under the auspices of Adolf von Harnack, Wilhelm Herrmann and others, to being an avid scholar of the traditional biblical hermeneutics.[6] While in Safenwil, Switzerland, Barth maneuvered radically away from anything humanistic in methodology that presupposes natural theology.[7] In effect, he became busy with the exegesis of Bible texts derived from its original language and immediate context alone.[8] He discovered that the Scrip-

2. The outbreak of World War I is not specifically regarded as the turning point of Barth's distaste against Liberal Theology. Härle, "Der Aufruf der 93 Intellektuellen und Karl Barths Bruch mit der liberalen Theologie," 220–24. Härle pinpoints that Barth's engagement with Leonhard Ragaz, Herman Kutter and Martin Rade, and significantly, the death of his father, Johann Friedrich Barth have made Barth suspicious of the Liberal Theology of the period between October 1910 and December 1911. Härle, "Der Aufruf der 93 Intellektuellen," 220–24. Wan, "Authentic Humanity in the Theology of Paul Tillich and Karl Barth," 6.

3. Johann Christoph Blumhardt (1805–80) and Christoph Friedrich Blumhardt (1842–1919) are German Pietist pastors that Barth personally met for a dialogue. See Winn, *"Jesus is Victor!"* 281. Barth was one of the theologians who felt as though the First World War had demolished the traditional Christian view of God.

4. Barth, "Letter to Rade," 132–35.

5. Barth's revisit of Scripture begins with his extensive work on the book of Romans. See *Der Römerbrief*. This is done with the help of his friend Eduard Thurneysen in pursuit of a theology detached from Schleiermachian influence. Colwell, *Actuality and Provisionality*, 15–16.

6. Adolf von Harnack promotes the historical-critical method of hermeneutics while Wilhelm Herrmann advocates religious individualism and anti-historicism—both of which eventually upset Barth. McCormack, *Karl Barth's Critically Realistically Dialectical Theology*, 22. Barth however carries over the theological themes in Herrmann, i.e., "the dialectical emphasis without a resolution but an emphasis on the mystery of God . . . [and] on the personality of Christ." Peterson, *The Early Karl Barth*, 46–47.

7. Barth had been a Reformed pastor in the town of Safenwil for ten years (1911–21). Here his theological thoughts have developed substantially and were shared in the pulpit. It was also in Safenwil where Barth was able to write the first and second editions of "The Epistle to the Romans" (*Der Römerbrief*) in the midst of the Great War. Busch, *Karl Barth*, 60.

8. Billings, "Scripture," 25.

tures's central theme is not anthropocentric but theocentric. In a profound way, Barth realized that the focus should not be on human's view of God, but rather, on God's view of humanity.[9] This represents the word of God which shows "the fundamental discontinuity between God and man."[10] Finally having a theocentric mindset (the *eureka moment* in his career), Barth admitted this is something denied him by liberalism.[11]

In 1922, Barth became engrossed with John Calvin (1509–64) when he commenced lecturing on Calvin at the University of Göttingen in Germany.[12] Barth explicitly said that, once he moved into the academy, he had to find something positive to say. That is why he started reading through the older Reformed and Lutheran dogmatics. Consequently, Barth began to think more deliberately as a Reformed theologian and immersed himself in classic Reformed theology.[13] In fact, he even confessed that his "theology had become more Reformed, more Calvinistic" than he had been aware of.[14] This line of thinking had informed Barth's understanding of the doctrine of election.[15] It is in this doctrine where Barth's yearning for a sovereign deity was satisfied. A Lord God who is not in any way confused and attenuated in human affairs.

Barth highlights the "discontinuity" or disconnect between God and humans in his lectures.[16] With this, he is on his way to rescue Western

9. Barth mainly exegetes the Gospel of John and Paul's Epistles. See §17 of *The Theology of John Calvin*. It does not mean that Barth has totally abandoned philosophical and scientific thought in favor of biblical hermeneutics. Barth merely makes a clear distinction between theology and philosophy making the former notably distinguished and respected. Barth's renewed seriousness in biblical hermeneutics is chiefly a reaction against the modern interpretation of Scripture headed by Friedrich Schleiermacher and a response to the epistemological inquiries of Emmanuel Kant. Smith, "Testimony to Revelation," 17–19.

10. Smith, "Testimony," 23. Barth's sustained interest in Reformed theology may have been triggered by Johannn Adam Heilmann's letter of invitation. See Barth, *The Theology of the Reformed Confessions*, vii.

11. Barth, *The Theology of the Reformed Confessions*, vii..

12. Calvin also inspires Barth to keep close to the biblical text and to "follow wherever it leads." Barth, *The Epistle to the Ephesians*, 8. Barth was the only Reformed theologian in a Lutheran faculty at the University of Göttingen. Galli, *Karl Barth*, 58.

13. Barth, *The Theology of the Reformed Confessions*, vii. Mark Lindsay comments that considering Heinrich Heppe's *Reformed Dogmatics* coupled with "two lecture series on John Calvin (1922) and the Reformed confessions (1923)," Barth's doctrine of election during this period was "thoroughly Reformed in nature." "Pierre Maury, Karl Barth, and the Evolution of Election," 110.

14. Busch, *Karl Barth*, 129.

15. Webster, *Barth's Earlier Theology*, 41.

16. In the Tambach lecture of 1919. "The Christian's Place in Society," 288.

"orthodoxy from the ravages of liberal theology."[17] Since then, Barth sees God to be entirely different from creation.[18] This conception is probably shaped by G. W. F. Hegel's philosophy that the divine is the "wholly other" in comparison to what is human; a vista which causes Barth to rethink his methodology.[19] He uses this alleged Hegelian thinking primarily, but not exclusively, to correlate his "systematic-theological reflection" and his hermeneutics.[20] Though Hegelianism or a quasi form of it is suspected to be the primary influence in Barth's thought here, it is actually Søren Kierkegaard who is instrumental in his understanding of God's uniqueness (even in the Son).[21]

Kierkegaard's notion of the "infinite qualitative distinction" clearly separates God (infinite) from humans (finite). Humans are seen incapable of fully comprehending God on their own accord.[22] This becomes the cornerstone of Barth's doctrine of God in which only God can make himself known, and God does this precisely through the Son.[23] Yet despite God's self-revelation through Jesus Christ, direct communication between the divine and human is still impossible because Christ appears to humans as *incognito*.[24] For Barth, "God's self-revealing is always *hidden*" even in revelation.[25] This approach (which owes more to Kierkegaard than to Hegel) saturates Barth's doctrine of election at this point in time. Moreover, Barth declines to accept Hegel's "dialectical method," a methodology which makes God's essential nature somewhat imprisoned in the "wholly otherness" of the divine being. Hegelianism disallows another way of looking at God in relation to creation, specifically to humanity.[26] It is in this departure of which Barth renders his interpretation of divine freedom in election.

Since God is absolutely free, explains Barth in his lectures, God cannot be said to be restricted even by the attributes perceived to be

17. Galli, *Karl Barth*, 1. Also see Schwöbel, *Karl Barth—Martin Rade*, 56.

18. Schwöbel, *Karl Barth*, 277.

19. Ward, "Barth, Hegel, and the Possibility for Christian Apologetics," 63.

20. Ward, "Barth," 63.

21. Barth confesses, "I believe that I have remained faithful to Kierkegaard's reveille, as we heard it then, throughout my theological life, and that I am so today still." Barth even adds that he could not go back to Hegel. Barth, "A Thank You and a Bow," 5. Cross, *Dialectic in Karl Barth's Doctrine of God*, 202–4

22. Cross, *Dialectic*, 202–4

23. Barth, "The Word of God and the Task of the Ministry," 199, 203.

24. Barth, *Theology and Church*, 254–55.

25. Lindsay, "Pierre Maury, Karl Barth, and the Evolution of Election," 111.

26. Barth, "Hegel," 304.

essentially divine.[27] For instance, God cannot be boxed-in to be atemporal, as in Greek mythology; God is said to have no categorical intervention in time. Another aspect to which Barth objects is the notion of God being distinct in an infinitely qualitative way to such a degree that even in Jesus Christ, God still remains fully unknown. Barth is disappointed with the received wisdom about God which is purely metaphysical and has nothing to deal with God's actual relations with humanity.[28] As a result, Barth recasts the notion of divine freedom geared towards the benefit of humanity vis-à-vis the divine grace.[29]

Being theocentric and having an eye for God's autonomy, Barth searches deeper for God's treatment of humanity.[30] Barth devotes his effort, not merely to re-examine the Scriptures, but likewise to investigate the Christian doctrines as taught in the Western tradition.[31] He mainly concentrates on the doctrines of God and predestination. Evidently, with a "tremendous respect for the past," Barth devises his own theology "in continuous dialogue" with the Fathers and the Reformers.[32] Still in 1922, Barth's view is also "subtly reconfigured" as he converses with his contemporaries.[33] Because he concentrates on the history of Christian thought, his theology becomes well-informed historically and also up-to-date.[34] One doctrine that indeed captures his imagination is Calvin's teaching on predestination.

1.1 Dual Predestination

With a rigorous attention to the doctrine of God, Barth endeavors to expound the notion of divine primacy and sovereignty. He is convinced that God is the Subject of the decision to elect. Barth follows Calvin's impulse on election in which God's decree is a clear manifestation of divine rulership over creation; God is free to decide the fate of humanity.[35] Barth also concurs with Calvin

27. Barth, *The Theology of John Calvin*, 9.

28. La Montagne, *Barth and Rationality*, 119.

29. Barth, in this regard, is likely influenced by Martin Luther, he suggests, "Listen to Luther himself. At Wittenberg in 1517 he said that the best and infallible preparation for grace, the only disposition for it, is God's eternal election and predestination." Barth, *Calvin*, 43.

30. Barth, *God in Action*, 42–43.

31. Klooster, *The Significance of Barth's Theology*, 28.

32. Thomas and Wieser, *The Humanity of God*, 5–6.

33. McDowell and Higton, *Conversing with Barth*, 2.

34. Torrance, *Karl Barth*, 9.

35. Goetz, "The Karl Barth Centennial," 458.

that divine sovereignty in election is grounded in God's liberty in himself; it is in no way dependent on human decision and action. The decree is solely based on God—it is for him, by him and in him. In this freedom, God is free to stand on his decision in eternity. Barth observes:

> For him [Calvin]—and again we must face the paradoxical connection—it was precisely the apparently uncertain thing that lies beyond us, predestination, the unconditional freedom of God's dealings with us, that gave him the possibility of taking firm steps in this world, and good reason to do so.[36]

Even though God's decree arises from divine freedom, Barth posits, such freedom is not capricious.[37] Rather, the divine freedom is reflective of God's compassionate character which is eternally unchanged; the decree can also be taken as immutably mirroring God's relationship with humanity.[38] Barth, in this circumstance, has reservations about the idea of election being "eternally fixed," where God had pre-ordained a *fixed* number of the elect in pre-temporal eternity. In other words, no human can change what had been predetermined simply because the decree is absolute, hence, permanent. This is why Calvin's doctrine of predestination is called *decretum absolutum* (God's absolute decree); an idea Barth wishes to avert.[39] Such an attitude leads to viewing a relational God of election.

Barth consents to Calvin's focus on divine freedom as long as it is God's relational actions and decisions for each person "that is in play."[40] Human decision and action merely shows God's compassionate preordination.[41] In this case, Barth deviates from Calvin in terms of the eternal predestination having to presuppose two opposite groups of people, namely, the elect and reprobate. If God's liberty were fundamentally based on divine pathos, Barth asks, then why would God discriminate in the first place? The thought of an eternal segregation of humans is at odds with Barth's rethinking of election.[42]

The "doubleness" of predestination is the *mystery* not only of election, but also, of salvation. How can a loving and gracious God let the reprobate

36. Barth, *Calvin*, 180.

37. Klempa, "Barth as a Scholar and Interpreter of Calvin," 38–39.

38. Webster, *Karl Barth*, 88–90.

39. Calvin, *Institutes* 3.21.1. On Barth's comments on Calvin's absoluteness of God's election, see Crisp's *Deviant Calvinism*, 161.

40. Lindsay, "Pierre Maury, Karl Barth," 111. Augustine of Hippo shapes Calvin's thought on this matter. Giberson, *Abraham's Dice*, 150. Cf. Augustine, *Confessions*, i–iv, 5.

41. Carson, *Divine Sovereignty and Human Responsibility*, 214–16.

42. Busch, *Barth in Conversation*. Volume 1, 257n69.

perish? Barth admits that the fate of the reprobate poses a serious challenge to Calvin's version of predestination.[43] Having faceless reprobate in the doctrine of election allows for the notion of a cold and passive deity. What Barth seeks is a relational God behind the decree. Although the decree is absolute, the God of the decree is not indifferent; what is fixed for Barth is the compassion of God. Aside from distancing from metaphysical injunction inherent in the hidden God, Barth goes beyond Calvin's worry of soteriological speculation. Barth does this by focusing on God's providence for the church.[44]

Barth revises Calvin's idea of a predestined "one church" by noting that God may, in fact, be actual in relating to the church.[45] Calvin insists that the "actual occurrence" of election with respect to the church is God's pre-temporal decision on who will believe him or not; and such actuality will only follow in time.[46] The electing activity is not exclusive to the event in which God reveals himself in and through the church's proclamation. God's calling of the elect and the non-response of the reprobate is merely a fulfillment of what has been eternally decreed.[47] On the basis of a reconfigured understanding of the relationship between eternity and time, Barth critiques Calvin's notion of a predestined church.[48] When God set forth his eternal and "fixed determination" in time, the decree, argues Barth, is already an actual occurrence.[49] Though God has the final say in who is elect and who is not, it does not mean that each person's destiny is already fixed in an apathetic manner. The invariability of divine foreknowledge is not in any way disassociated with human behavior or reaction. In other words, it is in the actuality of election where God's determination is said to be truly *at work* in each person's decision. Notably, the relational God in and of the election is highlighted.

Barth offers a distinct perspective on the actuality in time (happening and occurrence) of the individual response to God. It is not by the causality of what has been predetermined pre-temporally, but by God's active willing and doing to bring about positive response.[50] Here we can sense that

43. Busch, *Barth in Conversation*, 278–90.

44. Chung, *Karl Barth and Evangelical Theology*, 51.

45. Barth, *Calvin*, 178.

46. Calvin, *Institutes* 3.22.4.

47. Read Part II of Barth, *The Knowledge of God and the Service of God according to the Teaching of the Reformation.*

48. Barth's handling of time and eternity as it relates to election is evident in his lectures in 1936 and beyond.

49. Barth, *Calvin*, 386–87.

50. Chung, *Karl Barth and Evangelical Theology*, 51–52.

even though this conception indicates close affinity with Calvin in regards to God's primacy, Barth refuses the suggestion that divine sovereignty is essentially in and for God. This sovereignty is in and of God *on behalf* of humanity. And as Barth continues to find his own voice in rendering the election, he revisits this doctrine in light of the doctrine of God.

1.2 Predestination and the Doctrine of God

Although predestination, at some length, is intertwined with the being of God, it is not the case in Calvin's view.[51] Barth observes, "Calvin never connected the doctrine of predestination with that of God, whether directly or indirectly."[52] Albeit this statement comes after 1936, it is reasonable to presume that Barth's ambivalence towards Calvin's approach of separating predestination from the doctrine of God began, at least some time in 1921 prior to his lectures on Calvin.[53] After all, in Barth's thought, as Mark Lindsay puts it, "Election and its 'parent' locus of predestination most properly exist dogmatically in the closest possible relationship to the doctrine of God."[54] So despite Barth's admission of having Calvinistic inclination, it does not automatically follow that the doctrines of God and election are also separated in his theology.[55]

Calvin's position on God's unqualified sovereignty over creation, which Barth endeavors to avoid, lies in the unyielding stance on God's incomparability *ad extra*. This "incomparability" sits well with the theme of "discontinuity"; however the elements of *mystery* and *ambiguity* in election are amplified in such terms. It is in these terms that God's uncompromising freedom thrives in Calvin's doctrine of predestination. Notwithstanding the strong objections against the mysterious and ambiguous deity, God's absolute freedom nevertheless pervades Barth's doctrine of God.[56] After all, the absoluteness of freedom does not undermine a relational God, but rather upholds it.

51. Leith, *John Calvin's Doctrine of the Christian Life*, 120. *Göttingen Dogmatics*, xlvi.

52. *CD* II/2, 86. Note that in the *Institutes* 1.1, Calvin's presentation about the "Knowledge of God" has only covered three pages.

53. Chung, "Seeds of Ambivalence Sown," 58.

54. Lindsay, "Pierre Maury, Karl Barth," 109.

55. Evidently, Barth's stand on this matter becomes noticeable at the time of writing the *Göttingen Dogmatics*. His all-out proclamation of the connection between the doctrine of God and election is in *Church Dogmatics*. *CD* II/2, 77. Bender, *Karl Barth's Christological Ecclesiology*, 105.

56. McCormack, *Karl Barth's Critically Realistically Dialectical Theology*, 330.

The notion of God's absolute freedom should be at hand to better understand Barth's concepts of election and impassibility. Even if this direction is arguably less fruitful in probing his early understanding of election, such an attempt is reasonable in probing his formative understanding of impassibility. Since the discussion on impassibility principally deals with God's non-contingency and uniqueness, the unrestricted and unlimited God is pertinent in examining Barth's view of election. Correspondingly, it is also appropriate to see Barth's developing conception of God under two main categories, namely, the *transcendent* God and the *unknown* God.

Indeed Barth's early doctrine of God concerns divine transcendence.[57] In this, he is out to set God as immensely above the deities of the world, and its substitutes.[58] God, says Barth, is not to be "confounded with any high, exalted, force, known or knowable" in this world.[59] Barth shows the utter separation of the high God and the world; the two are totally unlike and exclusive. In other words, no part of the world is a manifestation or revelation of the infinite God.[60]

Barth endorses Calvin's take on divine *unknowability* with discretion. Even the knowledge which comes by faith, Barth asserts, cannot be valid in considering the election.[61] When God reveals himself to a person of faith, still that person is faced with a fact that God is, to a large extent, unknown. In other words, Barth is convinced that humans can never know God fully simply because what they seek after is an indescribable God.[62] The revealing and the revealed God is conceived to be above and beyond in all aspects: i.e., in time, space, concepts, and even all potentialities. God is the "wholly other" or the completely different even in his revelation.[63] Here Barth puts such "otherness" as implying exclusive separation:

57. Barth, *The Epistle to the Romans*, 30.

58. Barth, *On Religion*, 13. Barth rids himself of the philosophical and humanistic foundation and exposition of Christian doctrine because of the moral weakness of liberal theology as spearheaded by his respected professors in their war support for the Kaiser and Germany and the failure of humanistic optimism during the aftermath of World War I. Godsey, *Karl Barth*, 43–45.

59. Barth, *Romans*, 36.

60. We can sense here Barth's distaste for the analogy of being (*analogia entis*) in which God is known in what the created world offers. See Barth, "Fate and Idea in Theology," 33. Also Johnson, "The Nature of Barth's Rejection of the *analogia entis*," 83–119.

61. Barth, *Romans*, 276.

62. Barth, *Romans*, 91.

63. Barth, *Calvin*, 166.

> God, the pure limit and pure beginning of all that we are, have, and do, standing over in infinite qualitative difference to man and all that is human, nowhere and never identical with that which we call God, . . . the Lord, the Creator and Redeemer . . . that is the living God.[64]

God is seen to be unknowable and indescribable in Jesus Christ. This conception goes with the theme revelation-in-concealment in Barth's budding theology. Even when humans claim to know God, humanity's knowledge is of an incomprehensible reality. Consider, for instance, the personality of God. Although God is personal, says Barth, yet it is incomprehensible insofar as human perspective of this term is concerned.[65] God is personal in a transcendent way because even if God becomes personal in a fashion to which humans can relate, (for instance God being loving and gracious), these attributes remain insufficiently understood by the human mind.[66] Barth seeks to see the relational God within the transcendent-personal being, hence the term "the living God."

The idea of a true living God breaks the old barrier of seeing God as somewhat impersonal. Despite humans being completely different and totally alienated, God initiates to be the Redeemer. God in this way relates with humans, and more importantly, *gives* himself for their sake. This is where Barth centers his argument on God's self-revelation—when God reveals himself, God gives himself. But, at this stage, God's self-giving remains largely mysterious, especially in using the Reformed lens in looking at election. The incomprehensible transcendent deity overshadows the actual living and redeeming God. The hidden God remains hidden in the *incognito* Son.

The *incognito* Son is the stop-gap in the quest to further Barth's discussion on the self-giving deity; this is due to Calvin's persistent grip on Barth. The commitment to God's formidable-yet-compassionate being is unavoidable here in considering predestination.[67] However, Barth desires to see the divine outworking with an accent on God's compassion.[68] It is the locus of Barth's recasting of the doctrine of election; he does this by formulating the doctrine christologically.

64. Barth, *Calvin*, 330–31.

65. Barth, *Calvin*, 331. Also see Barth, *Anselm, Fides Quarens Intellectum*, 58.

66. Barth further comments on Rom 1:19–21 that "God is He whom we know we do not know." Barth, *Calvin*, 331.

67. Barth, *Calvin*, 275.

68. Roger Olson claims that Barth's intention for a christological concentration of election originates from his objection of a "hidden God behind Jesus Christ," especially in the context of the "German Christian movement which nearly deified Hitler and Nazi ideology." Olson, "Was Karl Barth a Universalist?" para. 23.

1.3 Jesus Christ's Role in Predestination

For Barth, the role of Jesus Christ in election is pivotal in communicating the divine grace through the church.[69] Barth's christological hermeneutics speak of election in ways beyond Calvin's attempt to be christocentric.[70] Yet despite the mention of Christ's role in the election of and through the church, Barth still echoes Calvin's thought on such connection; a connection that is not rigidly attentive to what Christ alone can do. Here Barth is swayed instead to highlight the election as *kerygma* rather than the Subject of the *kerygma* who is Jesus Christ.[71] The grace offered in Christ, in this case, is somewhat sidetracked because the election itself is given more attention. Later on, as Barth continues to modify his doctrine of election in view of Christ's role, it results in conceiving Christ as *the center* of this doctrine, therefore of the gospel as well. At this juncture, however, God's self-giving in election is still yet to be developed.

In order to understand Barth's Christology in view of predestination, it is necessary to deal with his conception of objectivism. God, being the "subject-matter" of theology provides the groundwork for a theological "objectivity" as opposed to human subjectivity.[72] But, even in Jesus Christ, God is still ontologically *unknown* and even *unknowable*. Accordingly, the more humans know of Jesus Christ, the more he is yet to be known.[73] And to understand Barth further, it is mandatory to be familiar with his method, i.e., constantly reiterating the dialectical "Yes" and "No" having complicated synthesis.[74] This method is obviously informed by Kierkegaard's diastasis between God and what is not God. Also, the Hegelian objectivity in Barth is still a challenge, especially in speaking of a relational deity.

I think Barth could have applied his dialectic method in a non-Hegelian fashion by strengthening the argument on God's free determination in Jesus Christ. Even if divine sovereignty is incorporated in the equation,

69. Barth, *Calvin*, 275–76.

70. Gibson, *Reading the Decree*, 27.

71. Barth, *Calvin*, 179.

72. Schwöbel, "Theology," 24–25.

73. It is to be noted that this notion is one of Kant's influence to Barth's theo-logical metamorphosis. God, the absolute objective, can only be accessed or understood in the *actus*, which for Barth, is the Godhead and not elsewhere. See Barth's 1930 lectures on Kant in *Protestant Theology in the Nineteenth Century*.

74. Hunsinger, *How to Read Karl Barth*, 58. The language of dialectic is that of *paradox*, in which the juxtaposition of an opinion alongside of it, implicated with it. In other words, the method of dialectic is to counter the "No" by its opposite "Yes": the thesis by the antithesis. But in this regard, Barth does not force such form of argument to produce a synthesis. Cross, *Dialectic in Karl Barth's Doctrine of God*, 91.

Barth can maneuver his argument to mean that God's essential nature is truly *pro nobis*. In spite of the fact that God is still ontologically *unknown* in self-revelation, God does not rigidly remain *unknowable*. Barth is yet to learn how to skillfully apply the beauty of the Yes alongside the No to formulate a christocentric election as evident below:

> The one thing we must not do, . . . is ignore Christ as we put the question. Any secondary guarantee of our election that ignores the origin, the revelation, would instead provoke God's wrath against us, and as we plunge into the abyss of his majesty we could only be crushed by his glory.[75]

Barth sees Jesus Christ merely as the Subject of election, and humans being the object, even of "God's wrath."[76] Though assurance rests on Christ alone, Barth sympathizes with Calvin on the issue of the objective knowledge in election. Humans can never be "too sure" of what exactly is the election, but rather, "only by humility, objectivity, and worship we learn not to ask whether we are elect."[77] So even if the incarnation, life, and death of Christ speak of the God of election, the argument of Barth in the end inescapably recoils into Calvin's thought.[78]

Here the weakness in Barth's christocentric position is on the object of election. Despite Jesus Christ being the Redeemer, Barth falls short of this theme since Christ is merely represented as the *object of faith*, but, not the *object of election*.[79] Barth's attempt to be christocentric in conceiving the election is still weak. Jesus Christ not being the object of election hinders Barth from recognizing an eternally self-giving God. The inexorable Otherness and incomparability of the electing God preserves the notion of immutability, and

75. Barth, *Calvin*, 180.

76. Barth seems to agree with Calvin that "it is a fearful thing to fall into the hands of the living God" (Heb 10:31) using this passage in the context of predestination.

77. Barth, *Calvin*, 180.

78. This is due to Barth's attempt to articulate more cogently what he wishes to contend; which is, the fact that God's supremacy does not invalidate human relative choice and responsibility to seek after God. Barth, *Calvin*, 182–84. The proof of election is evidenced by a lived life of the human subject rather than on Christ's life *per se*.

79. Even if he is to regard Christ as the Representative of humanity, such representation only applies to the forgiveness of sins, not to the actual taking of the place of humans as reprobate. Barth puts it, "Christ represents those who in him believe in the promise of God, and that means the forgiveness of sins, not an alteration in us, but the unheard-of and incomprehensible thing of an alteration in God's attitude to us. This alteration is the point of the sending of Jesus Christ." Barth, *Calvin*, 184.

also, impassibility in Barth.[80] This is reinforced in Calvin's insistence on the immutability of the Logos.

Calvin is one of the forerunners in Europe to strictly argue for the Logos to be immutable, hence also, impassible.[81] He refers back through the canons of Chalcedon to the formulations of the Fathers, wherein both the Alexandrian and Antiochene schools were agreed at least upon such presupposition.[82] Unlike Calvin, Barth at this point did not address in any depth the question of the hypostatic union. It appears that Christology, or the lack of it, shapes Barth's formative thought on impassibility.[83] We can only be certain that, at this point, in the hopes of developing his theology, he does not attempt to *historicize* the being of God.[84] To do this is to significantly impact Barth's view on either immutability or impassibility, which, is logically presupposed to be close to what Calvin has in mind.

Because of the firm hold of the "wholly otherness" of God, the young Barth is reluctant to accommodate a "common history" between the divine and human.[85] By historicizing the being of God, he would have abandoned "classical theism" in favor of a divine ontology relative to time. Thus by deduction, the Logos remains unhistoricized, untouched by Christ's humanity. If Barth has thought otherwise, he would be compelled to "historicize" (or perhaps even abandon) many of the attributes classically ascribed to God, i.e., immutability and impassibility.[86] Ultimately, election as Barth understands it, remains arguably speculative rather than actualistic, for, at least, the remainder of this period of his lectures on Calvin.

Here Barth quite easily slips back to being Calvinistic, i.e., strong emphasis on divine transcendence, than having his own brand of theology. Although he is already attracted to God's compassion for humanity, his commitment to the transcendency of God persists. In Barth's quest to present a deity as truly for humanity, he is still dragged by the notion of an infinitely qualitatively distinct/other being. This allows for an acceptance of mystery in God's decision which casts a shadow on the unrestricted self-giving God. Thus an electing God who is willing to suffer is unaccommodated

80. Hector, "God's Triunity and Self-Determination," 247–51.

81. Calvin, *Institutes* 2.14.

82. Calvin, *Institutes* 2.14. See also Gregg and Groh, *Early Arianism*, 68–70. The Chalcedonian Formula states that the *Logos* and Jesus Christ are one and the same yet acknowledged in two natures. This is expounded in chapter 3.

83. von Balthasar, *The Theology of Karl Barth*, 30–39.

84. Historicizing the being of God would come later as reflected in *CD* IV/1.

85. Read Chételat, "Hegel's Philosophy of World History as Theodicy," 215–30.

86. Nimmo, "Karl Barth and the *concursus Dei*—A Chalcedonianism Too Far?" 60–61.

at this period. The implication of the revealing and the revealed God in Jesus Christ remains considerably ignored. That is why despite Barth's effort to advance his own version of election, the weight of the mysterious God takes a heavy toll on his developing theology.

1.4 Barth and Calvin on Election

Barth discovers in Calvin an exciting approach to theology as shown above. For him, Calvin brings forth the gospel in the doctrine of election to develop further. Barth is indeed indebted to his predecessor's theological framework substantially and formatively.[87] Calvin has influenced Barth in these aspects: first, in ascribing great importance to the doctrine of predestination; secondly, in the insistence on God's primacy, lordship and autonomy as well as the conundrum in election; thirdly, in maintaining the doubleness of predestination in the sense of which election and rejection are two aspects of the decree; and lastly, in highlighting that election must be understood in the self-revelation of God as attested in Scripture. In other words, as William Klempa puts it, "For the most part, Barth took his stand with Calvin and spoke of predestination as "eternal, unconditional and twofold."[88]

Though Barth's doctrine of election is in some ways similar to Calvin's, it also shows development in the following facets: the "doubleness" of predestination; the timing or *occurrence* of election; the relationship between the doctrines of predestination and of God; and, more importantly, clarifying and prioritizing the role of Jesus Christ in the decree. These sharp contradistinctions are the outcome of Barth's reinterpretation of Calvin's doctrine of predestination.[89] It indicates that Barth eventually has worked out his own theology to speak of election as truly out of grace.[90] For this reason, John Webster asserts that the 1922 lectures on Calvin drive Barth to have a profound reflection on the biblical interpretation of election in the Göttingen period and beyond.[91] As a result, the *Göttingen Dogmatics* ushers in a fresh approach to Reformed confessions, including an attempt to reinvigorate Christology.

87. Chung, "Seeds of Ambivalence Sown," 55.

88. William Klempa, "Barth as a Scholar and Interpreter of Calvin," 38–39.

89. Webster comments that Barth's 1922 lectures were a "rough document." *Karl Barth*, 34.

90. True learning, according to Barth, is to think beyond what is already learned. Lee, *Double Particularity*, xvi.

91. Webster, *Word and Church*, 92.

After inspecting Barth's initial take on divine suffering, we will be in a better position to look for any engagement with impassibility in his first attempt to write dogmatics at Göttingen.

2. 1924 *The Göttingen Dogmatics*

While giving lectures at the University of Göttingen (Germany) during the period between April 1924 to October 1925, Barth also began a cycle of dogmatics.[92] The first of which is later known as *The Göttingen Dogmatics*.[93] It is important to note that this is the only cycle he ever finished.[94] This is his first account of a sustained engagement with the doctrine of election; it is also foundational in understanding the christological development of Barth's theology.[95]

In the *GD*, Barth keeps the theme of divine primacy and lordship. At this stage, he seems to attempt to reconcile his views on divine immutability and autonomy.[96] Barth here understands God to be relational, i.e., at work in human affairs. This impacts the notion of immutability as it relates to the decree. God's decree is not fixed insofar as the number of the elect and their fate are not immutable. Barth puts it:

> [E]xclusively a basic description of God's dealings with us, of his free and actual use at every moment of the possibility of saying Yes or No to us, of electing or rejecting us, of awakening us to

92. "Preface," in Barth, *The Göttingen Dogmatics*, ix–x. Hereafter, the abbreviation *GD* will be used. Barth had been a Professor of Dogmatics and New Testament Exegesis at the University of Münster in Germany from October 1925 to March 1930. Haley, *The Humanity of Christ*, 75n50.

93. It is originally entitled: *Instruction in the Christian Religion* (*Unterricht in der christlichen Religion*). In order to know the reason for the title revision, read *GD*, vii. Barth was not able to see the ET of the *GD* because it was published posthumously in 1991.

94. Barth wrote only the first volume of the *Christian Dogmatics* when he was at Münster. It is due to the fact that "historically and materially," this work lacks depth in context. Also, Barth's theology has developed to a point where he could no longer say the same things as before. "Author's Foreword," in *Church Dogmatics* I/1, trans. G. T. Thomson (Edinburgh: T&T Clark, 1936), vii. Unless otherwise stated as revised (rev.), this is the version used throughout for *CD* I/1. The *Church Dogmatics* is also considered an unfinished work. Barth failed to write the fifth and concluding volume of *CD* due to old age and failing health. In fact, he was only able to write fragments of *CD* IV/4 in 1967 before he died on December 10, 1968 at Basel, Switzerland. "Editors's Preface." *CD* IV/4, vi; "Preface." *CD* IV/4, viii.

95. McDonald, *Re-Imaging Election*, 31. This shift from soterio-eschatological view began at Göttingen. Wu, *The Concept of History in the Theology of Karl Barth*, 99–101

96. See Goetz, "The Suffering God," 385–89.

> faith or hardening us, of giving us a share in the hope of eternal salvation or leaving us in the general human situation whose end is perdition.[97]

Barth cements his argument that the "actual" response of a person to the gospel shows who is, and who is not, elect. Though Barth agrees with the "twofold possibility," he nonetheless is convinced that there exists "the simultaneous presence and succession of faith and unbelief in different individuals or even in the same individual."[98] The actualized freedom of God in every moment of possibility reconfigures Barth's doctrine of God. Here God is said to lord *with* (not lord over) human beings. In other words, God shares himself with humankind. It does not negate Barth's position on how God reveals himself since the direction of such sharing is from above to below.[99]

The acknowledgment of election as the *extension* of knowing God in God's outworking is foundational in this period. That is why Barth solidifies his position that election and the doctrine of God are inseparable:

> Thus, if the doctrine of predestination is correct, it may be said that it rightly belongs here as a continuation of the doctrine of God, both in relation to the dead point beyond which it leads us and in relation to what follows, which puts it in a proper light.[100]

Basically, a correct estimation of God's being is the corollary to a proper understanding of election. In fact, predestination as the execution of the first and principal decree, argues Barth, affects all humanity; "God creates humanity immediately and originally with the destiny of manifesting his glory by manifesting mercy and righteousness."[101] Nevertheless, Barth concedes that humans are still accountable for their actions.[102] God's self-sharing does not lead to the progressive understanding of the divine self-giving. In this case, the issue of impassibility is still unengaged in Barth.

I think Barth's effort to interconnect the election and God's being is quite premature at this point to effect a strong onto-soteriological formulation. The fact that Barth already alludes to God's sympathetic freedom in his Calvin lectures, and now stresses God's mercy and righteousness, then he

97. *GD*, 455–56.

98. *GD*, 443–44.

99. *GD*, 442. Barth's hermeneutic methodology is consistently "from above to below" (*von oben nach unten*). Diller, "Karl Barth and the Relationship between Philosophy and Theology," 1036.

100. *GD*, 445.

101. *GD*, 447.

102. *GD*, 447.

could have pushed this insight further. An insight which shows the decree as positive since God's essentialities in consideration are also positive. The hidden God having an ambiguous decree is slowly side-tracked to give way to God's full self-revelation in Jesus Christ. The revelation in Jesus Christ is "identical in subject and object."[103] Here Christ is simultaneously the Subject and Object of revelation. It is in this regard where Barth advances the transcendent-yet-relational God of election. It is also in such theme where divine self-determination is expounded.

2.1 God's Self-determination in Election

In Barth's conviction, God's self-determination is conjoined with the desire to save the elect. This soteriological drive is primary at this point, yet the concept of the condemnation of the reprobate is nonetheless retained. Barth sustains his position on divine transcendence, but, positively. The pure negation arising from the actual response of individuals is dominated by the actual love God invokes to humankind. God's self-determination, as opposed to human participation, is what Barth deepens in articulating the election:

> At this point, the doctrine of election comes into play, because it can function as a systematic-theological reflection of the particular determination of God's acting toward and upon human beings. It points to the distinction between the statement that "God lives, God knows, God wills" and the statement that "God does this very specific thing, he is the God of the gracious choice."[104]

This time, at least structurally, Barth locates the doctrine of election at the end of the doctrine of God. It stands at the transition from the reflection on God's being to the reflection on God's acting. Here we can sense that the novelty of Barth's approach consists in a renewed understanding of the relation between the concepts of election and God.[105] Even at this junction, the Otherness of God is re-emphasized by positing that God reveals himself as a real person; a real person to effectively relate with humanity. This person is "absolutely unique"—the man Jesus of Nazareth.[106] The distinction between human concepts of God and God's real being in this man is integral in Barth's theology. In other words, his doctrine of election serves as the

103. *GD*, 95.

104. *GD*, 444.

105. Gockel, *Barth and Schleiermacher*, 136–37.

106. *GD*, 368.

concise explanation of such distinction, and then becomes the "apex" of the doctrine of God.[107]

In the *Göttingen Dogmatics*, the mystery inherent in God's self-revelation is reconsidered in terms of the "veiling and unveiling" of God in Jesus Christ.[108] God is seen to dialectically reveal himself to humankind. Barth states, "[I]f veiling is the content of God's veiling and unveiling the point of his veiling, we are obviously set under a twofold possibility grounded in God himself."[109] Notice that only here Barth introduces the dialectic phrase "veiling and unveiling" of God in self-revelation.[110] Another interesting facet is that God's twofold revelation is relative to the twofold possibility of the elect and the reprobate. Correspondingly, the doubleness is in the dialectic pairs in election, namely, Creator and the creature; eternity and time; and also, death and resurrection.

In the divine intervention in Jesus Christ, argues Barth, the Creator breaks into creation without being confounded with creaturely reality.[111] This idea is strengthened since eternity and time are conceived as two distinct realms: a chasm between God and humans. All creatures are bound by time; God however is eternal, therefore, he extends beyond time. Divine reality, Barth reasons, is totally different from creaturely reality. In the great gap between two realities, there is no way from humanity to God. There is a way, however, from God to humanity—through Jesus Christ. It is in Christ that the dialectic pairs are viewed harmoniously:

> This means that even though he [God] is nontemporal and nonspatial he stands in a positive relation to the limit of time and space and to what they enclose as his creatures, without himself being limited by them as the infinite is by the finite. . . . Eternity is the quality of God in virtue of which he contains in himself the meaning of time. Eternity is simultaneous duration. We recall the biblical saying: 'My times are in thy hand' (Ps 31:15).[112]

For Barth, eternity is not incompatible with time. Eternity contains time because the eternal God makes himself known in Jesus Christ.[113] Even if

107. *GD*, 214. Apex in this context is not synonymous with the central theme from which all doctrines find affinity. Gockel, *Barth and Schleiermacher*, 141.

108. Barth has carried this through from the paradoxical language of 1922 *Der Römerbrief*, 346–53.

109. *GD*, 440.

110. *GD*, 440.

111. *GD*, 441.

112. *GD*, 435–36.

113. Hauerwas, *With the Grain of the Universe*, 162.

eternity is to be distinguished from time, eternity coexists with time by giving meaning to it. Here Barth talks about God's turning to creation through empowering and commanding creation.[114] Despite the diastasis between God and humanity, the transcendent-yet-relational God is developed. It is through and in Jesus Christ that the infinite God reaches out to finite humanity. Thus when the Creator comes into contact with creation, the gap between eternity and time is reconciled.[115]

In light of the compatibility of eternity with time, the present is taken with the future; hence the two are seen as one successive event, e.g., death and resurrection wherein the former leads to the latter thus the two are inseparable.[116] Death is treated as no longer an end in itself since resurrection comes as a result of death by virtue of the death-and-resurrection of Jesus Christ.[117] This is how Barth understands the "simultaneous duration" of eternity as it points to the harmony between two realities as a result of the intervention of the incarnate God.

The simultaneity of eternity with time speaks of the being of God. For Barth, divine transcendence is converged with divine immanence, which means that the Creator God is understood in the creature Jesus Christ.[118] This understanding however is not something that humans can fully grasp because Christ intersects the world vertically "from above."[119] When Barth discusses God's self-unveiling in Christ, it is coincident with the *veiled* humanity of Christ.[120] In other words, the revealed God (*Deus revelatus*) remains the hidden God (*Deus absconditus*).[121] The hidden God, at this juncture, though still indescribable, is not inclined to suspicion. Although God is still sovereign over what is not God, such sovereignty is properly conceived to be truly *for* humanity. In fact, in Barth's view, Jesus Christ

114. Yuen, *Barth's Theological Ontological of Holy Scripture*, 110.

115. Barth, "The Doctrinal Task of the Reformed Churches," in *The Word of God and the Word of Man*, 256–57.

116. This conception is found in *Romans* where the world of the Creator touches the creation "as a tangent touches a circle." Barth, *Romans*, 31. In other words, the redemption of humanity has begun *and* it is still ongoing. Redemption, Barth proposes, is conceived in terms of the "not yet" and "already so," a conceptuality fully developed in *CD* IV/1, 646–61.

117. *GD* 149–50.

118. *GD*, 388, 437.

119. Barth, *Romans*, 30.

120. Langdon, *God the Eternal Contemporary*, 60–61.

121. *GD* 186. For a different perspective on the revelation of the God-self; cf. Brian, *Covering Up Luther*, 107–8.

"places Himself in front of us, covering and justifying and liberating us."[122] It is in this line of thought that humanity somehow finds surety in election. Barth is no longer critical of divine hiddenness since he considers it in view of Jesus Christ. I think the key to the mystery behind the electing God and the election itself is in the demonstration of Christ's humanity.

It is only at Göttingen that Barth becomes interested in the question of the hypostatic union.[123] James Haley points out that the language of veiling and unveiling "anticipates the language of *anhypostasis* and *enhypostasis* that Barth would soon discover."[124] This development gives Barth the necessary linguistic tools for his later engagement with the doctrine of impassibility. In dealing with Christ's humanity, the uniqueness of Jesus Christ is underpinned. Jesus Christ is unique in his humanity because it is the humanity of God. In God being human in Christ, the divinity is not compromised.[125] Christ's humanity cannot be said to be that which is obvious in humankind; hence absolute creaturely reality. In spite of Christ being fully human, he is also fully God. Barth's Christology comes into play here not only in matter of revelation, but also in matter of salvation.[126] The events of revelation, and more importantly salvation, are events from God and *in* God.[127]

Interestingly, God's revelation through concealment, as Barth revisits this matter, is no longer much on the evidence of the life of the elect. The focus is shifted from general humanity to Christ's humanity.[128] In this respect, the election of humanity is now based on how Jesus Christ lived his life as the *Representative*. The analogic pattern of Jesus Christ being the Representative as the Redeemer, and vice-versa, underlines the divine self-giving. The Son gives himself but this does not equate to viewing that God's self suffers. In other words, this self-giving does not mean that the Son gives himself up. It has repercussions in understanding Barth's doctrine of election at this point, and how this intermediary election inspire his thoughts

122. Barth, *The Word of God*, 277.

123. Haley, *The Humanity of Christ*, 5. Haley adds that Barth has learned the concepts of *an-enhypostases* from reading Heinrich Heppe's *Reformed Dogmatics* and Heinrich Schmid's *The Doctrinal Theology of the Evangelical Lutheran Church*. Haley, *The Humanity*, 5. Heppe's thoughts are contributory to the shaping of Barth's doctrine of reconciliation. Brouwer, *Karl Barth and the Post-Reformation Orthodoxy*, 149.

124. Haley, *The Humanity*, 3. *Anhypostasis* indicates that the humanity of Jesus had no subsistence apart from the incarnation of the Logos, and *enhypostasis* indicates that the enfleshed Logos is the pre-temporal Son of God.

125. *GD*, xlviii. Marga, *Karl Barth's Dialogue with Catholicism in Göttingen and Münster*, 137.

126. *GD*, 473.

127. Gockel, *Barth and Schleiermacher*, 154.

128. Hunsinger, *Disruptive Grace*, 131–33.

on impassibility. Though he signals an allowance for divine passibility, he never, at least at this stage, forces such trajectory.

As the material shows, Barth appears uninterested to discuss divine suffering *per se*, albeit he carries the thought of self-giving in God's revelation. The divine self-giving is limited only to God being human in Jesus Christ without any theopaschite inclination. In his christocentric tendency, Barth gives more weight on God being merciful.[129] Even if God remains hidden, God's concern *ad extra* is advanced without hesitation. Divine sovereignty is reconceived in Jesus Christ. With this development in place, Barth is able to reformulate his view on the God of election in his own terms, i.e., rigorously christocentric. So for now, we will keep focused on his dynamic rendition of the *uniqueness* of Christ's humanity. It could expose what Barth thinks of immutability.

But before we scrutinize Barth's conception of the humanity of Christ, we have to first examine how he looks at the being of Jesus Christ through the triune God.[130] This is due to the cohesiveness of the doctrines of God and of election. Election, Barth stresses, is a triune decision.[131] Thus Barth's reworking of Christology with the doctrine of election is always in view of the Trinity. It indicates how Jesus Christ is considered in conjunction with the Godhead. The transcendent-yet-relational God of election is truly taking shape here. The electing God is true to being in and of himself in eternity according to Barth. Though such a claim precedes the teaching of divine simplicity, he however reinvents it in the context of the unity of the Godhead. Barth qualifies:

> Worthy of being put first here is the concept of God's unity, which carries with it the two thoughts of his uniqueness and simplicity. In absolute mystery there stands behind each relative attribute the truth that God is both unique (*unicus*) and simple (*simplex*).[132]

This assertion of God being simple is not simplistic insofar as the uniqueness of God is concerned; especially in considering the triune activity (*perichoresis*). Barth, in this context, gives more attention to the Son of God manifests in Jesus Christ. Despite this schema, Barth still largely holds the notion of divine simplicity as taught by the Fathers. This position disallows any form of sharing or communication of properties between Christ's

129. *GD*, 461.

130. Barth's extensive work on the Trinity however came only after the Göttingen period. Moseley, *Nations and Nationalism in the Theology of Karl Barth*, 89.

131. *GD*, 428.

132. *GD*, 428.

two natures (*physis*).[133] The Godhead being in "one essence, and of equal dignity within this essence" is sustained amidst the reworking of Christology. This is why Barth does not go further into the implication of the nexus between the Son of God and Jesus Christ. The hiddenness of the triune God is strong in Barth that he somewhat disassociates the Father from the Son in articulating the divine inner life.[134] Nonetheless, because the uniqueness of the Son's humanity is derived from the hiddenness of God, Jesus Christ is not to be conceived in a simplistic manner. Even in Jesus Christ, God is sovereign over creation.[135] This ensures God's ontological distinction from creation.[136] Here Barth revisits the importance of the Logos in election. Also, how the Logos is not affected in the incarnation.

2.2 Election and Christology

To begin, Barth is against the nineteenth-century kenoticism.[137] He criticizes the surrender of the divine omni-attributes in the self-emptying of the Logos. The nineteenth-century kenoticists argue that such surrender is a pre-condition to incarnation. It results in the proposition of *kenosis* by subtraction, i.e., the notion of God's self-deprivation.[138] Conversely, Barth views the *kenosis* to take place by addition; through the addition of the human nature.[139] Thus, in the *Göttingen Dogmatics*, he initially alludes to the idea of participation between the two natures (*genus tapeinoticum*), but in a provocative fashion. It is only to question if the nineteenth-century Lutherans were not more consistent than their seventeenth-century forebears in accepting the interpenetration of natures.[140] Barth discards such formulation wholesale because

133. *GD*, 429.

134. *GD* 17–20, 105.

135. *GD*, 439.

136. This idea is prominent in *CD* IV/1–2 where Barth centers his argument on Christ as the Lord (and Servant), contrasting it to the permeating "idolatrous confusions of God with other 'lords' and 'masters'" that happened during Nazi Germany and also, perhaps in the surging Communism. Olson, "Was Karl Barth a Universalist?" para. 23.

137. McCormack, "Karl Barth's Christology," 243–46.

138. McCormack, "Karl Barth's Christology," 246.

139. Remarkably, even in *CD* I/1 which was written in 1932–34, Barth's stance on God taking the human form is "something new in God." See page 316. This however is no longer tenable in *CD* IV/1 in Barth's historicization of God's self-condescension.

140. *GD*, 49. *Genus tapeinoticum* is the notion of a "two-way" sharing of the attributes between the *Logos* and Jesus of Nazareth, hence, the *Logos* shares the divine attributes with the human Jesus and at the same time latter shares the human attributes with the former. G. W. Bromley observes, "In the staunch Lutheran centre that was

he is conservatively Reformed at this period.[141] This kind of theological attitude furthers disinterest in (im)passibility.

Despite Barth's attempt to stress the significance of the Logos in reconceiving the election, it is, to a large extent, still deficiently christocentric.[142] This is so because the being of the Logos and Jesus Christ are treated separably in *kenosis*. The notion of immutability persists in such a way that blocks any suggestion of divine affliction in the self-emptying of Christ. Respectively, even the event of the incarnation, or Christ's death as the Redeemer, does not sway Barth to allow for a theopaschite theology.[143] We will investigate why such reluctance in Barth's theology remains, and crucially, where it originates.

It is also at Göttingen where Barth articulates dogmatically the distinction between *anhypostasis* and *enhypostasis*.[144] According to Bruce McCormack, Barth's initial take on *an-enhypostasia* is "a watershed" in his theological revolution.[145] This is crucial to his christological revision of election from 1924 to 1938.[146] On the one hand, Barth continues to gain a critical distance from the dogmatics of classical Protestantism.[147] On the other hand, his *an-enhypostatic* Christology takes another function. Barth no longer construes Christ's humanity in a fundamentally instrumental way—as the mere veil under which God is revealed. Instead the revisit of the *an-enhypostasia* prefigures a way to view the Logos to be indirectly identical with Jesus Christ.[148]

The *an-enhypostasia* is indeed invaluable in Barth's progressive Christology. He now had a language at his disposal to express his christological inclination without breaking away with the Reformed tradition.[149] In dealing

---

Göttingen, Barth could not escape the originality and vitality of the great first-generation reformer, Luther." "Preface," in Barth, *Calvin*, ix. We will discuss this in depth in chapter 3.

141. McCormack, "The Doctrine of the Trinity after Barth," 106. Nevertheless, Barth employs the *genus tapeinoticum* in *Church Dogmatics*, IV/1 in particular, to underscore the *kenosis* in historical context.

142. Barth exclaims, "We did not elect God . . . God elected us." *GD*, 450.

143. *GD*, 439.

144. Haley, *The Humanity of Christ*, 10.

145. McCormack, *Critically Realistically Dialectic Theology*, 366.

146. Jones, *The Humanity of Christ*, 25–26.

147. *GD*, 456.

148. Terry Cross concludes that in the *an-enhypostasia* model, "Barth found he could say the Subject of revelation is the *Logos* veiled in human flesh, while at the same time truly say the Subject was *in human history*." *Dialectic in Karl Barth's Doctrine of God*, 97. Sumner, *Karl Barth and the Incarnation*, 94.

149. Barth, *Revolutionary Theology in the Making*, 185. Barth's Christology has

with Christ's humanity, Barth keeps the notion of a one-person Christ. It means that Christ's humanity was not that of a human person (*hypostasis*) before the incarnation; the incarnation is not a uniting of a human-kind with the Son of God, but a union of the Logos and specifically of Jesus Christ.[150] In other words, the humanity of Christ had no independent *hypostasis* from the Logos. If there were a human person to whom the person of the Son of God was added, there would have been two persons in Jesus Christ. Necessarily, though Barth allows for the notion of addition in *kenosis*, he however holds that Christ's humanity has never existed independently from the Son of God.[151] Thus the Son of God is always the Son of Man.

Barth's revisitation of *an-enhypostasia* does not have significant part in his modification of the doctrine of election. Here God's "free activity" in the incarnation is fundamentally sustained; so the Reformed and Lutheran conceptions of God inform Barth's flourishing Christology.[152] The notion of *an-enhypostasia* simply does not force Barth to tackle the question of impassibility. He does not contest the Western orthodox account on impassibility (only Christ's humanity suffered, not the divinity) due to his agreement with "some of its presuppositions."[153] However, the discontinuity between divinity and humanity is logically revamped because of the two natures of Jesus Christ. The free activity of God does not discredit the relational God but rather builds it, especially as it relates to the church.[154]

I agree with McCormack's observation that the *an-enhypostasia* is a "watershed" in Barth's developing Christology. Yet Barth does not solidify the union of the two natures to make a statement, at least on immutability, if not on impassibility.[155] If Christ's divinity is the One self-same God as Christ's humanity is the One self-same human, it is fair to interject that the experience of Jesus Christ could also be referred to be that of God. This formulation could have impacted how the election displays God's eternal

---

always been largely sympathetic with Chalcedon as well (the Logos and the human Jesus are in one person in two natures). This is discussed in depth in chapter 3.

150. Nimmo, "Karl Barth and the *concursus Dei*," 61–63.

151. Hunsinger, "Election and the Trinity," 93–95.

152. Lindsay, "Pierre Maury, Karl Barth," 113.

153. Migliore, *Introduction to the Göttingen Dogmatics*, liii. Refer to *GD*, 408.

154. Barth, *The Great Promise*, 27–28.

155. Surprisingly, Barth already alludes to the importance of the Logos in speaking of the nature of God, beginning in 1925. According to McDowell, Barth says that the *Logos incarnandus* can be taken as "the form that the hominization of God's Self takes." This means that the Logos is essentially immutable in eternity because the Logos is always in himself as himself pre-temporally and in time. McDowell, "Afterword," in *Election, Barth*, 163. Barth, *Witness to the Word*, 21, 31.

self-giving in Jesus Christ. So the word "watershed" is strictly limited to Barth's Christology, not to his doctrine of election.

What is true of the Göttingen period is that Barth makes several substantive maneuvers in his doctrine of election with the following features: (1) The establishment of the doctrine of election within the doctrine of God. (2) The consideration of the twofold possibility of predestination in the context of God's veiling and unveiling. (3) The reinvigoration of Christology in the hopes of decoding the enigma behind the electing God and the election. Based on what has been laid out so far, Barth is closer to reinventing himself as an innovative theologian than being rigidly Reformed.[156] In addition, he has gone a long way from merely being largely Calvinistic to slowly finding his own voice in discussing predestination. It came mainly as a result of connecting the conception of God to election or vice-versa. Any trail of theopaschite theology however remains hardly recognizable. Even if there are traces of mysterious distress in God, i.e., *kenosis*, it is largely disclosed in the shroud of primacy and majesty.

Having discovered that there is barely any engagement with the doctrine of divine impassibility at Göttingen, we will now turn to investigate whether or not Barth eventually tackled this topic in his theo-logical awakening in Geneva.

3. 1936 Pierre Maury's Lecture in Geneva

After his professorship at Münster, Barth moved to Bonn, Germany, where he taught systematic theology from 1930 to 1935.[157] Unfortunately, Barth was deported from Germany in June 1935 after refusing to swear unqualified allegiance to Adolf Hitler and went back to Switzerland. He was appointed chair of systematic theology in his hometown in Basel at the University of Basel from 1935 up until his retirement in 1962.[158]

156. Barth puts it, "My conscience is clear that the dogmatics is Reformed in spite of my serious departure from the tradition and all its implications, . . . though naturally we cannot hide the fact that all doctrine, and not just the doctrine of predestination, takes on a different appearance as a result of the correction." *GD*, 456.

157. Zellweger, "Karl Barth," para. 5. It is in Bonn where Barth began to write the *Church Dogmatics*, the first half-volume of *CD* was published in 1932. Guretzki, *Explorer's Guide to Karl Barth*, 181.

158. In David Guretzki's account, Barth was one of the government employees who were required to swear allegiance to the *Führer* Hitler. He says that "Barth did not refuse to give an oath of loyalty but did ask that his oath be qualified in such a way that he would swear allegiance to the *Führer*" only within his commitment to Jesus Christ and to Scripture. Guretzki continues, "His [Barth's] proposal was presented to the appropriate officials but was turned down, after which his position as professor was suspended.

Because parts of the German Protestant Church attempted to align with the Third Reich in 1934 through the German Christian movement, Barth spearheaded the writing of the Barmen Declaration that same year.[159] This confession of faith rejects the pressure of the National Socialism (Nazism) on German Christianity by emphasizing that the church's allegiance should be to the Lord Jesus Christ alone. Any other lords, i.e., the *Führer* Adolf Hitler, ought to be resisted in matters of ecclesiastical polity and beliefs.[160] This mindset follows after the theme of *Romans* in which the revealed God in Jesus Christ overthrows any attempt to ally God with human government. Since the Nazi ideology contradicts the Christian gospel, Barth set himself against Nazism through the Barmen Declaration.[161] He did this by asserting the authority of the Word of God, hence, any other source of authority for the church is subservient. Jesus Christ is the Word, and only in and from him comes the message and governance of the church. This means that the state should not rule over the church, and also, the church is subordinate to the Word.[162]

The context above provides a critical picture to the way in which Barth approaches his task in knowing who is the God in and of the election. Barth's passion for a sovereign yet merciful God is undeniably intensified by the events in his life. The election of God, as opposed to the determination of any secular or religious power, might become Barth's source of comfort for what had been a very unsettling condition for him.[163] Thus it is solely in Jesus Christ where Barth seeks firm grounding for his unstoppable emerging theology.

He was tried before three judges, found guilty, sentenced, and eventually dismissed from his post, after which he was required to leave Germany." Guretzki, *Explorer's Guide to Karl Barth*, 34–35. Such taxing and shameful experience might have contributed to Barth's distaste of a *worldly* type of rulership which oftentimes brings misery.

159. Barth largely wrote the Barmen Declaration with the aid of two Lutheran theologians—Thomas Breit and Hans Asmussen. Barth personally mailed this document to Hitler which showed how bold Barth was at that time. This was one of the founding documents of the Confessing Church (spiritual resistance against state manipulation of religious affairs) where Barth was elected as a member of its eldership council, also known as the Brethren (*Bruderrat*). Galli, *Karl Barth*, 86.

160. Allen, *Karl Barth's Church Dogmatics*, 5–6.

161. Noticeably, this declaration does not mention (explicitly or implicitly) the opposition against anti-Semitism because there was no consensus within the Confessing Church about it. For many, the issue was restricted to the treatment of Jewish Christians. For another view on this matter; cf. Barnett, *For the Soul of the People*, 55.

162. *Book of Confessions*, 357–58.

163. Dolamo, "Karl Barth's contribution to the German Church struggle against National Socialism," 239–40.

At the dawn of the 1930s, in formulating a truly christocentric doctrine of election, the Subject (God) is no longer ambiguous as the focus transitions to the birth, life, death, and resurrection of the Son.[164] The mystery of divine freedom to damn the reprobate is somewhat resolved since the notion of the twofold possibility is creatively redefined in election. In turn, the Subject is Jesus Christ, the second person of the Godhead; Jesus Christ is also the Object of election. He is the Representative of humanity as both the *Elect* and the *Reprobate.* On both counts, Jesus Christ is determinative of being human.[165] It is in this context that God's determination, in view of relative sovereignty, is understood to take effect. Barth's near-mature doctrine of election gradually allows engagement with impassibility. Here, the living God lives in *intimate relationship* with humankind.

Another valuable facet of this near-mature doctrine of election is the sufficiency of divine grace. Grace is fully expressed in election, not just in theory, but also in praxis as accounted in *human history.*[166] Hence for Barth, the incarnation, crucifixion and glorification of Jesus Christ are integral in comprehending the decree. And while the twofold possibility is no longer viable in Barth's thought at this stage, he nonetheless innovatively retains the duality of predestination by making Jesus Christ the Object of election as well. All humanity is *elected* because Jesus Christ had taken the condemnation of humans by being the *Reprobate* on their behalf. Here the living God self-gives to demonstrate his relationship with humankind. God, in this relationship, is the One who is condemned in eternity in order for humanity to have eternal life.[167] The unveiled-yet-veiled God is hidden as the Subject but revealed as the Object. The onto-soteriological impact of such formulation is a breakthrough in conceiving the God of the decree. Thus Jesus Christ is the self-same God in and of the election. This thought is derived from Barth's encounter with Pierre Maury, one of the renowned Reformed theologians in the 1930s.[168]

164. See Althoff, "Freedom and Love in the Thought of Karl Barth."

165. Nolan, *Reformed Virtue after Barth*, 38.

166. Jenson, *Alpha and Omega*, 148–54.

167. Barth's treatment of election is a powerful means of hope for the entire humanity, and, could be, especially for the Jews under the cruelty of Nazis. Gorringe, *Karl Barth: Against Hegemony*, 148.

168. In the foreword by Suzanne McDonald, *Election, Barth, and the French Connection*, xi.

3.1 Reconsidering Jesus Christ in Election

In the summer of 1936, Barth attended the Calvinist Congress in Geneva, Switzerland.[169] There, he was inspired by Pierre Maury's unconventional lecture on "Election and Faith" in which a greater christological emphasis on election was made as never done before.[170] The profound impact of Maury's lecture on Barth's thinking is crucial in informing his later Christology. In Barth's foreword to Maury's *Predestination and Other Papers*, he described Maury's lecture as, "one of the best contributions made towards the understanding of the problem. . . . [It] was he who contributed decisively to giving my thoughts on this point their fundamental direction."[171] Barth followed Maury's theological direction in making Jesus Christ both the Subject and the Object of election.[172]

Barth, commenting on the significance of Maury's 1936 lecture, says this surely made him rethink his Christology which led to his theological revision of election.[173] Maury's lecture itself precedes the publication of *CD* I/2 by two years, and so it is certain that it took Barth some time to work out the full impact of christocentric election on his larger project.[174] In the autumn of 1936, Barth gives consecutive lectures in Debrecen, Hungary expounding on "God's Gracious Election."[175] These provide the basic framework for his full-scale treatment of election in *Church Dogmatics*; however, his thoughts on the subject in 1936 are still in progress.[176] It is not until *CD* II/2, some time between the autumn of 1939 and the summer of 1941 that Barth has a breakthrough articulation on election. In this, he concludes

169. Note that Barth "in all likelihood" missed Maury's delivery of the lecture itself and Barth merely read the manuscript. See Barth, *Pierre Maury: Nous qui pouvons encore parler . . .*, 94.

170. This lecture is published also in 1936 in the review *Foi et Vie* and translated in German in 1940 in the *Theologische Studien*. Maury, *Election, Barth, and the French Connection*, 28.

171. Maury, *Predestination and Other Papers*, 16. See also *CD* II/2, 167.

172. Lindsay, *Barth, Israel, and Jesus*, 90.

173. Maury, *Predestination and Other Papers*, 15–16.

174. Sumner, *Karl Barth and the Incarnation*, 88.

175. Smythe, *Forensic Apocalyptic Theology*, 16.

176. McMaken and Congdon, *Karl Barth in Conversation*, 203. Matthias Gockel has shown that in the Debrecen lectures it was the "eternal God and thus also the eternal Son of God [who] is the *electing* God" for Barth, and likewise for Maury. See *Barth and Schleiermacher*, 161. Charlotte von Kirschbaum, who Barth met at Göttingen, assisted him in writing the *Church Dogmatics*.

without reservation that Jesus Christ is indeed the Subject and Object in and of the decree.[177]

In fact, Barth claims that Jesus Christ truly represents God and humanity by simultaneously being the electing God and the elected Man. This advanced notion makes this doctrine truly an election of grace; God is self-determined to represent humanity as the Elect and the Reprobate. The freedom in grace is relocated at the forefront of this doctrine through the divine outworking of Christ.[178] It shows how Barth's God is more determinative in self-giving. God, in this context, self-gives without restraint while upholding the God-self. Thus the transcendent-yet-relational deity is maintained but with more emphasis on the divine substitutional act. This also starts signalling the constitutive element of such an act in speaking of the God behind the decree. As a result, the Logos is taken consistently with Jesus Christ.

The renewed emphasis here critically affects Barth's revised understanding of the role of Jesus Christ in election. From that time on, Barth began to critique the classic doctrines of predestination as not being adequately and fundamentally christocentric.[179] Again, this can be better construed in his early thoughts on the Logos and how it develops in light of God's ontology. Employing the *an-/en-hypostatic* formulation, Barth asserts something of God's inner life, insofar as he affirms that Jesus Christ has no independent existence apart from the *union* with the Logos. Not only does this speak to the identity of Jesus Christ, but it also argues for a very particular character of the eternal Word of God who is bound to *this* Man.[180] This can be seen as a substantial evolution to Barth's Christology in which previously, the emphasis is on the distinction between the two.

Barth further modifies his doctrine of election by reinterpreting the nexus between God's being and election. God's sympathetic autonomy is now articulated rigidly. It is not only central to unlock the mystery in and of God, but more importantly, foundational in discussing the state and future of humankind.[181] In this case, the primacy of the Logos is determined to be in solidarity with human beings. Jesus Christ signifies how serious God is in reuniting with humanity. Thus, the person of Jesus Christ is critical for Barth in knowing the identity of the electing God. Here the Electing God is always

177. *CD* II/2, 164.

178. *CD* I/2, 2–3.

179. Busch, *Karl Barth*, 278.

180. *CD* I/2, 163. F. L. Shults claims that Barth misreads the Patristic formulation of *anhypostasis* and *enhypostasis*. See "Dubious Christological Formula," 433, 445.

181. *CD* I/2, 849.

seen in the Elected Man, hence election itself can never be articulated apart from the election of Jesus Christ. This formulation is indispensable as Barth recalibrates his theological trajectory to be truly christocentric.

The impact of Jesus Christ's soteriological identity on election shows the full thrust of Barth's developing theology. Maury's proposal that there is no knowledge of the electing God (and election itself) apart from the true knowledge of Jesus Christ is groundbreaking for Barth. But he goes beyond Maury by making Christology "speak directly and controversially, to the eternal being of God himself" in light of election.[182] In other words, election and rejection are being "fully realized in Christ" and not elsewhere.[183] Barth's thought proves beneficial in developing a theopaschite theology. Jesus Christ being both the Subject and Object of election marks the beginning of an allowance for the actual-yet-mysterious suffering of God. Christ being the Representative surely speaks of a self-giving God; a God who is not potentially, but deterministically takes to himself what is human's. Barth explicates:

> We understand it now as the freedom and sovereignty of the divine work and action consummated in God's revealed Word, as the way which God has *taken, takes and will take* with man in the person of Jesus Christ.[184]

Barth's inclination to speak of God in terms of being in full solidarity with humanity becomes stronger. The self-determination of God in Jesus Christ shows how Barth has progressed in his Christology. With Maury's aid, Barth finally finds his own voice in discussing the doubleness of predestination.[185] Certainly, a reinvigorated Christology constructs a way beyond the impasse of Calvin's notion of a twofold possibility. Barth, in this respect, links the gap

182. Lindsay, "Pierre Maury, Karl Barth," 113.

183. Barth here picks up the theology of Athanasius concerning the election rather than following the footsteps of Augustine and Thomas Aquinas. Athanasius accords the representative aspect of election to Christ's divine *and* human natures whereas Augustine and Thomas accord such representation to Christ's human nature only. Barth explains that in Athanasius's mind, the eternal, complete and active being of Jesus Christ is foundational in the proper treatment of the decree itself. Barth expresses his dismay that the Reformers "ignored altogether" the Athanasian view of election by giving their full attention to the teachings of Augustine and Thomas on election. *CD* II/2, 106–11.

184. *CD* I/2, 856–57. Italics mine.

185. The result, however, accurately speaking, is mutual. John McDowell notes, " . . . the influence of Barth on the Parisian pastor [Maury] should equally not be underestimated, and this suggests that what Barth may have taken from Maury has been a particular sharpening of his own theological trajectory." "Afterword," in *Election, Barth,* 158. For an alternative insight on this topic; cf. McCormack, *Orthodox and Modern,* 263.

between the final decisions in the decree, and, who makes the decision in the first place. The *kerygma* is now concentrated on Jesus Christ—the God of election. Hence, the election is no longer a source of discomfort but of hope. In spite of Barth's preservation of the "Yes" and "No" in predestination, the latter is emphasized under the former. Also in this schema, the Son's humiliation in the incarnation is given more weight. Jesus Christ can be taken to be truly and undoubtedly the Representative of *all*.[186] Thus Jesus Christ does not only represent humanity, but crucially, it is in him and through him whereby the essence of the God of election is constituted.[187]

Formulating God's being in view of God's act is taking a firm hold on Barth's theological structure. Although Barth's voice at this juncture is controversial, it is so only in terms of its force in speaking of election beyond the tradition. The notion of God's Yes over the No is oftentimes perceived as problematic. It is not controversial insofar as the essential nature of God is concerned. The insistence on *who should God be*, instead of discovering *who God is*, likely dismisses the gracious and compassionate God in and of election. For Barth, seeing God unreservedly in Jesus Christ is the way forward in understanding the election. In effect, immutability and impassibility are slightly placed under re-examination.

For this reason, I subscribe to the idea that even if Barth builds his argument on the shoulder of Maury, he nonetheless exceeds Maury by fortifying the actualization of the divine act.[188] Barth nourishes his christological view of election by arguing that Jesus Christ's substitutionary act is totally rooted in the decree. In many regards, Barth has the necessary component to articulate an actualized election that is systematically theopaschite. Here, Calvary plays an important part:

> That which happened on Calvary for us and upon us and became manifest on the Easter Day is our eternal election, although it

186. Stephen Williams criticizes Barth's rigid christological interpretation of election by saying, "[T]o think theologically in Christ and to think Christ in all our theology, is substantively determined by a material Christology which, I believe, is unbiblical and has no legitimate purchase on theology so long as that material Christology includes the belief that all are elect in Christ." Williams, *The Election of Grace*, 197.

187. The use of the term "constituted" in speaking of the essence of God means that God determines himself to be what God is, i.e., for the benefit of humanity. Although this particular term is usually associated with Bruce McCormack's reading of Barth's view on God's ontology, I do not suggest that God's decision brings about God's being (the former pre-exists the latter), but rather I argue that God's being *coincides* with God's decision. In other words, God is eternally in himself in God's being-in-self-determination. See Paul Molnar's discussion on this issue in "Can the Electing God be God Without Us?" 199–222.

188. Lindsay, "Pierre Maury, Karl Barth," 113.

> happened in time. And God's decision, as it has been made once and for all in Jesus Christ, is our life's predestination.[189]

The mystery which envelops the electing God and the election itself is also given light at this juncture. The God who elects, and, the receiving end of election are no longer left hanging simply because both find their fulfillment in Jesus Christ. The inevitable questions of *who is elected* and its flip side *who is rejected* are answered in Christ. Christ being the real and actual Representative, in Barth's view, is a strong case to put forward a suffering God without minimizing the indescribability of such suffering.

When Barth connects Calvary with election, it signals openness to the discussion on impassibility. The ontological ramification of the text is substantial in understanding how Christology shapes his dogmatics. The themes of sovereignty, determination and representation are employed christocentrically. Now, Barth situates the being of God more closely with Jesus Christ's being.[190] Predestination is no longer inimical to the discussion of divine suffering because the subject-object motif in election fits properly with the transcendent-yet-relational deity.

3.2 The Suffering of the Electing God

From underpinning God's freedom rooted in mercy and solidarity, Barth advances his argument on God's self-determination in the Son.[191] The decree is no longer unknown on the basis of its knowability derived from the divine act in Jesus Christ. Barth rivets his christological presuppositions by positing that election is not only determinative of what God does, but also constitutive of who God is. God is in what God does; and what God does is demonstrated in Jesus Christ. In other words, what has been eternally decreed can never be known apart from what has been shown in Jesus Christ. Thus the decree does not only point to God's foreordination but to God's essentiality too. Respectively, the being of the electing God can never be divorced from divine suffering. Since Barth highlights Calvary as central in election, therefore, crucifixion has eternal implications too. Calvary can speak of who God *is* in revelation, as well as before it.

Divine self-revelation is revolutionized by reconsidering the God before creation. In this way, the revealed God is not confined to Jesus Christ

189. Barth, *Gottes Gnadenwahl*, 46.

190. This seems to be the product of Kierkegaard's "Truth in the form of personal being" locating the Incarnation at the forefront of God's objectivity countering the illusion of finding the truth within humanity. Torrance, *Karl Barth*, 45.

191. *CD* I/2, 873, 875.

but it also includes the Logos. The inseparability between the Logos and Jesus Christ denotes what the electing God wills for humankind. It is in this willing that Calvary finds its meaning because Christ's substitution is an actual act which arises from an eternal act. So the Revealed speaks of the Revealer; and the Revealer does not remain independent from the Revealed. Barth finds that the suffering at Calvary tells about the ontology of God. There is no longer an Electing God shadowed by the Elected Man. In fact, the latter brings into view the former.

Inasmuch as the being of the electing God is taking a reconception in terms of the divine substitutionary act, Barth still, at least at this stage, appears quite hesitant to engage with impassibility. Even if he has the tool to formulate a theopaschite theology, he does not venture on it, perhaps because suffering itself is largely linked to Christ's humanity alone. Barth however ventures on the intersection between divine and creaturely realities. Yet in this intersection, the notion of the God-self is not lost, rather reinforced. The self-giving God is still the self-determined God.

God's self-determination for and with humanity is primary at this junction.[192] Barth is now ready to formulate a more robust Christology that can support (without being limited to soteriological concerns) the abiding union of the Logos and Jesus Christ; and also, the link between God's history and human history. Here the question on how an atemporal God can interact with a temporal creation is dealt with. The conception of time and eternity, in Barth's view, is now informed by the incarnation.[193] As a result, the decree and its execution in Jesus Christ are progressively understood to be a juxtaposed event, hinting at a systematized actualistic election. In order to better appreciate it, we have to examine how Barth has progressed in his conception of time *in* eternity in speaking of God's actuality. It is also here where God can be seen, to a limited degree, sovereignly suffer.

After leaving Göttingen, Barth views eternity and time in the sphere of "contemporaneity."[194] It means that any happening in time is the fulfillment of what God has predetermined.[195] Though Barth places human history in a formal category, distinguishing it from God's history, yet he articulates

192. Hector, "God's Triunity and Self Determination," 246–61.

193. *CD* I/2, 881, 883; II/1, 21–22.

194. Creaturely time is not yet infused in God's eternal time. See *GD* 17–18. Barth finds it difficult to break from German idealism which promotes an eternal antecedent "reality" over against temporal subsequent "realities." However, his renewed treatment of the relationship between eternity and time is far from his former dialectic view of the "eternal Now" during the *Romans* period. Roberts, "Karl Barth's Doctrine of Time: its Nature and Implications," in *A Theology on Its Way?* 17–20.

195. Wu, *The Concept of History*, 9.

eternity and time inseparably. This makes the divine revelation and human history knitted together but having the latter contingent upon the former.[196] God's history superimposes human history in the being of Jesus Christ. It is in this framework where Barth puts forward God's independence even in subjecting himself in time.[197] The appropriation of the dual histories works positively in formulating an actualistic election, but precludes any allowance for the actuality of divine suffering.[198] It is due to Barth's view of the "eternalization" of revelation which results in the superimposition of the divine-eternal over the human-historical.[199]

The dominion of what is eternal over the temporal makes time part of creation according to Barth.[200] So the actuality of divine suffering is somehow confined to the life of Jesus Christ, not to the inner life of the Godhead. Even if Christology is considered in conjunction with the doctrine of the Trinity, the notion of suffering is still relative to Jesus Christ only. The role of the Logos in understanding divine suffering is yet to be unpacked here. Barth's focus is on Jesus Christ in making a statement about the sacrificial act in substitution. It is due to the proximity of Jesus Christ to time rather than before time. Though he (by anticipation in the decree) precedes creation, the flesh however, is irrefutably part of creation.

Clearly God creates time, says Barth, albeit God treats it in relation to eternity since he works in time.[201] Such a dynamic perception of time is made positive because of Christ's being. Even if Barth sees God as distinct from creation, with the aid of time, he can speak of God as truly in solidarity with humans. This assertion begins with the revisit of the *an-enhypostasia* in the *Göttingen Dogmatics* wherein eternity and time are reconstructed.[202] Jesus Christ being fully God and fully human in one person points to Barth's emphasis on time in revealing who God is and what God wills in eternity.[203] But in the activity within creation, God remains the Creator; One who is immutable in the outworking of the decree.[204]

196. Wu, *The Concept of History*, 45.

197. McGrath, *The Making of Modern German Christology*, 110.

198. Higton, *Christ, Providence, and History*, 43.

199. Ogletree, *Christian Faith and History*, 227.

200. Barth, *The Word of God*, 277. *CD* I/1, 539, 544.

201. *CD* I/2, 47. For Barth, time is constituted by God's eternity, a concept that is distinct from Hegel's supposition that God's eternity is realized in time. Griswold, *Triune Eternality*, 248–49.

202. McCormack, *Barth's Critically Realistic Dialectical Theology*, 328.

203. McCormack, *Barth's Critically Realistic Dialectical Theology*, 328.

204. *CD* I/2, 50.

Barth does not linger on any notion of impassibility even in divine outworking in time. Rather, he is attentive to the contemporaneity of eternity in time as he reconfigures his Christology. For Barth, Jesus Christ, the eternal Revealer, is also the temporal Receiver because he is the source and order of time. Jesus Christ is said to be the link between eternity and time as the "one divine act of repprochement."[205] Moreover, Barth views the incarnation as the turning of God's time with what is created.[206] Even if God is not subjugated by time (God remains transfinite within creation), he nonetheless chooses to be subjected to time.[207] But when God is in time, God remains atemporal.

3.3 Excursus on Eternity and Time

Barth sees the relation of time and eternity in God's interaction with creation, so such interaction is understood as a divine event. The divine event, in Barth's formulation, is the outworking of God's freedom for humanity:

> But this different time is the new, third time, which arises and has its place because God reveals Himself, because He is free for us . . . without ceasing to be what He is, He also becomes what we are. God's revelation is the event of Jesus Christ.[208]

God's time with human beings signifies a determination *pro nobis*. It is in divine proximity to time, "the third time" where the event in Jesus Christ finds its meaning.[209] This event is the point of ontological contact between divine reality and creaturely reality where the two are said to be occurring concurrently.[210] Eternity and time is but a continuous duration in Barth, so time is also conceived to demonstrate the being of God. It is a functional being since "God's time *in* our time" is duration for and with humans.[211] Because Jesus Christ indeed intercedes for humanity in the eternal self-determination, the divine existence and the creaturely existence are also conceived in a continuous duration.[212]

205. Cassidy, *Karl Barth on Time, Eternity, and Jesus Christ*, 4.
206. Qu, *Concrete Time and Concrete Eternity*, 134.
207. *CD* I/2, 45.
208. *CD* I/2, 49.
209. *CD* I/2, 52.
210. Busch, *The Great Passion*, 81, 265.
211. *CD* I/2, 49.
212. Kojiro, "God's Eternal Election in the Theology of Karl Barth," 67.

Barth's notion of the third time is an ingenious expression to uphold God's sovereignty over creation, but, in the flesh. In the event in Christ, God is not lost in time; what is lost in time is the notion of an ambiguous and capricious deity. God, who creates time, dominates it under eternity by making time engulfed in the being of Christ. In Christ therefore, humanity not only make sense of eternity, but also, find solace in time. God makes time for humanity and such time corresponds to the predestined time of the Subject and Object of election.

In being so, God has not become inimical to his eternality. According to Barth, God remains atemporal in interacting with the world. This formulation becomes more pronounced in the subsequent volumes of *Church Dogmatics*. God in time remains atemporal because, Barth affirms, "God's eternity . . . is a quality of His freedom."[213] God exists in a "pure duration" even in time which is why he never stops being himself. Since God chooses to be in Jesus Christ, time itself becomes instrumental in demonstrating the contemporaneity of the eternal act. It is in divine freedom in duration, Barth postulates, Jesus Christ is said to have been a predominant being:

> Time is the form of creation in virtue of which it is definitely fitted to be a theatre for the acts of divine freedom. In order that in His outward relationships too God may be the eternal and may act as such, time is required as a determination of creation. If creation were eternal instead of temporal, God, as the Eternal, could not be eternal in the creation, i.e., He could be not be free, sovereign and majestic, nor could He act accordingly.[214]

In Barth's talk of divine activity, time can never be apart from eternity because God wills it to be. Time is a divine instrument to determine creation because God uses time (the third time) to manifest his action. Respectively, although time is created, it precedes the creation of the world in view of God's willingness to be known.[215] In this sense, time becomes the platform for the divine outworking. God not only creates time but crucially, he also determines time itself and "all its contents" in the execution of divine constancy.[216] For Barth, the contents of the third time are the contents of eternity since this time reveals what it is in eternity.[217] So time cannot be said to be anti-God simply because in it, God truly displays

213. *CD* II/1, 608.

214. *CD* II/1, 465.

215. *CD* II/1, 61–62.

216. *CD* II/1, 156.

217. *CD* II/1, 616.

his sovereignty. Sovereignty in this scenario is relative, i.e., sovereignty in terms of being coincident with creation.

Barth makes the connection between eternity and sovereignty in God's life. Eternity is the "simultaneous possession of life" in God's sovereign movement.[218] Thus eternity is not only conceived as the supreme life of God, but also, it is inseparable from God himself. God is eternity, hence God is called the eternal One.[219] Eternity becomes the quality of divine sovereignty.[220] That is why divine sovereignty is a pure duration in which the "beginning, succession and end" are conceived as one simultaneous event without "separation, distance or contradiction."[221] Any notion of divine self-determination is treated against God's eternality.

In a sense, eternity is not time, yet God's time is eternity.[222] Barth argues that time is distinguished from eternity insofar as pure duration is considered. In fact, eternity is not simply an "extension of time both backwards and forwards."[223] God's eternal time is what Barth refers to the third time to differentiate it from the created time and the fallen time.[224] The third time is God's time for human beings and it is in it where the eternal One is said to co-exist with creation.[225] Here divine existence is not only that which is atemporal but also, God in his sole decision, takes creaturely form in the flesh.[226] Jesus Christ reveals God as "supremely temporal" in using his liberty to be self-limited in time.[227]

Noticeably, such self-limitation is not something new to God because, as in the Göttingen period, Barth thinks that whatever divinely transpires in the temporal reflects what is eternal. In the contemporaneity of eternity and time, Jesus Christ is taken as constant with the eternal Logos. The Revealer and the Revealed is one and the same being in view of God's outworking. Ultimately, Barth's previous idea of the divine-eternal over the

218. *CD* II/1, 608.

219. Garr, *Christian Fruit—Jewish Root*, 364.

220. *CD* II/1, 608.

221. *CD* II/1, 608.

222. *CD* II/1, 608.

223. *CD* II/1, 608.

224. *CD* II/1, 613. This is Barth's three-dimensional view of time. The created time is the time when God creates and the fallen time is the time when Adam and Even fell into sin. Qu, *Concrete Time and Concrete Eternity*, 92. For critique of Barth's view of time, see Farrow, *Ascension and Ecclesia*, 291.

225. *CD* II/1, 608, 614.

226. *CD* III/1, 67. Barth's mature framework of time as it relates to eternity is presented in §47 of *CD*.

227. *CD* III/2, 437.

human-historical is reframed to an affirmative articulation. The being of the Son of God is simultaneously actual with that of Jesus Christ. God is no longer seen negatively in terms of his dealing with time. In Jesus Christ, God can be said to have determined himself to live with humanity. This, I think, is the real positive account of time. For Barth, God not only creates time to his advantage, but also, it is to God's disadvantage because it is in time in which God sovereignly offers himself. It showcases the divine revelation and human history as indivisible events in the form of Christ's substitution. An act which does not sacrifice the divine essentialities.

Here Jesus Christ is said to be the Lord of time because despite assuming flesh, he nonetheless remains the Lord.[228] The being of Christ is "supremely temporal" because the Almighty God wills to live in time.[229] Barth alludes to God's eternality in this terms:

> He [Jesus Christ] was the concrete demonstration of the God who has not only a different time from that of man, but whose will and resolve it is to give man a share in this time of His, in His eternity.[230]

God elects himself to be in time to make it part of the divine event. It is in this event where God unconditionally fellowships with humankind; a fellowship which is eternally set yet temporally occurred. Barth continues the theme of God sharing his time with humans by highlighting the meaning of "God with us."[231] Barth asserts:

> [A]s indicated by the biblical concept of eternity—God is historical even in Himself, and much more so in His relationship to the reality which is distinct from Himself.[232]

We have an indication here of God willing to be in a "relationship" with that which has a different reality. This notion is a far-cry from the incompatible realities of the eternal and the temporal in the *Göttingen Dogmatics*. What is incompatible has now become compatible in the being of Jesus Christ. Such formulation is given weight in Barth's dialectic articulation:

> The eternity which He [God] Himself is true time and the Creator of all time is revealed in the fact that, although our time is that of sin and death, He can enter it and Himself be temporal

228. *CD* III/2, 440.

229. *CD* III/2, 437.

230. *CD* III/2, 450–51.

231. *CD* IV/1, 8.

232. *CD* IV/1, 112.

> in it, yet without ceasing to be eternal, able rather to be the Eternal in time.[233]

For Barth, God is not only the source of time but has become time. In becoming time, God is still eternal because even in subjecting himself to creaturely reality, God's divine reality remains. This is concretely demonstrated in the reality of Jesus Christ. God being time, Barth clarifies, is a temporal being without detriment to God's eternality. This is the epitome of what Barth calls the "supra-temporal" (*überzeitlich*) where God is said to be self-consistent in self-revelation.[234] In conceiving the tight connection between eternity and time, Barth is able to speak of a truly consistent God of election. Nevertheless, Barth's treatment of the relationship between eternity and time is not at all consistent in *Church Dogmatics*; an observation which differs from James Cassidy's position on this matter. According to Cassidy, Barth has a "consistent and coherent" treatment of eternity and time throughout *CD*.[235] Although I agree with Cassidy that eternity and time relation is a concurring theme in *CD*, yet there are substantial nuances that need to be considered in each volume.

In *CD* I, Barth's focus is on the doctrine of revelation. Here he redefines eternity in a dynamic perspective wherein eternity is described in a contemporaneity *and* non-contemporaneity with time. So in order to advance his Christology within such description, Barth conceptualizes the notion of the third time—God's time for human beings in his self-revelation. In other words, what Barth endeavors to convey is that despite the gap between God and humanity, the fact is: "God's time for us" (*Gottes Zeit für uns*) and God shows himself to be so through what Barth calls the revelation time (*Offenbarungszeit*).[236] In this respect, Barth allows eternity and time to interfaced with each other in God's self-revelation.

In *CD* II, Barth's attention is on the doctrine of God. We can see here the progress of Barth's notion of a dynamic eternity wherein eternity is viewed to be in *contingent* contemporaneity with time. In the election of Jesus Christ, God is said to have determined time to consummate the eternal decree. In this regard, Barth "fills out the content of pre-temporality" which informs the following volumes of *CD*.[237] This step is necessary in

233. *CD* IV/1, 187–88. Prior to this text, Barth also argues that despite God being "absolute, infinite, exalted, active, impassible," God is not "His own prisoner." *CD* IV/1, 187.

234. *CD* II/1, 621. *KD* II/1, 702.

235. Cassidy, *Karl Barth on Time*, 1.

236. *CD* I/2, 45. *KD* I/2, 50.

237. Langdon, *God the Eternal Contemporary*, 76.

order to articulate the constancy of God in being above time and also in time. Moreover, this strengthens the omnipotence of God in and of election whereby the eternal God is in the Now of human time.[238]

In *CD* III, Barth concentrates on the doctrine of creation. The main point here is God being the Creator and Source of time. Time therefore is dependent on eternity because time is only a creation of the eternal God. In spite of Barth's continuance of the theme of election, the accent is on the Creator becoming a creature. However, in voluntarily subjecting himself to creaturely time, God remains the source of time. It is in this backdrop where Barth presents a series of encounters between the Creator and creatures, and it is where Jesus Christ is said to be truly the Lord of time.

In *CD* IV, Barth intends to expound his doctrine of reconciliation. The contingent contemporaneity between eternity and time is reinvigorated by the historicization of the divine being in the being of Jesus Christ. Here God's time not only determines creaturely time, but also, God is truly conceived to be time himself without any association to the Hegelian conception of history. Barth intensifies his argument that God is said to be absolutely free in time by being time. Barth does this by arguing that God shares his time with humans by having them reconciled with God. The third time is concretely evidenced in the incarnation because the created time is infused in God's time. It is so because, in Barth's mind, creaturely time is incapable of containing God's being or act because whatever is created can never fully contain what is not created.[239] Furthermore, the idea of the eternal God repeating himself in the temporal realm is accentuated. Thus for Barth, Jesus Christ is indeed the reference of the dialectical yet actualistic relation between eternity and time.[240]

In other words, when he left Göttingen, Barth, strictly speaking, had slight variations in rendering the relationship between eternity and time from 1932 to 1967. The difference is with the notion of contemporaneity. Barth, in the infancy of his thought in *Church Dogmatics* shows the remnants of the *Göttingen Dogmatics's* idea of the irreconcilable antithesis of eternity and time. For this reason, Barth formulates the contemporaneity-non-contemporaneity of the two. But in reconceiving the doctrine of election, Barth puts forward the contingent contemporaneity of eternity and time, thus silencing (not eliminating) the aspect of non-contemporaneity. Concomitantly, the relationship of eternity and time is positively articulated especially in *CD* III and *CD*

238. Pokrifka, *Redescribing God*, 273.

239. *CD* III/1, 5–11. For Barth, the incapability of creaturely time is in the sense of it being *created*, hence distinct from God, and not of it being the "fallen time," i.e., being marred by sin. See Cassidy, *Karl Barth on Time*, 4.

240. Cassidy, *Karl Barth*, 2–3.

IV. It is also important to note that Barth's progressive thought exhibits traces of Platonic conception on this matter which stresses the dominion of eternal reality over the temporal reality.[241]

The supremacy of the eternal over the temporal does not undermine Barth's wish to present a self-giving God of election. The actuality of *sovereign* suffering is seen as God's exercise of unrestricted sacrificial act in time, hence the terms contingent contemporaneity and supra-temporality. These terms are elegantly and effectively accommodated in the notion of the third time in order to sustain a constant God even in assuming flesh. In this way, Barth has overcome the antithesis between the transcendent God and the immanent God.

3.4 The Elected Time of Suffering

The elected time is where the Godhead is properly understood in relation to its actualization in and of time. In being supremely temporal, the Godhead determines its continuous duration (also known as pure duration) with creation. The traditional tension is resolved in collating God to time by looking at the eternal time through Barth's doctrine of the Trinity.[242] As a result, God's history encapsulates past, present and future.[243] The recasting of the divine activity with the eternal time strengthens Barth's proposal of a constant God in temporality.[244] We can interject that whatever God is in time *is* the same God of eternity. If this is true in Barth, the divine ontology is made meaningful in Jesus Christ. This formulation is the foundation to relating the experience of Jesus Christ with that of the Logos. It becomes corollary to the discussion on the sovereign suffering of God. Thus Barth's reconstruction of eternity and time leads to a theopaschite-inclined conception of election.

As regards God's self-revelation in election, Barth is convinced that God's self-giving nature is eternally consistent. One might ask if this consistency, at least in Barth's works, could be regarded as parroting the canonical concept of immutability. Based on my investigation, the answer is more likely in the negative. God indeed *does not change* in himself since Barth advocates divine aseity. Evidently, however, when Barth sees God to have been unchanged in God's self, this notion should be taken in view of his rethinking of election. God is constant in himself as it pertains to God being

241. Roberts, *A Theology on Its Way?: Essays on Karl Barth*, 17.

242. Langdon, *God the Eternal Contemporary*, 21.

243. Langdon, *God the Eternal Contemporary*, 24.

244. Jenson, *God after God*, 69.

consistent with the decree. It is in this sense that we can understand what Barth means by God being above human conditioning, i.e., immutability, impassibility, simplicity, etc. Similarly, whenever such ascriptions of God are applied, Barth more often than not use them in his own terms as he sees fit in the grand scheme of his take on predestination. For example, God is supremely temporal in an atemporal duration due to God's capacity to self-change (in self-giving) in view of the decree.

For Barth, there is no ontological change in God in time because God has self-determined who he would be from incarnation to crucifixion.[245] Barth cannot speak of election apart from Jesus Christ's self-deprivation as the Lord. Divine self-sacrifice does not counter the tradition, whether Patristic or Reformed; the immutability of God's decree itself speaks powerfully of the God who makes the decree. In other words, God is conceived to be immutable in Jesus Christ. This is possible because in eternity God has already chosen to be in Christ, notwithstanding the *kenosis* involved. Even if God is said to have been incomparably afflicted, this affliction is fully and in all respects voluntarily actualized in divine reality.

The divine reality therefore informs what actualization means for Barth. Even in such reinvigorated Christology, Jesus Christ remains the source and identity of creaturely reality; not otherwise. Barth's refusal to separate the Logos from Jesus Christ, and likewise, Christ from the Trinity, results in a reconsideration of God's essential nature. What is the upshot of this reconsideration? The consideration of *an-enhypostasia* could have led Barth to reappraise his view on impassibility.[246] Yet he is equivocal about Jesus Christ being the reality of God, perhaps because such conception is disassociated with the infinitely qualitative being of God.[247] What is clear at this point is that Barth is poised to re-investigate this matter, with consideration of course, to divine essentialities. But he does not necessarily agree in full with the tradition in order to sustain the theological momentum in modifying the election.

245. McCormack, "Grace and Being," 98–99. This is an expression of his "actualism."

246. Chung, "A Bold Innovator: Barth on God and Election," in *Karl Barth and Evangelical Theology*, 71.

247. Barth, "Paradoxical Nature of the "Positive Paradox": Answers and Questions to Paul Tillich," in *The Beginnings of Dialectic Theology*, ed. J. M. Robinson, 152. McCormack even says that Barth, in this period, is never tempted to venture on "a strict identification of the second person of the Trinity with the human Jesus." McCormack, "The Doctrine of the Trinity," 91–92.

Evaluation

After considering the evolution of Barth's doctrine of election in 1922 to 1936, it is fitting to assess its relevance for our second concern, namely, the issue of impassibility. Based on my investigation, Barth, at least in the early 1920s, stands within the Protestant orthodoxy on impassibility. But when Barth's christological development of the doctrine of election was at its full swing, his understanding of election took an alternate course. The implications as such on impassibility can be appreciated in view of his restructured doctrine of God. Here, the revisit of the Logos in election allows Barth to review his take on immutability.

Accordingly, the Logos is no longer seen as strictly transcendent since it is consistently seen in relation to Jesus Christ. As a result, the *Logos incarnandus* becomes a springboard in which God is conceived to have been always with humanity. In this way, the election begins to be robustly christocentric. It is the outcome of the given political, social and theological events in the early to mid-twentieth century that have shaped Barth's mind.

Also, the self-giving of the electing God starts to be developed. Barth's argumentation moves in the direction that is indeed relationship based. God gives himself to establish a relationship with humankind. In addition, God's substitutionary sacrifice demonstrates divine determination in this relationship. The transcendent-yet-relational deity of election is argued with richness and intensity within God's mediation in the third time.

What is further enhanced is the compassionate God behind the election. Since election becomes interconnected with the doctrine of God, it becomes more actualistic, and, less speculative. It is actualistic as a concrete *event in time*, not a stand-alone reality in pre-temporal eternity. It is less speculative since the emphasis veers from theocentricity to christocentricity. It is christocentric in the sense that the attention shifts from the seemingly detached God to the real-person in real-time Jesus Christ. Christ's entry in time is therefore pivotal in Barth's near-mature thought on election.

Barth's qualitative differentiation between eternity and time paves the way for a dualistic ontology between God and humanity. In effect, God's revelation in Jesus Christ is viewed dialectically in terms of the divine outworking. I also observe that Barth is not only dialectic but also analogic in appropriating Christ's history as the *actual portrayal* of the eternal God. Both methods are employed to emphasize God's direction to creation.[248] Such self-determination is conceived in detail in God's willful condescension in human history. This act, of course, hinges on God's free compassion. So the incarnation becomes fundamental to the understanding of God's self-disclosure in hiddenness in Jesus Christ.

248. Allen, *Karl Barth's Church Dogmatics*, 8.

Barth sees no ontological change in God even in Jesus Christ's suffering because the immutable decree reflects the immutable author of the decree. Sovereignty is accentuated in God's self-determination with and for humanity. The actuality of God's sovereign suffering is derived from the immutable mercy of God in eternity. It implies though that the impassible God of pre-temporality is the same impassible God of temporality. This, however, is not spelled out clearly from the lectures on Calvin up until the commentary on Maury's lectures in Geneva. Why? It is because Barth only attempts to actualize the election without historicizing the being of God; and also, he does not tackle the idea of impassibility because it is not an issue for him.

So does Barth have a doctrine of divine impassibility? My answer is obviously negative on the basis that it neither challenges nor aids his developing doctrine of election; and, it is true likewise to his reconfiguration of Christology. But if the question is, does Barth advocate impassibility? then my answer would be yes and no. Yes, on the basis wherein he strongly argues in favor of immutability, which has classically been the handmaid of impassibility. Therefore impassibility is viable in his progressive theology. No, on the basis that Barth's actualization of election inevitably implicates an actualization of God's being—a consequence of incorporating election into the heart of the doctrine of God. This dialectical reply reflects Barth's cycle of stressing either the "resistant" or the "relational" side of the Subject-Object of election. Even in the being of Jesus Christ, the Creator-creature diastasis is well maintained. To think otherwise would be hypothetical, simply because the material itself does not allow any other conclusion, but only allusion.

Furthermore, is Barth's view of impassibility influenced by his revision of Calvin's teaching of predestination? The answer is more likely negative as well simply because there is no solid evidence to prove Barth's deviation from the Western tradition. Therefore, there is neither a doctrine nor a substantial statement on (im)passibility in Barth's writings from 1922 to 1936 to warrant an affirmation, or, denial of the Reformed orthodox view on impassibility. In Barth's quest to find his own voice in reconceiving the election to be undeniably christocentric, his theology could never be the same again.[249] The christological concentration signals a sovereignly self-sacrificing God in and of the election. The same concentration could also potentially lead to surprising results in conceiving God in this way.[250]

249. Godsey, *Karl Barth*, 43–44.

250. Eberhard Jüngel writes, "What is systematic about [Barth's] theology is that it resolves to make progress precisely by constantly correcting, or else completely changing, its direction." Jüngel, *Karl Barth, A Theological Legacy*, 27.

Chapter II

Election and Divine (Im)passibility in Barth's Theology between 1938 and 1942

I HAVE ARGUED THAT it was only after 1936 that Karl Barth's formulation of the transcendent-yet-relational deity placed divine impassibility under re-examination. This is the result of situating the doctrine of election within the doctrine of God. I have also argued that, in Barth's theology, God orientates himself *ad extra*; God's act of election is out of supreme commitment to humankind. This act is central to the eternal decree, which indicates a God who wills to give himself without giving up God's essentialities.

In the *Church Dogmatics,* especially in volume II, Barth expounds upon the self-giving of God in Jesus Christ in considering impassibility.[1] I shall argue that the identity and purpose of Jesus Christ in election is key to the question of whether or not God is essentially impassible. In order to do so, the following have to be addressed: first, what prompts Barth to discuss impassibility, and to what extent does he engage with it?; second, what is specifically indicated in the decree which shows God's suffering?; and last, how does Barth's developing doctrine of election impact his treatment of divine suffering?

Two texts will be under consideration, namely, in *CD* II/1, 491–92 and in II/2, 163.[2] Here we will be able to examine what God truly wills by electing

1. This is made clear when Barth explains his schema in treating his doctrine of election as having primary importance in dogmatics in terms of making it integral to the doctrine of God and superior to the doctrines of creation, providence, sin and reconciliation. *CD* II/2, 77–84.

2. Chronologically speaking, the text in *CD* II/1 should come first, but I thought it appropriate to make it follow instead the text in *CD* II/2 to adopt Barth's schema, i.e., God is known in God's act. So the topic: The eternal will of God in the election of Jesus Christ will be tackled first before considering the topic: The constancy of God. See §§33.2.3 and 31.2 of *CD*.

Jesus Christ (in connection with suffering) which will help us to understand Barth's handling of impassibility against the reality of God.[3]

We will now investigate how Barth initially discusses impassibility in election.

1. Barth's Treatment of Impassibility

The first text begins with a direct engagement with impassibility.[4] Barth asserts:

> In giving Himself [God-self] to this act He *ordained the surrender* of something, i.e., of His own impassibility in face of the whole world which because it is not willed by Him can only be the world of evil.[5]

Barth renders his interpretation of impassibility in light of God's self-surrender. God in pre-temporality had given up his impassibility in effect of his foreordination.[6] This conception is a radical move from Barth's earlier objection to the idea of abdication of the divine omni-attributes in *kenosis*.[7] The accommodation of God's surrender of his impassibility is the product of Barth's progressive doctrine of election.

In *CD* II/1–2, the role of Jesus Christ is pronounced in speaking of God's foreordination. In the foreordination, the subject-object theme of election is foregrounded. God is the One who acts and God also is the One who is acted upon.[8] For Barth, it is in the person of Jesus Christ that the Electing God is said to be orientated to humanity; and likewise, it is in Christ that the Elected God's person is said to be one with humanity. It is God's will to do whatever it takes to be a God for human beings even it entails self-sacrifice.[9] We can see here not only a truly christocentric view of election, but more importantly, a truly pro-human God of election.

Another facet that needs clarification as regards foreordination is its relationship to creation. When Barth says that God relates himself to

3. In seeking the collapse of the Third Reich, Barth, in this period, stresses the reality of God in his decree that can never be impugned by anyone or anything. Gorringe, *Karl Barth: Against Hegemony*, 145

4. Barth cites Rom 8:30; 9:19.

5. *CD* II/2, 163. Italics mine.

6. *CD* II/2, 163. Johnson, *The Mystery of God*, 61.

7. Specifically in the Göttingen period.

8. *CD* II/2, 163–64.

9. *CD* II/2, 164.

creation, it is a self-determined act without any notion of contingency for God.[10] God wills to act in this way, and, he acts as such without coercion. However, God's acting happens in a place where he does not will to be so. In other words, though God willed to be acted upon, he does not will the location where it takes place. Whatever God wills, is of God; and whatever is not willed by God, is of evil.[11] That is why Barth calls the location where God is acted upon as the "world of evil."

Even in the world, the subject-object theme pervades Barth's view of election. God being the Subject gives direction to the world, whereas God being the Object gives something of himself in the world. Apparently, the notion of divine self-giving is strengthened in this scenario. Barth goes deeper into the divine self-giving by describing it in terms of surrender. God's act of surrender (*aufgegeben*) is set before creation.[12] Impassibility is of God but which he had given up by being acted upon. This conception is the corpus of Barth's re-examination of impassibility. But what precisely prompts the allowance of the notion of self-surrender concerning impassibility? We will investigate such radical step by considering the continuation of the above text:

> In Himself God cannot *be affected* either by the possibility or by the reality of that will which opposes Him. He cannot be affected by any potentiality of evil. In Him is light and no darkness at all.[13]

There are three outstanding observations in this passage crucial to Barth's conception of impassibility. First, God's impassibility is God not being affected *ad extra*. Second, God *in se* is not affected by a pressing evil, and also, cannot be affected by a potential evil. Third, there is no evil in God, which makes him *immune* to evil.

Barth conceives of impassibility as God's preeminence in and of himself. In formulating God as unaffected, it means that God will not and cannot be affected by creaturely reality.[14] God does not will this reality rather it opposes him because it is of the fallen world. According to Barth, even if God is in the world, God is *in se* not affected by any sort of evil. This is the God of election because God is in his act and God's act opposes what he does not will. We have here a diastasis of the opposition involved in election: something which

10. *CD* II/2, 164–65.

11. We will discuss how Barth defines evil in the section "God Wills to be Affected by Evil."

12. *KD* II/2, 178.

13. *CD* II/2, 163. Italics mine.

14. *CD* II/2, 156, 495.

opposes God, and, something which God opposes. For Barth, there is no evil in God because evil is something external of God.[15] Since God's being is in his act, thus God's being is not evil because his act is not evil. God's eternal being is in opposition to evil because God always opposes evil in his act. This is the reason why God is said to be immune to evil. Such framework is helpful in investigating what comes next:

> But when God of His own will raised up man to be a *covenant-member* with Himself, when from all eternity He elected to be one with man in Jesus Christ, He did it with a being which was not merely affected by evil but actually mastered by it.[16]

The intersection between the reality of God and creaturely reality is obvious. Accordingly, the unaffected God wills to be affected by letting the opposition of evil take place in him, specifically in Jesus Christ. We can say that God's self-surrender of his impassibility is made manifest in Jesus Christ. It is the result of the divine decision to be in solidarity with humankind.

Barth views this decision in covenantal terms. The election of Jesus Christ in this regard is an election to be in covenant with human beings. God commits himself to represent humanity "in the union of his Son with Jesus of Nazareth."[17] In other words, God institutes this covenant in Christ; in Christ also, God orientates himself towards humankind.[18] On the one hand, in creaturely reality, there is no binding agreement between God and humanity, hence no covenant. On the other hand, in divine reality, there is an existing transaction between the two. Since Barth conceives the election within the intersection of realities, the covenant in mind is made between the Logos and Jesus Christ. It is in this perspective where Barth views the covenant history to have consummated the shared histories.[19] Because Barth puts forward the dominion of divine reality over that of creation, then, in actuality, the covenant is binding in time and in the world.

Barth grants that God alone sets the value and the jurisdiction of this covenant. The value lies in the identity of Jesus Christ and the jurisdiction transcends the boundary of time and space.[20] Jesus Christ is identified in this case as the covenant-Partner.[21] Although the scope of

15. *CD* II/2, 122, 164.

16. *CD* II/2, 163. Italics mine.

17. *CD* II/2, 8.

18. *CD* II/2, 9.

19. *CD* II/2, 9. Ogletree, *Christian Faith and History*, 161.

20. *CD* II/2, 10, 11. For a different perspective on Christ's covenant; cf. Berkhof, *Christian Faith*, 160.

21. *CD* II/2, 53.

the covenant is within creation, the covenant is not bound by it.[22] In this covenant, God gives himself when the covenant-Partner has moved into the world.[23] Thus, when God commits into this covenant, God commits to give himself. God nevertheless does not lose or undermine himself in this commitment, Barth qualifies, because God is the *Lord* of the covenant.[24] The fact that God institutes and executes the covenant so the divine self-giving within the covenant is under God's terms.

Also, it is in God's terms where God foreordains humans to be "covenant-members" by virtue of Jesus Christ's representation. Again, we can see here the subject-object theme. Jesus Christ is the Subject of the covenant being the Executor; whereas Jesus Christ is the Object, being the One upon whom the covenant is executed. It is in this context where Barth tackles impassibility—Jesus Christ is acted upon in the world by the execution of the covenant. In God's voluntary surrender of his impassibility, Jesus Christ is seen to be affected. More on this matter later as we probe how Barth interprets God ontologically and lexically in relation to the covenant.

1.1 Ontological Study

The primal decision (*Urentscheidung*), in Barth's thought, is God's determination to be *affected* in the covenant.[25] It denotes a decree constituting an *affected* God "from and to all eternity."[26] This, however, does not sit well with the Western tradition, especially as Barth reconfigures the discussion on impassibility. He writes:

> There is a link here with the particular conception of the fathers and scholastics frequently touched on in the first part of our doctrine of God—a conception now appropriated afresh by the older Protestant orthodoxy. According to this conception God is everything in the way of aseity, simplicity, immutability, infinity, etc., but He is not the living God, that is to say, He is not the God who lives in concrete decision. God lives in this sense only figuratively. It is not something which belongs to His proper and essential life, but only to His relationship with the world. Basically it may only be "ascribed" to Him, while it is believed that His true being and likewise His true Godhead are to be sought

22. *CD* II/2, 54.

23. *CD* II/2, 53.

24. *CD* II/2, 9, 12.

25. *KD* II/2, 8, 15, 53–54.

26. *CD* II/2, 79. See Jones, *The Humanity of Christ*, 80.

> in the impassibility which is above and behind His living activity within the universe.[27]

For Barth, the rendering of God in terms of aseity, simplicity, immutability, infinity and other divine attributes is at odds with his own conception of God. This stereotyping of God makes God imprisoned in himself to a point where God *no longer lives*.[28] In other words, such human conditioning of God creates an impersonal, "figurative," and thus not real, deity. Barth, by contrast, insists on God being personal; hence, *a living God*—full of vitality and autonomy, as opposed to being unnecessarily choked or confined from within and from without.

A living God, Barth clarifies, is the One who lives in "concrete decision" *by* exercising absolute independence. This concrete decision is the election of grace in which God has "proper and essential" life in relation to the world; not over and beyond it. In fact, Barth asserts the idea of the divine being-in-action in the "world of evil." So what is God's concrete decision in this context? God's concrete decision is the election of Jesus Christ on behalf of humankind.[29] God wills to reach out to the fallen world.

What Barth is strongly proposing here is to see God in this decision because it speaks of the God of election. Barth argues, "God is He who is not only to be found alone in His act, but is to be found alone in His act because alone in His act He is who He is."[30] In other words, any conception of God without reference to the divine will is merely figurative with Barth. His commitments to the notion of a dynamic God, as well as his departure from the traditional view of impassibility are outcomes of a reconstructed doctrine of election. Consequently, Barth can no longer allow for an impassible God in which such a locus is forced into the essential life of God without regard to the primal decision.

The argument on divine essence is integral to understanding God's self-determination (*Selbstbestimmung*).[31] Since Barth's God is pre-temporally affected, this indicates God to be neither simple nor pure in essence consequent of election. On the contrary, God is *complex* and *composite* in the nature of Jesus Christ in pre-temporal eternity because in being so, the unity of God

27. *CD* II/2, 79.

28. *CD* II/1, 303.

29. *CD* II/2, 161–63.

30. *CD* II/1, 272.

31. *KD* II/1, 742, 760; II/2, 18, 32.

with humanity finds its realization.[32] Jesus Christ, argues Barth, is the fullness of God in election.[33] So the suffering God is the covenantal God.

The being of Jesus Christ in the covenant does not merely signify a God who is affected, but valuably, it characterizes a God who is *not exclusive*. For Barth, God is inclusively complex (composite); albeit this God is in his eternal being.[34] Barth elucidates that God remains the altogether God of the covenant—even if the divine essence is united with a human being. The complex and composite God in solidarity with humanity is what God truly *is* in eternity. This makes Barth an advocate of the *pre-temporal* Christ (the Son of God is synchronous with the Son of Man). Such formulation is pivotal to this study because it shows how Barth's reconception of election impacts his doctrine of God.[35]

God's inclusiveness is with respect to God's decision to have "fellowship with man for Himself."[36] In a sense, God is seen to have sacrificed his inner life without detriment to his lordship in the covenant. With Barth, God's self-sacrifice is not only situated pre-temporally, but also, it is located in the "bosom" of God.[37] It means that God takes the rejection, condemnation, and death of humanity unto himself.[38] God is in himself in act (of suffering) and being (as *the* sorrowful One) in election.[39] God, in being so, remains sovereign and free. God is still sovereign in his willingness to be one with humanity, and God is still free in the inclusion of humankind in God's being. For this reason, Barth comprehends the divine self-determination as unconditional (*unbedingter*).[40] Here God is not so determined by anything other than God; and God does not simply exist as One who must be with humans (a need which would transgress divine self-sufficiency).

Thus in Barth's theology, the true being of the true Godhead can be viewed properly in and through the divine outworking within creation. The

32. God is complex and composite because Barth indicates, "The multiplicity, individuality and diversity of the perfections of God are those of His simple being, which is not therefore divided and then put together again." *CD* II/1, 332; *CD* II/2, 162. For a more nuanced view concerning God's complex nature; cf. Jenson, "Cur Deus Homo?"

33. *CD* II/2, 123–25. This formulation has biblical support in Heb 1:2, 3 and 2 Cor 4:4.

34. Barth asserts, "In God multiplicity, individuality and diversity do not stand in any contradiction to unity." *CD* II/1, 332.

35. Gunton, *Theology Through the Theologians*, 73. Also "The Doctrine of God: Karl Barth's Doctrine of Election as Part of his Doctrine of God," 381–92.

36. *CD* II/2, 162.

37. *CD* II/2, 167.

38. *CD* II/2, 167.

39. *CD* II/2, 167.

40. *KD* II/2, 108, 193, 241.

essential life of the triune being is made concrete in the life of Jesus Christ. This is what Barth means by stating that the God of election is "the living God inwardly as well as outwardly, a quality expressed and attested in concrete decision."[41] God must be understood *only* in such terms precisely because God does not will to exist otherwise.

We will better understand Barth's conception of the primal decision by examining the actual words he used in articulating the electing God in view of impassibility.

1.2 Lexical Study

The translators of *Die Kirchliche Dogmatik* in English do not necessarily allow variations in nuance of the German words Barth originally used to convey "immovability" or being "unaffected"; they merely employ the conventional term "impassibility" or "impassible."[42] For instance, page 163 of the ET translates as "impassibility" the word *Unangerührtheit*, which expresses the idea of immovability:[43]

> In giving Himself [God-self] to this act He ordained the surrender of something, i.e., of His own impassibility [*Unangerührtheit*] in face of the whole world which because it is not willed by Him can only be the world of evil.[44]

Barth grants that impassibility is God's immunity to evil. He thinks of God as immovable or unaffected by anything that is not God or anti-God.

On page 79 of the ET, Barth uses a different German word which carries a similar idea as just explained. In this text, the term translated as "impassibility" is *Unbeweglichkeit*, which might be rendered as immovability.[45] He postulates:

> Basically, then, it may only be "ascribed" to Him [God], while it is believed that His true being and likewise His true Godhead are to be sought in the impassibility [*Unbeweglichkeit*] which is above and behind His living activity within the universe.[46]

41. *CD* II/2, 79.

42. Translated by G. W. Bromiley, J. C. Campbell, I. Wilson, J. S. McNab, T. H. L. Parker, W. B. Johnston, H. Knight, J. L. M. Haire and R. A. Stewart. McCormack, "Divine Impassibility," 152.

43. *KD* II/2, 178. ET stands for English Translation.

44. *CD* II/2, 162.

45. *KD* II/2, 85.

46. *CD* II/2, 79.

In this circumstance, Barth describes God in a unique fashion, hence at variance with the Western tradition. God in his "true being" is immovable in himself unless God decides to be moved *ad extra*. In other words, it can be interjected here that God transcends impassibility.

While the first two German words are utilized as nouns, this one on page 166 of the ET is used as an adjective, "impassible" translates *unangerührten*, which means unmoved:[47]

> He [God] could have remained satisfied with Himself and with the impassible [*Unangerührten*] glory and blessedness of His own inner life. But He did not do so.[48]

God is seen as categorically unmoved in his glory. It is pertinent to acknowledge that in this respect, impassibility is articulated metaphorically. Barth endeavors to picture a *what could have happened* scenario as he construes God's decision to make humankind a covenant-partner.[49] According to Barth, God could have remained in himself, i.e., immovable and unaffected, but God decided otherwise. Rather, God chooses to share his glory with that which is external of, and unlike, God.

The translators's employment of the conventional term "impassibility" or "impassible," I think, does not do justice to what Barth has in mind—to engage with impassibility in the context of the covenant. It can either misdirect the reader to treat the notion of impassibility akin to tradition; or limit his ontological formulation of God's immovability or being unaffected.[50] The usage of the two alternative terms (for the same English word) indeed has theological importance, not only in Barth's doctrine of God, but also especially in his doctrine of election. Likewise, the translations of the German words above have critical consequences in how the primal decision is related to impassibility.

It is unfortunate yet challenging to accept that there is no precise English equivalent for Barth's own rendition of impassibility. In effect, I am left to either be satisfied with the translation "impassible" or "impassibility," or rather be creative to fill in the gap. It is the position of this study to exercise the latter, mainly because Barth appears to have meticulously

47. Barth in this circumstance uses the phrase "impassible glory" or "unaltered glory" (*unangerührten Herrlichkeit*). *KD* II/2, 181.

48. *CD* II/2, 166.

49. Barth could have been informed by Caspar Olevian's concept of covenant in God's relation with humanity. *De substantia foederis gratuiti inter Deum et electors* (Geneva, 1585).

50. *Unangerührtheit* and *Unangerührten* have the same root *Unangerührt* which basically means untouched.

selected *Unangerührtheit*, *Unbeweglichkeit*, and *Unangerührten* to individually address each facet of his articulation on the covenantal act and being of God. For instance, when Barth employs the word *Unangerührtheit*, he underscores God's self-consistency within the covenant, despite the presence of that which opposes God. By employing the word *Unbeweglichkeit*, Barth in this case accentuates God's innate transcendence over what is created. And with the usage of the word *Unangerührten*, Barth amplifies God's desire to share the divine being with what is external. In other words, in each and every occasion Barth utilizes such German word, there is a commensurate theological weight which should not be taken for granted. So to take these synonyms in the context of the covenant is necessary to properly understand Barth's God. In the covenant, God is immovable as the Executor as God is unmoved in being executed upon.

Barth's likely agenda for this approach is to convey God's deliberate relation with creation. On the one hand, although God relates himself in time and in the world, such immanence does not compromise the God-self. On the other hand, despite the fact that God is over and beyond creation, such transcendence does not diminish the desire to be with humanity. Because Barth intentionally uses the cited words in the context of election, I am challenged to handle these words consistently, vis-à-vis the God in and of the covenant.[51]

Even though Barth specifically addresses the act and being of God as just mentioned, he does not, however, employ those German words against the issues posed by the notion of impassibility. Even if Barth discusses divine immovability, hence immutability, he still does not approach impassibility head on. What is obvious in this theological decision, particularly in the reconception of election, is the potency and dynamism *in* God relative to creation. Despite Barth's occasional allusion to God's self-giving, it does not in any way infringe God's sovereignty. This resonates, in a sense, with Barth's positive approach to the idea of immutability. God is not only capable of being moved in himself, but more importantly, God *determines* himself to be so in the decree.

In spite of the fact that being unaffected *per se* is not what exactly captures Barth's thought on impassibility, yet in the interest of what has been laid out, we shall have to be content (at least for now) in considering Barth's God in this fashion. There is no avenue, at this junction, to examine impassibility in view of the God of election apart from the notion of the unaffected God. But, as a caveat, being unaffected is logically accommodated as long as the balance between transcendence and immanence is

51. Also see McCormack, "Divine Impassibility," 183.

sustained within the covenant.[52] This thought shores up Barth's dialogue with the Fathers, Scholastics, and Protestant theologians (particularly in the Reformed tradition).[53]

1.3 God of Election and Impassibility

In his conversation with the Church Fathers regarding the suffering of God, Barth argues with a balanced view of impassibility.[54] God's self-demonstration and self-affirmation is in the differentiation-in-communion with something distinct from himself; something which is not usually associated or ascribed to God as in the tradition.[55] For Barth, the accommodation of the notion of divine impassibility should not be detrimental to the notion of God's voluntary self-giving. Understood in this sense, the term impassibility is closely, but not entirely, linked to the traditional doctrine of immutability. In Barth's reasoning, immutability connotes God's unchangeableness in his being, perfections, purposes, and promises even in view of the life of Jesus Christ.[56]

It is noteworthy to mention that impassibility (*apatheia*) is not classically interpreted as something negative as portrayed by some contemporary theologians.[57] To the Fathers, *apatheia* is something positive which

52. For lack of a better term plus the challenge of fully capturing Barth's dialectical thought on the affected God. Also see Ticciati, *Job and the Disruption of Identity*, 181.

53. *CD* II/1, 444–45, 549, 562, 610, 614.

54. Barth expounds this topic in *CD* II/1, 490–607.

55. *CD* II/1, 491–93.

56. *CD* II/1, 493–94. Grudem, *Systematic Theology*, 163. In order to appreciate Barth's reaction to the Fathers's teaching on impassibility, we have to deal with how impassibility has been classically interpreted. The term "impassible" (Greek: *apathēs*) had more than one literal meaning in the early post-apostolic era. Grant, *The Early Christian Doctrine of God*, 112. Augustine likewise engages in the discussion on impassibility by referring to the Greek term ἀπάθεια (*apathēia*). See Scrutton, *Thinking through Feeling*, 42–45. For instance, Origen connects impassibility to the phrase "among other things" (Latin: *inter alia*) resulting to a complicated definition of impassibility. For example, seeing a compassionate God without actual feelings of compassion. It could be a description of a deity devoid of emotions; or reflecting a God entirely unperturbed and motionless. Clement of Alexandria has his own interpretation of *apathēs*—conceiving God as insusceptible to distraction by the pleasures of the flesh. In other words, such conceptions initiate the denial of any form of real affliction in God. Webster, *The Possibilities of Theology*, 9.

57. For example, Jürgen Moltmann states that a "God who is incapable of suffering is a being who cannot be involved." *Crucified God*, 222. Also, according to Wolfhart Pannenberg, the unaffected God (the Father) cannot be said to be a God of love if his is not affected by the passion of the Son. *Systematic Theology*. Volume 1, 314. In J. K.

connotes being "purified of all selfish desires" or "freedom from suffering and irrational impulses." In fact, *apatheia* is thought to be the ancestor of *agape* (unselfish love).[58] This is why impassibility is plausible in Western orthodoxy because God is never portrayed as gloomy and detached, albeit the concept of perfection describes God as rigidly aseitic.[59] Nonetheless, the idea of suffering is seen as utterly incompatible with God regardless of whether it is externally caused or self-determined.[60]

Although Barth also denies a contingent deity, however the un-necessitated God of election orientates himself to creation. While it is evident that Barth sees God as eternally for humanity, being so does not mean being unwillingly subjected to creation. God in the beginning is not dependent on creation, however, God in eternity has determined himself *with* humankind. It is not out of necessity, but rather, it is a self-initiated subjection to creation out of compassion. We can sense here the delicate equilibrium between transcendence and immanence.[61] Respectively, Barth thinks of divine suffering as something God wills yet unnecessary insofar as the Godhood

Mozley's evaluation, the idea of an unaffected and unsympathetic deity could be the impetus for critical theologians to move away from the classic notion of impassibility. *The Impassibility of God*, 121–22. Also read Hart, "No Shadow of Turning," 185, 193–94.

58. Gavrilyuk, "God's Impassible Suffering in the Flesh," 136–37. Evagrius of Pontus, *Praktikos*, 81. See also Dennis Okholm's exposition of ascetic theology in *Dangerous Passions, Deadly Sins*, 3–5.

59. For example, Thomas Aquinas argues that God has no passions and that God's perfection rules out his negative emotions, i.e., sorrow, fear, envy, or anger. See Leftow, "God's Impassibility, Immutability, and Eternality," 173–74. Cf. Fronda, *Wittgenstein's (Misunderstood) Religious Thought*, 127. In a Thomastic account, aseitic is an "operative word" denoting God to be the "ultimate cause." Leftow, "God's Impassibility," 173–74.

60. Barth differs from some of the old positions on impassibility. One example of which is the position of Irenaeus of Lyons (c. 202). Irenaeus characterized God not to be passionless, but rather, expressing emotions. The key to this handling of impassibility is in the proper understanding of creation. For Irenaeus, God is impassible (incapable of feelings) yet at the same time, God is in fact *expressing* emotions in a different ontological order from creatures. Irenaeus, *Haer*, 2.1.1, 3.8.3 (PG 7 [1857]: 709–10, 867–68). Another example of an old position on impassibility is from Anselm of Canterbury (1093–1109). Anselm allows for the notion of God to be merciful despite being impassible. Davies and Evans, *Anselm of Canterbury*, 91. Notably, Anselm conceives of God being somewhat incapable of having the "experience" of feelings (despite God being merciful). Anselm, *Basic Writings*, 59.

61. It is also in this context wherein Barth states, "By existing in this way is not subject to any necessity, as though He must first exist in order to be who He is. But by His existence He simply reaffirms Himself." *CD* II/1, 306.

is concerned.[62] Indeed, the very essence of God is viewed in light of God's voluntary condescension in creation.[63]

Barth, true to his foundation of theology, approaches the question of impassibility on biblical grounds, but he is somewhat philosophical in explicating how God can be seen to have suffered in Jesus Christ. With Barth, his only affiliation with anything human in dealing with impassibility is the human Jesus in election. It is substitutionary or representative and not conventionally literal, but, dialectic in expression. When Barth says that God is eternally merciful, God's mercy or his "feelings" of mercy is purely independent on external actions and events.[64] In other words, God's mercy is not insusceptibility to what is outside of God, but rather, it is a decision to be one with humanity in all aspects, including suffering. This is obvious in Barth's treatment of God's mercy with justice; God's mercy is just insofar as evil is treated with seriousness by "taking to Himself the *torment* that that which is inexcusable must inevitably carry with it."[65] God is viewed as truly in intimate relationship with his creatures. Barth elucidates:

> But the personal God has a heart. He can feel, and be affected. *He is not impassible*. . . . God is moved and stirred, yet not like ourselves in powerlessness, but in His own free power, in His innermost being: moved and touched by Himself . . . to compassion to another's suffering.[66]

For Barth, God's heart *can feel*, i.e., feeling of divine sorrow, as in divine affection. This feeling is not fluctuating (as in creaturely feelings) but an eternal feeling for humankind.[67] Here God is not rigidly impassible, which by implication includes having compassion with *the* sorrowful.[68] Moreover, God is understood to have a "wounded" heart by allowing himself to "feel the pain of our sin."[69] Correspondingly, God is conceived to be self-moved, self-touched in the covenantal being of Jesus Christ. A very good example of someone in whose theology there is the notion of a self-moved God is seen in John Calvin's concept of divine impassibility.

62. *CD* II/2, 180. Barth exclaims of God, "He speaks of His suffering, not as a necessity laid upon Him from without, but as something which He Himself wills." *CD* II/2, 180.

63. Nimmo, "The Compassion of Jesus Christ," 79.

64. *CD* II/2, 167.

65. *CD* II/2, 167. Italics mine.

66. *CD* II/1, 370; *KD* II/1, 416. Italics mine.

67. *CD* II/2, 171–72. Barth, *Dogmatics in Outline*, 37.

68. Again, the sorrowful in Barth's articulation of election is Jesus Christ.

69. *CD* II/2, 166; II/1, 399. Kitamori, *Theology of the Pain of God*, 46.

Calvin claims that while God is impassible, it is also true that God has emotions.[70] Thus for him, God is impassible with respect to comparing *God's emotions* to human experience. For instance, concerning divine repentance, Calvin explains, "whenever we hear that God is angered, we ought not to imagine any emotion [i.e., passion] in him, but rather to consider that this expression has been taken from our own human experience."[71] Calvin's allowance for any divine emotion ends up being mere divine expressions and not, in reality, feelings akin to what humans undergo.[72]

Calvin's notion of a self-moved deity is presupposed by an advocacy of divine sovereignty. God's *expression* of emotions is the divine countenance *in se* and not at all caused *ad extra*. After all, he has no problem with God expressing emotions simply because God has absolute freedom to do so. What Calvin disallows is the notion of an actual suffering in and of God because, for him, "God certainly has no blood, nor does He suffer, nor can He be touched."[73] Thus even in the treatment of the economic Trinity, Calvin argues, "the Son has all of God's essential properties, such as impassibility."[74] This is definitely not the case with Barth because he sees the Father (in the Son) to have been suffering from and to eternity. Although he likewise advocates the absolute sovereignty of God demonstrated in absolute autonomy, God's willingness to suffer precedes the divine sacrificial act. Barth puts it, "The impassibility of God cannot in any case mean that it is impossible for Him really to feel compassion. Where grace is manifest and effectual, it is always a question of the misery of man."[75] In this assertion, impassibility is reconsidered in view of God's active relation with human beings.

Barth, in continuing the discussion on divine repentance, alludes to the actuality of God's emotions.[76] In reference to Peter Barth's thesis on predestination, Karl Barth argues that God is not bound to any human presuppositions about God.[77] God is free *at every moment* which is why "God's

70. Calvin argues for full impassibility via biblical accommodation. See Calvin, *Institutes* 1.17.13.

71. Calvin, *Institutes* 1.17.13.

72. In this manner, Calvin's thought parallels to some degree with Ireanaeus's expressivist view of divine emotions.

73. Calvin, *Institutes* 2.14.2.

74. Helm, *John Calvin's Ideas*, 62.

75. *CD* II/1, 371; *KD* II/1, 417.

76. Refer to the excursus in *CD* II/2, 188–89.

77. Peter Barth is Karl Barth's younger brother. Peter Barth's thesis is entitled: "The Biblical Basis of Calvin's Doctrine of Predestination," presented in the same 1936 Calvinist Congress in Geneva where Pierre Maury delivered his breakthrough study on election. *CD* II/2, 188.

repenting cannot be thought away from the biblical presentation of God's thinking and action."[78] God's emotions are said to be actual because God relates with humankind within creaturely time.[79] It means that in relating with humans, God is not imprisoned in and of himself in his foreordination. God's eternal will, Karl Barth claims, "is not left behind by time but precedes every moment of time."[80] This is what he calls the "living will" of God; a will which corresponds to a covenantal relationship.[81] With this conception, any mechanistic exposition of predestination is shunned, and also, God's grace is underlined in the freedom of God.

God, in the "freedom of His grace," is seen to be a God not of whim or caprice, but rather, of love and mercy.[82] In this respect, Karl Barth conceives of divine sovereignty in a way that is in "unforeseen and astonishing developments" as God works supremely in time.[83] It means that God's decree is "living and progressive" because it is understood not as "something which happened once and for all," but rather, as "something which continues to happen."[84] In other words, the God of election is self-moved as God moves in time. Although he supports Peter Barth's correction of Calvin's teaching on predestination, Karl Barth further points out that it is only in Jesus Christ where the electing God is properly known, not elsewhere.[85] In this case, the life of Jesus Christ is indicative of how God is seen to be truly active in and by himself.

Karl Barth seeks the eternal predestination in God's temporal dealings by asserting: "We must be taught by Scripture that God has entered into a mysteriously living relation to us men."[86] In this way, Barth manages to resolve what appears to be the irreconcilable facts about God, i.e., God is immutable *as* God is capable of repentance or change in emotions between "wrath and forgiveness."[87] To put it another way, God's movement in time speaks of a deity who wills to be also *emotionally involved* in the affairs of human beings. It is so because God chooses to be in an intimate

78. *CD* II/2, 188.

79. *CD* II/2, 193.

80. *CD* II/2, 193.

81. *CD* II/2, 194.

82. *CD* II/2, 188, 192.

83. *CD* II/2, 188.

84. *CD* II/2, 192.

85. *CD* II/2, 191–92. Karl Barth says that his brother's thesis is "intrinsically correct" but it needs improvement in articulating God's freedom in order to avoid any form of synergism. *CD* II/2, 190–91.

86. *CD* II/2, 189–90.

87. *CD* II/2, 189.

relationship with humanity yet such willingness does not allow for God to be conditioned by humans or any creaturely reality.[88] That is why Karl Barth treats the doctrine of predestination as understanding the "mysteriousness and life" of God in relation to humanity.[89] It is achieved if the eternal life of God is understood in the life of Jesus Christ.

The life of Jesus Christ, in a sense, demonstrates how God's anger and compassion are feelings of autonomy and sovereignty. When Barth says that God is free to punish, and also to repent such act, this shows a living God and not a static God. A living God is One who is totally unrestricted in conducting Oneself despite being in time. Nevertheless, a living God is also One who thinks and acts selflessly.[90] The God of election has the power to freely express the divine feelings consistent to the divine being. That is why God's freedom, Barth posits, is indeed a freedom *in favor* of humanity. The decree shows God's willing, affirming, and loving humanity.[91] The decree is viewed to be "mysterious" insofar as God's decision to be in covenant with humanity is concerned, while the decree is viewed to be "living" insofar as it corresponds to this intimate relationship.[92]

We can deduce that when Barth sees God to be *active temporally* in God's dealings in the world, the doctrine of impassibility is indeed reconsidered in strict view of Jesus Christ. So the metaphysical, anthropological and expressivist approaches to impassibility are, at length, incongruous with Barth's God. It is due to the covenant schema in Barth's theology in which God is seen as constant in being unmoved, but also, God is constant in willing to be self-moved. It is in the being of the immovable-yet-self-moved God where Barth puts forward the notion of divine suffering.

Barth differs from his predecessors's position on impassibility because he speaks strongly of the God in solidarity with creation, human beings in particular.[93] There is no other God behind and above this God in Barth's doctrine of election. Colin Gunton evaluates the received formulation of impassibility as an "unfortunate breach between act and being" of

88. *CD* II/2, 191. This is Karl Barth's contribution to "activist predestination" as presented by Peter Barth. For more insight about Karl Barth and activist predestination, see Henry, *God Who Stands and Stays*. Volume VI, 94–95.

89. Excursus in *CD* II/2, 190.

90. *CD* II/2, 193.

91. *CD* II/2, 192.

92. *CD* II/2, 191. Karl Barth notes that Pierre Maury is also in support of Peter Barth's thesis on the basis of conceiving predestination in connection with God's redemptive work. In this regard, Barth asserts, "It is impossible, then, to separate the doctrine of predestination from Christology and soteriology." *CD* II/2, 191.

93. Heron, "Karl Barth: A Personal Engagement," 301–2.

God.[94] In reaction, I would say Barth has successfully bridged the lacuna inherent in the aforementioned conceptions of impassibility by sustaining God's sovereignty in self-giving.

It is imperative for Barth to conceive God as the living God of the covenant. To treat the being of God in terms of the divine works *in and through* creation (as opposed to being transcendently above the world) is Barth's ingenious way of handling impassibility without detriment to the transcendent-yet-relational deity in election. In other words, he keeps distance from the canonical conception of impassibility as a result of his christocentric direction. Barth even up to this point, does not categorically support or deny impassibility, whether incidentally or deliberately. What we can obviously learn from him, thus far, is that the decree speaks of a God who is willing to suffer.

2. Election and Divine Suffering

We continue the exposition of our first text by exegeting the latter part in order to find out the reason for Barth's conception of God's willingness to suffer.[95] He points out:

> But when God of His own will raised up man to be a covenant-member with Himself, when *from all eternity* He elected to be one with man in Jesus Christ, He did it with a being which was not merely affected by evil but actually mastered by it.

On this account Barth is qualifying the rationale behind his claim of God having chosen to be affected by outside events and actions. He thinks there can be no election without God willing to be affected, not only externally, but also crucially, from and to eternity (pre-temporal, temporal, and post-temporal).[96] It is clear in Barth's argumentation that the divine activity is directed to humankind.[97] Accordingly, the section below will discuss *when* God determines himself to be affected, followed by considering *what* God wills to affect himself.

94. Gunton, *Act and Being*, 126.

95. *CD* II/2, 163. Italics mine. This is the second part of the main passage.

96. *CD* II/2, 79; II/1, 370. See te Velde, *The Doctrine of God in Reformed Orthodoxy*, 373. This study approaches the study of election from pre-temporal, temporal and post-temporal angles of divine decision to arrive at an unbiased conclusion. Lindsay, "Ecclesiology and Election in the Early Fathers," 74.

97. Read Tseng, *Karl Barth's Infralapsarian Theology*.

2.1 God Wills to be Affected in Eternity

Ontologically speaking, the phrase "to be affected" does not denote a future reference; Barth's God is always affected from pre-temporality through which time began in creation.[98] He says God's decree to give Oneself is not only ascribed to an "actual event" but as something *eternally foreordained.*[99] It implies Barth's recognition of God's will as not merely in its manifestation in time, i.e., the incarnation, but in God's "bond and commitment" (*Bindung und Verpflichtung*) as reflected in the decree.[100] Hence, this section is divided into two parts: (i) the affected God in pre-temporal eternity, and (ii) the affected God in temporal eternity.

Barth emphatically states that God commits to be incarnated:

> If it is indeed the case that the divine good-pleasure which was the beginning of all things with God carries with it the risk and threat of negation, then it is so because the Son of God incarnate represents and Himself is this divine good-pleasure.[101]

This "beginning" is itself *in* God whereby created things or beings come into existence. Barth describes that in the beginning of all things God has appropriated "the risk and threat of negation" unto God's self.[102] We will understand what this means with the aid of Barth's conception of the Logos: The Logos was in the beginning with God.[103] It is God himself who identifies with the Logos.[104] The divinity of God is attributed to the Logos (*Gottes identifiziert, daß gerade die Göttlichkeit des ὁ θεός auch dem ὁ λόγος zugeschrieben wird*).[105] For this reason, Barth sees the Logos as "the same" with God.[106] In fact, the Logos is "like God Himself."[107] The Logos is like God himself in the sense that it "partakes of the divine essence."[108] In other words, whatever is ascribed to God is also ascribed to the Logos.[109] It can be

98. Sergius Bulgakov echoes this concept in his notion of the "metaphysical Golgotha." *Lamb of God*, 232.

99. *CD* II/2, 161. Also see Jenson, *God after God*, 152 and *Alpha and Omega*, 79.

100. *CD* II/2, 183. *KD* II/2, 200.

101. *CD* II/2, 163.

102. *CD* II/2, 163.

103. Excursus in *CD* II/2, 96.

104. *KD* II/2, 103. Cf. *CD* II/2, 96.

105. *KD* II/2, 103.

106. *CD* II/2, 96. "The same" in the ET is "this was" (*Dieser war*) in *KD* II/2, 105.

107. *CD* II/2, 95.

108. *CD* II/2, 98.

109. Whatever is ascribed to ὁ θεός is also ascribed to ὁ λόγος. *CD* II/2, 96.

inferred that whatever is ascribed to the Logos is also ascribed to God if we follow Barth's impulse in using the term "the same."

"The same" was with God and "the same" was God.[110] Who is this "the same" called the Logos? The Logos is Jesus Christ.[111] Barth writes, "He was in the beginning with God; Jesus was" (*Er war im Anfang bei Gott; Jesus war es*).[112] This "the same," is Christ, having the same ontological essence and legitimacy of the creatorship as God. Now, if the Logos is Christ and the Logos is God, then Christ is God. Christ is with God, and is God eternally. Barth even affirms the fourth-century exposition concerning the Logos: "There was no time when it was not."[113] Though Barth does not necessarily involve the Logos's assumption of flesh, its anticipation, i.e., God's committal, is deemed as if it has taken place already in divine reality (already-but-not-yet embodiment).[114] In other words, since the Logos has its own reality which "stands completely outside the series of created reality," the *not yet* of the flesh is conceived as the *already so* in Barth's thought.[115] It makes the ontological significance of the *Logos incarnandus* inhospitable to the suggestion of the *Logos asarkos*. The former is where Barth accommodates his theopaschite tendency making the latter insignificant in this context.

According to Barth, God in pre-temporality already carries the danger of the negative side of predestination (reprobation) because of the election of Jesus Christ. God's committal is already binding, hence the term "bond and commitment." This implies the precedence of such negation, or has already happened (past) insofar as God is concerned.[116]

It is interesting to note that despite Brian Asbill's exposition of God's self-binding in Barth's doctrine of election, he nevertheless maintains that in speaking of divine objectivity, the God of Barth, in the beginning, is a God *in and for himself*. Asbill writes, "Barth is insistent that God's life not be limited to God's life with creatures. Since God is the eternal trinity, there is a proper sense in which God is 'in and for himself'. Furthermore, Barth draws on divine aseity in conjunction with divine self-preservation in order to protect God's divinity in all that God is and does."[117] I am aware of Asbill's intention to explain the concept of pronobeity (the treatment God's

110. Excursus in *CD* II/2, 98. *KD* II/2, 105. Barth exposits John 1:1–2.

111. *CD* II/2, 98.

112. My own translation of *KD* II/2, 105.

113. Excursus in *CD* II/2, 95.

114. *CD* II/2, 97–98. Cf. *CD* IV/2, 43. Lee, *Trinitarian Ontology and Israel*, 23.

115. Excursus in *CD* II/2, 95.

116. However this same danger of negation anticipates the incarnation of the Son.

117. Asbill, *The Freedom of God for Us*, 192.

aseity with God's being *pro nobis*) in Barth by indicating God's lordship in the act of self-binding to humanity, hence this lordship is rightly portrayed as Immanuel.[118] Here, aseity is not taken as distant from creation, i.e., it has nothing to do with a relational God.[119] The incarnation, life, death, and resurrection of Jesus Christ are self-necessitated events in the God-self. Without such self-driven outworking, God remains ambiguously transcendent.[120] I completely side with Asbill in this matter.

However, I part ways with Asbill in saying that Barth has a notion of "divine self-preservation" in God's being and act wherein God is truly and fully in himself *first* before being in the world. Yet Barth has no intention of upholding God's self-preservation or keeping of divine objectivity by muting God's revelation of eternal love in and through the Son.[121] Thus God is truly and fully God, and wholly in himself in his bond and commitment in Jesus Christ. Of course, God does not need creation to be in and of himself, but what God does, according to Barth, is to attach God's self to creation.[122] God's life is *altogether* the eternally foreordained life of Christ.[123] This is not an abstract view of divine aseity; it is how Barth conceives of what it means for God to be *in se*. Because the human subject of election, first and foremost, is Jesus of Nazareth, this line of thinking cannot be taken as anthropocentric or pantheistic, but rather far from it. God decides, proclaims, and lives to be this God alone—the incarnate God.[124]

Asbill's attention to the idea of "God's own" in considering the trinitarian event of "knowing and loving" draws inspiration from Barth's conception of the living God:[125]

> The fact that God is means that from all eternity God is active in His inner relationships as Father, Son and Holy Ghost, that He wills Himself and knows of Himself, that He loves, that He makes us of His sovereign freedom, that He maintains and exercises this freedom, and in so doing maintains and demonstrates Himself. . . . His being and activity ad extra is merely an overflowing of His inward activity and being, of the inward vitality

118. Asbill, *The Freedom of God for Us*, 192.

119. Asbill, *The Freedom of God for Us*, 120, 176.

120. Asbill, *The Freedom of God for Us*, 184.

121. Barth puts it, "There can be no doubt that in His overflowing glory God is sacrificial love; love which seeks not her own but the things of others." *CD* II/2, 173.

122. *CD* II/2, 171–72.

123. Read excursus in *CD* II/2, 106–8.

124. *CD* II/2, 176.

125. Asbill, *The Freedom of God for Us*, 177, 199.

> which He has in Himself. . . . This is no less activity than in His own way God in Himself is activity and in a different way His whole work in the world is activity. It is the transition from the one to the other: from God's being in and for Himself to His being as Lord of creation.[126]

It is tempting to sympathize with Asbill regarding Barth's articulation of the reality of the living God if we fail to consider the following: first, God's love in this context is a *sacrificial love*, not God's love to and for God's Self; second, what overflows from God's inward activity and being cannot be properly understood apart from Barth's conception of the Son of God who is also the Son of Man; third, the living God "in a different way" is not at all different from how Barth views the life of God revealed in Jesus Christ.[127] God's self-binding commitment to humanity therefore, in essence, is real for God.

For Barth, the "risk and threat" God carries is in God's *reality* in eternity—that which has transpired. That is why in Barth's assertion, the election of grace is the *beginning* of all things including the beginning of God's suffering: "In the very fact that from all eternity He willed to suffer for us."[128] God's eternal decision *is* God's external action; God's being is always and only ever being-in-action. The God of Barth is a being before and after this act. This God therefore is someone who has risked himself and has been threatened within the covenant; it is the essence of predestinating Christ. In Christ, Barth continues, there is already, in origin and from all eternity, this twofold reference, i.e., divine and human.[129] The divine and human in Jesus Christ accentuate the covenant model of election.

Barth's usage of the covenant model brings us to discuss this passage in full:

> From all eternity God *could have* excluded man from this covenant. He could have delivered him up to himself and allowed him to fall. He could have refused to will him at all. He could have avoided the compromising of His freedom by not willing to create him. He could have remained satisfied with Himself and with the impassible glory and blessedness of His own inner life.

126. *CD* II/2, 175.

127. *CD* II/2, 173–77. Barth attests, "The eternal will of God which is the predestination of all things is *God's life* in the form of the history, encounter and decision between Himself and man, a history, encounter and decision which are already willed and known from all eternity, and to that extent, prior to all external events, *are already actual before Him* and for Him." Italics mine. *CD* II/2, 175.

128. *CD* II/2, 165, 169.

129. *CD* II/2, 162.

> *But He did not do so.* He elected man as a covenant-partner. In His Son He elected Himself as the covenant-partner of man.[130]

Barth highlights God in and of the covenant by negating the thought wherein God, in the sovereignty of his liberty *per se*, could have been detached and indifferent from anything external. God is essentially and eternally complete in himself. Barth shows here that God could have remained exclusive in his inner life; hence, be a God in and for himself. Nonetheless, this is not who God is—God chooses to be a God for humanity so he will always be with humanity. God decides to be this God only because he is God *in* the covenant. This is why God gives himself and could not be in any way impersonal or sterile and, in this sense, immovable. Barth speaks of God as inclusively *outward-looking*; a God who is utterly interested with what befits humanity.[131] The vivid evidence of God's inclusivity is the decree to include humanity in his eternal covenant.

Another aspect of this particular passage is God being a great risk-taker. Notwithstanding his omniscience, God still foreordained to create humans; humans who are susceptible to the corruption of evil and poignantly, who have already been "overtaken" by evil, as Barth puts it.[132] Despite this fact, God nevertheless made himself exposed to danger by being allied with humans, and more so, by being *affected* in the first place. For Barth, this is not due to God's suitability with creation (that God belongs to the same ontological order with it), but God simply chooses to be in it as a self-moved, self-touched deity.

What Barth sees in the ever-binding committal is God's self-surrender of his own impassibility. The preordination to give-up a divine attribute is linked with God's self-giving in election. So if we are to follow closely Barth in this regard, he is not speaking of God as being affected in time only, but crucially, also before time—in God's committal.[133] When God commits (self-obligation) to suffer in the covenant, in the Platonic sense, God is already affected (self-obligated).[134]

The covenant implies an eternal exchange between God and humanity. It is in this framework where Barth stresses the enormity of God's self-sacrifice. The eternal sacrificial exchange is set against a distorted conception

130. *CD* II/2, 166. Italics mine.

131. *CD* III/1, 3, 5.

132. *CD* II/2, 164. This matter will be dealt with in the subsection: "God Wills to be Affected by Evil."

133. *CD* II/2, 187.

134. *CD* II/2, 183.

of sovereigty; a sovereignty outside the covenant.[135] In the decree, Barth alludes, God loses and humanity gains as a result.[136] How did God lose in this eternal exchange? According to Barth, God has ascribed to himself perdition.[137] But how did humanity gain in this eternal exchange? God has ascribed salvation to humanity, says Barth.[138] Even though such determination is a divine self-take, it is always in relation to humankind. God's will is precise (*in concreto*) and also it is strictly revealed (not *in abstracto*). Thus Barth is convinced that God lives in a concrete decision which makes God indeed a "living God"—the One who dynamically self-gives.[139]

In this study of Barth's modification of election, the challenge is to attend (equally) to what God wills *to remove from humanity*. This is where we need to locate Barth's handling of impassibility in view of the substitutional sacrifice. On the side of humanity, the eternal exchange does not simply convey humanity gaining as a result, but dialectically, humanity losing too. In the decree, humans gain by giving up something they incur (by choice) upon themselves by living against God. If God allows the ultimate consequence of human choice, then humanity's ruin is inevitable. But God rather sacrifices himself than to sacrifice the future of humankind.

The internal action of this decision, posits Barth, inevitably involves the sacrifice or abandoning of *something in God*. This something is in connection with the discarding of *something* from humankind. In this scenario, Barth argues for this "something" as a concrete indication, not what God *has* but rather what God *is*. It is likewise true with humanity. God is understood to have abandoned what he is in eternity, i.e., impassibility, in order to discard from humanity its state of being, i.e., condemned.[140] Here a *deficient* or *incomplete* God does not confront us because Barth's God does not cease to be fully God (even if the language of abandonment is right). In other words, in God's committal, God remains committed to himself by committing humans unto himself. In Jesus Christ, God remains the covenant-Partner so that humans can be God's covenant-partners.[141] By extrapolation, however, there is no pri-

135. Also see Hunsinger, *Reading Barth*, 167.

136. *CD* II/2, 162.

137. *CD* II/2, 162.

138. *CD* II/2, 162.

139. *CD* II/2, 79.

140. *CD* II/2, 167.

141. We can interpolate that in Jesus Christ, God and humanity are deemed as simultaneous covenant-keepers.

mal decision without sacrifice because what is ascribed to God by virtue of election is the negative character of predestination.[142]

There is a "disproportionate relation between the divine taking away and the divine giving."[143] The former pertains to the humiliation of God or rejection and the latter pertains to the exaltation of humanity or election. Barth's seemingly unfair-yet-proper rendition of predestination is better appreciated in the context of *what* God truly wills in electing Jesus Christ. Barth, however, presents the resolution of disparity in the eternal exchange between God and humanity. In Barth's own words, the negative character in election "will relapse more or less automatically into a relation of proportion or equilibrium."[144] The eschatological implication of the covenantal affected God in Jesus Christ is here attested.

At this point, we have to deal with the second part of God being affected in eternity, i.e., in time, to examine Barth's notion of the effected equilibrium in election.

2.2 The Affected God in Time

Barth's thought of God's self-giving prior to creation entails God as being internally affected in the decree.[145] We will move on to probe his explanation of God being affected in *time*.[146] Since the decision to self-sacrifice is eternally foreordained, it covers both pre-temporality and temporality. The latter is what he describes as an "actual event."[147] Having the decree as the reference, this actual event indicates a *point in time*—the Christ event.[148] Barth sees God as decreeing "the risk and threat of negation" as God's own in Jesus Christ. This negative appropriation to God's self is again, due to the role of the

142. Thus, this eternal exchange is both amazing and glorious in the context of the suffering of God. It is amazing in regards to God's determination to lose as a result of the "No" of election and God's determination for humankind to gain as a result of the "Yes" of election. It is glorious in regards to God's sacrifice for in such sacrifice, God's glory is revealed to humankind and triumphed over the world of evil. Hence, the crux of the matter in this eternal exchange is that God's suffering in his decree is a *glorious sacrifice*.

143. Excursus in *CD* II/2, 174–75.

144. Excursus in *CD* II/2, 175.

145. Though this notion is at odds with Augustine's idea of a limited movement in God wherein God can never be affected internally. te Velde, *The Doctrine of God*, 386.

146. For additional insight on Barth's conception of the temporal eternity, refer to §14 and §47 of *CD*.

147. *CD* II/2, 161.

148. *CD* III/2, 438.

enfleshed Word.[149] This point in time signifies the incarnation of the Son of God wherein the Son of God is revealed in Jesus Christ.

Barth begins his articulation of God being affected in time when "God sent forth His own Word" into the world.[150] The sending of the Word is thought of inseparably in the willing of the Word. Barth asserts, "It is, therefore, a true and objective knowing and willing, a personal Logos, (*persönlicher Logos*) which, since it is the Logos of God, is also omnipotent."[151] It is in this omnipotent sending and willing to be sent is where Barth concentrates his theopaschite rendition of time. The personal Logos therefore is always objectively viewed with Jesus Christ. This is the reason behind the Logos being "the self-communication proceeding from person to person and uniting God and man."[152] The personal Logos is the medium whereby "the Word of the cross" (*das Wort vom Kreuz*) is spoken.[153] Indeed the personal Logos is "God Himself, and in His revelation is known as Jesus."[154] That is why this Word of the cross is vividly portrayed in the crucifixion of Christ. In this way, the Word is certainly heard in the outworking of divine omnipotence.

Thus the omnipotence of God is conveyed properly in the Son's obedience to the Father.[155] It is also in this omnipotence wherein Barth upholds the eternality of divine suffering. There is no purport of collapsing the Trinity since Barth underscores that in this scenario, the Father *was with himself*; hence with the Son.[156] In other words, God *is* in Jesus Christ in the time of the incarnation. This is the vivid demonstration of God's primal decision to be God in time. What has been decreed eternally (personal Logos) has been actualized temporally (the Word of the cross) because God wills it; and more significantly, God has the power to consummate his will.[157]

What makes the election thoroughly concrete, Barth postulates, is God's choice to make the decree be acted upon in time: "the man Jesus of Nazareth who was born in the cradle of Bethlehem and died on the cross of Golgotha and on the third day rose again from the dead."[158] This epochal series, namely, the birth, life, ministry, death, and resurrection of

149. *CD* II/2, 163.

150. *CD* II/2, 163.

151. *CD* II/1, 605. *KD* II/1, 683.

152. *CD* II/2, 97.

153. Excursus in *CD* II/1, 605. *KD* II/1, 683. Barth cites Rom 1:16 and 1 Cor 1:18.

154. Excursus in *CD* II/1, 607.

155. *CD* II/2, 162.

156. *CD* II/2, 162.

157. *CD* II/2, 162.

158. *CD* II/2, 174.

Jesus Christ are parts of the single and indivisible foreordination of God's sacrifice. In the covenanted exchange, the "removing and refusing took place in Jesus Christ" according to Barth.[159] What God had gone through in Jesus Christ encompasses the dual realization (divine reality and human reality) of the primal decision.

This primal decision, argues Barth, is an actual decree as revealed in time. It is in time in which God has made *known* what he has obligated for himself (in eternity). We can say therefore that the divine self-giving is above and beyond time, yet also, within and through time.[160] In qualifying time in eternity, Barth thinks of the decree as predisposing time (advance disposition), and it also disposes time.[161] While it is obvious that Barth's thought on the implication of eternity on election, or vice-versa, is far from being straightforward, there is however a vehicle to understand this—through the divine activity.[162]

Barth considers the decree in terms of the *divine activity* in "history, encounter, decision" between God and humanity.[163] Because Barth utilizes the terms "history" and "encounter" in view of humankind, he speaks of this divine activity as covered by time. Yet the context shows that the "history, encounter, decision" between God and humanity as *prior* to time; and already *actual* in God.[164] This is viable in the covenant model. Barth understands such "history, encounter and decision" as "already willed and known from all eternity; and to that extent, *prior to all external events, are already actual before Him and for Him*."[165] The history in this context, is not human history but divine history actualized in Christ's event.

It would have been clearer, in my estimation, if the term "eternal history" (*Geschichte*) were used in the ET rather than simply translate it to "history" (*Historie*) to avoid any misunderstanding.[166] Also, in Barth's formulation of divine suffering, he does not make it plain that God, in this case, is passible. Perhaps what he grasps at this stage is a twofold theopaschite motif—God is internally impassible, but in relation to what is external,

159. *CD* II/2, 174.

160. *CD* II/2, 173

161. *CD* II/2, 155.

162. *CD* II/2, 175.

163. *CD* II/2, 175.

164. Barth orders it as such as "history, encounter, decision" with the intention not to confuse it with God's actions and participation in time. For insights on Barth's treatment of history, see Wu, *The Concept of History in the Theology of Karl Barth*.

165. *CD* II/2, 175. Italics mine.

166. For Barth, God wills his history to be in commonality with human history. *CD* IV/1, 7.

God is passible.[167] Thus, Barth explicitly alludes to the fact that God is self-moved because the suffering involved in the incarnation, and thereafter is purely God's choice. Even if it is pointed out that the actuality of God's sacrifice can be traced pre-temporally, Barth nevertheless does not argue in direct engagement with the issue of impassibility. What is axiomatic in Barth's writings, at it refers to God's self-giving, is the distinction in divine reality insofar as the *will* and the *reference* is concerned.[168]

Having understood that in eternity God determines to be affected, we will now move on to investigate *what* God wills to affect himself.

2.3 Affected by Evil

In answering what God wills to affect himself, we have yet to discover a more compounded reason behind such will. To locate the question of impassibility in Barth's doctrine of election, we have to qualify what evil *is* according to him. So this section is divided into two parts: (i) God's will for fallen humanity, and (ii) God wills to be "mastered" by evil.[169]

It is foundational in Barth to view the decree as God's self-giving.[170] It is the will of God to give himself in Christ's event. Christ's event gives grounding to the Christ-event. The former is the realization of God's committal while the latter encapsulates the eschatological result of such committal. In combining the two, we can see the content of the covenant in function.[171] This is God's will as understood in covenantal sphere. The rendering of God's will is focused on humans who "are created and fallen away" from God; hence, God's decision is to resolve the fall of humanity.[172] It is not and it will never be the will of God, or part of such will for his creatures to sin. So, it is here where Barth devises his own concept of what is evil in view of the covenant.[173]

167. Shippey, "The Suffering of God in Karl Barth's Doctrines of Election and Reconciliation," 165.

168. *CD* II/2, 167.

169. These divisions are derived from Barth's own thought and terminology found in *CD* II/2, 161, 163. The study of evil in Barth's theology is beyond the scope of this book because he discusses evil in depth in §50 of *CD*.

170. *CD* II/2, 161.

171. See Collins, *Trinitarian Theology, West and East*, 20–22.

172. Barth states that God's will (in all eternity) "is and only" for fallen humanity. This is the *content* of the "eternal predestination." *CD* II/2, 161. Lauber, *Barth on the Descent into Hell*, 20.

173. Evil for Barth is "nothingness" (*das Nichtige*), in the sense that God, according to Barth, did not will it and will never will it simply because it is not included in the

Barth construes that the will of God is twofold; it is dialectic in its form and substance.[174] This duality in the decree is what is known in the Reformed tradition as the double predestination (*gemina praedestinatio*), however Barth renders it with a twofold object and twofold content which derive its meaning and fulfillment in Jesus Christ.[175] Barth seeks to clarify that there is a "Yes" and a "No" or the positive and negative facets of election.[176] In other words, the twofold object-content is understood as God's alliance with fallen humanity.[177] Correspondingly, Barth stresses that in such alliance God *jeopardizes* his own honor.[178] God takes the negative character of election as *his own* (Christ's event); whereas humans are conferred with the positive character as *their own* (Christ-event) in effect of the covenant. The No in the decree is reserved to God and the Yes is reserved to humankind.[179] The conception of God's self-jeopardy is quite tricky; although these verbs are not used as self-inflicting, yet they could be taken, to some extent, as self-incriminating.[180] It is so because Barth sees the covenantal suffering in the function of the content. Hence the verbs in discussion are deemed as concession, and also, submission (*propensus* on God's part) to something which opposes God *but* willed by God.[181] Because God has committed to human beings who are "overtaken by evil," we have to examine what God has compromised in this context.[182]

Predestination, in Barth's reasoning, speaks of the complete and unconstrained covenantal act.[183] In this act, God is said to have compromised himself by permitting the *thought of evil* (being human) to enter into God's

decree. In other words, evil is what God did not determine in himself, therefore, evil is what God has passed over and *not willed*. Barth does not even associate evil to a proper existence, i.e., creature, but he rather simply considers evil in his doctrine of election as a non-being (yet real). In sum, *das Nichtige* is deemed as a "paradoxical and negative language." McDowell, "Much Ado about Nothing," 319.

174. Barth in this case articulates the form and substance in terms of the twofold aspects of the object and content of election.

175. *CD* II/2, 162. Morrison, *Karl Barth in Plain English*, 98.

176. *CD* II/2, 161. This is what Barth calls the "quality of God's will." *CD* II/2, 161. Also see te Velde, *Paths beyond Tracing Out*, 266–68.

177. Van Kuiken, *Christ's Humanity in Current and Ancient Controversy*, 22, 23.

178. *CD* II/2, 163.

179. *CD* II/2, 166.

180. *CD* II/2, 161–63.

181. Refer to excursus in *CD* II/2, 165.

182. *CD* II/2, 162–64.

183. *CD* II/2, 162–64.

being.[184] This thought of evil is what Barth calls the "shadow" of God's glory.[185] This shadow is not only what God does not decreed, but also vitally, it contradicts the covenant itself.[186] On the one hand, the covenant is the avenue whereby God is said to be fully in himself. On the other hand, the covenant is also the avenue whereby God is said to be self-compromised. So how do we come up with a synthesis of these seemingly contrasting hypotheses? The clue lies in the participation of God and humanity in the intersected realities. In the content and function of the covenant, the divine self-compromise accentuates the God-self, not otherwise. It is so because of the identification of the dual participation in and of Christ. Here the subject-object theme is again helpful.

In the covenant, humans participate by exclusion (fall away); whereas God participates by inclusion (solidarity). God is said to have compromised himself by *being* in the covenant because such a being has permitted the integration of human beings. Thus, in the being of Jesus Christ, humankind is fully integrated. That is why all people find their identity in Christ; and, it is in this identification where they see their purpose. However, in this self-compromise, God does not compromise his essentiality because humanity's participation is overlapped and overridden by God's participation. We can see here a shaping of a theopaschite view of election.

Barth strengthens this theopaschite view by utilizing another intriguing term which gives weight to the notion of God's self-compromise.

2.4 Mastered by Evil

When Barth argues for a self-compromised God, it is taken with the idea of hazarding oneself.[187] God's will as hazardous to God *in se*; such conception is something awfully grievous. In election, Barth sees God to have been "not merely affected by evil" but in actuality, has been "mastered" (*Überwältigt*) by it.[188] It is very important to recognize that the word "mastered" is an unfortunate translation having the potential of initiating serious confusion. In addition, the context where the term "mastered" is set against is somewhat vague as well. Let us review:

184. *CD* II/2, 162.

185. It is in this context where Barth asserts, "God *wills* evil only because He wills not to keep to Himself the light of His glory but to let it shine outside Himself, because He wills to ordain man the witness of this glory." *CD* II/2, 170. Italics mine.

186. *CD* II/2, 164.

187. *CD* II/2, 162, 164.

188. *CD* II/2, 164. *KD* II/2, 178. Italics mine.

> He [God] elected to be one with man in Jesus Christ, He did it with a being which was not merely affected by evil but actually *mastered* by it.[189]

Barth's use of the term *Überwältigt* is better understood as being "overwhelmed" or "overcome." Either way in these translations, he concedes no ground on the autonomy and sovereignty of God even in God's own being *Überwältigt* by evil. Nevertheless, his point is clear—God suffers and he suffers terribly as the Substitute. Also in German, the Subject of the overwhelming or overcoming of evil is not indirectly indicated but directly. Barth writes, "This man is not only touched by evil, but is overwhelmed by it" (*dieser Mensch ist vom Bösen nicht nur angerührt, sondern überwältigt*).[190] Thus the being in consideration is the humanity of Christ. Barth specifically associates the phrase "mastered by evil" to "this man"—Jesus Christ.[191] That is why Jesus Christ is the Representative of human beings in the covenant.

The overwhelming of evil is the epitome of what Barth calls the negative character of predestination. In God's self-determination, reprobation, and death come as a result. God's decision to give himself on behalf of humanity is a *real threat* to God, even if it is actualized in Jesus Christ. Barth thinks when God gave himself up, God "hazarded" himself in the person of Christ.[192] What is involved in this hazard is the endangerment of the divine "power and status."[193] In doing so, Barth construes, God has given away "all the *prerogatives* of His Godhead."[194] Yet in hazarding Oneself, God does not put his essentiality into peril. The risking of power and status is associated with the offering of the divinity, but, God's freedom to love is upheld. In Jesus Christ, God indeed is jeopardized yet such jeopardy is not twofold, hence, not a case of double jeopardy.[195] Though Christ jeopardized his divinity, God did not jeopardize his humanity. This may seem quite odd, . . . let me explain.

In Barth's view, the jeopardizing of divinity is actualized in the self-emptying and self-abasement of Jesus Christ vis-à-vis the *kenosis*.[196] At the same time, Christ cannot jeopardize his humanity because it is in this

189. *CD* II/2, 163. Italics mine.

190. My own translation of *KD* II/2, 178.

191. The context also suggests that Barth is speaking of fallen humanity in general. See excursus in *CD* II/2, 158–61.

192. *CD* II/2, 161.

193. *CD* II/2, 162.

194. *CD* II/2, 173.

195. *CD* II/2, 163.

196. *CD* II/2, 165.

being where humanity identifies itself. Here, the sacrificial act of God is a determination to appropriate damnation to himself rather than having humankind damned forever.[197] Even if we treat Christ's divinity and humanity in a unified being, Barth insists that God cannot imperil what he himself is eternally obliged to. Though Christ died at Calvary, such death is regarded to the flesh (Christ's event), not to the identity of humanity itself (Christ-event). This is what I call the majesty in the death of Jesus Christ.[198] For this reason, Barth argues that God could have remained in impassible glory, but God did not. God rather gives up the blessedness of his inner life so that humankind will be forever blessed.[199]

Now there appears to be a discrepancy arises from the arguments above. If Jesus Christ is the One overwhelmed by evil, and, if the divinity is that which is jeopardized, then how can we reconcile these formulations? The key is with Barth's engagement with impassibility in view of Christology. Barth discusses the surrender of impassibility as evident in the life of Jesus Christ—fully human and fully divine. In other words, God is affected in Christ in *kenosis*; as such refers to God's capacity to be affected *in time* is Jesus Christ.[200] This however does not disregard the twofold reference of the divine will. Therefore, it is in this twofold reference where the twofold theopaschite motif in Barth's dogmatics is properly understood.[201] Alan Lewis confirms, "God own majesty and mysterious incognito are preserved in the very event of their jeopardizing."[202]

Although the God of election, at this juncture, is still largely revealed in hiddenness, but in the discussion of God's suffering, Barth is quite unhampered. In the fullness of God in Jesus Christ, Barth reasons, God is said to have experienced the "actual onslaught and grasp of evil."[203] Thus there is no instance in eternity, or no phase in time whereby God is said to be immune from suffering. The God of Barth in his doctrine of election is a self-giving God, an *affected* God. In fact, the electing God is *already overwhelmed* by evil; this is the result of the self-activated will of God. Yet in this manner, God's primacy and lordship remain.

197. *CD* III/3, 289–90. Yet Barth explicates that *das Nichtige* "constantly threatens and corrupts" humankind.

198. For a more nuanced interpretation of Christ's death; cf. Drury, *The Resurrected God*, 114–15.

199. *CD* II/2, 166.

200. *CD* II/2, 164.

201. More on this topic in the next chapter.

202. Lewis, *between Cross and Resurrection*, 186.

203. *CD* II/2, 164. As such is the backdrop why Barth says that the Trinity has abdicated its entire prerogatives.

We will see below how Barth manages to articulate, in the first place, God's primacy and lordship without undermining God's grace and compassion. Barth does this in a direct yet dialectical fashion by positing a sovereign God who freely and lovingly suffers.

3. God's Sovereignty in Sacrifice

We have now come to discuss the second text:

> But as the living God, He is not Himself subject to or capable of any alteration, and does not cease to be Himself. His life is not only the origin of all created change, but is in itself the fulness of difference, movement, will, decision, action, degeneration and rejuvenation. . . . He does not do this of necessity but in freedom and love, or, one may say, with the necessity in virtue of which he cannot cease to be Himself, *the One who loves in freedom*.[204]

In order to apprehend clearly Barth's view of God's sacrifice, we have to trace what prompts him to treat divine love with divine freedom. In *CD* II/1, he expounds love in connection with freedom in the context of God's perfection.[205] For Barth, God's freedom cannot be aptly defined without love; and God's love cannot be amply understood without freedom. God is free in love and God loves in freedom. This free love is foundational to conceiving God's sacrificial decision and action. God is free to act on God's decision to sacrifice in Jesus Christ; also, this sacrifice is an act of love. The election of Jesus Christ shows how God freely loves humanity.[206]

God is seen to be truly dynamic because "He lives and loves" freely and it is in this being wherein God is said to have been repeating himself.[207] This is Barth's way of strengthening his stance on God's self-demonstration and self-affirmation in the differentiation-in-communion paradigm. In fact, it is in such paradigm where Barth views God's lordship because for him, divine sovereignty is about God living in free love.[208] This is God's omnicausal and autocratic (*Allwirksamkeit und Alleinherrschaft*) treatment of creation.[209] The

204. *CD* II/1, 491–92. Italics mine.

205. §30 and §31 of *CD*.

206. *CD* II/1, 274–75.

207. *CD* II/1, 301.

208. *CD* II/1, 301. Surprisingly, Barth neither converses nor cites Gustav Aulén with the latter's notion of the "sovereignty of divine love" against creaturely existence vis-à-vis time and space. Aulén however cites Barth on the Word as a "means of grace." *The Faith of the Christian Church*, 128, 149, 323n1.

209. *KD* II/1, 605.

divine freedom in "active relations" with creation is grounded in the loving being of God.[210] In this sense, God is said to be "the free Creator, the free Reconciler, the free Redeemer."[211] The correlation between divine love and divine freedom, as Barth sees it, is in terms of unity and distinction:

> Therefore, explicitly or implicitly, when we speak of the love of God we shall have to speak also of His freedom, when we speak of His freedom we shall have to speak also of His love, and of all others. But if we do not wish to deviate from Scripture, the unity of God must be understood as this *unity of His love and freedom* which is dynamic and, to that extent, diverse.[212]

In this regard, divine love and divine freedom are inseparable, yet each maintains its distinctive characteristic. This distinction must not be comprehended to factor in a variation in God's being, i.e., divine freedom accentuates "God in Himself"; while divine love accentuates "God for humanity."[213] Barth thinks that this is the mistake in orthodoxy, notably in the Reformed tradition. It is so because freedom is usually associated with sovereignty, hence essential to God; as opposed to love which is somewhat regarded as unessential to God due to its nonproximity with sovereignty.

For Barth, the love and freedom God has should be taken not only in tandem, but more importantly, on an equal footing.[214] To think otherwise is to fall into the Reformed misconception of God.[215] To ensure a consistently appropriate view of the two, says Barth, the strict application of God's transcendence over against God's activity must be avoided.[216] God is indeed personal because he lives in sovereign love and supreme freedom. God cannot be other than this God because he cannot be other than a free-loving being.[217] In sovereign love, God is seen to be perfect in the world. Barth writes, "God is He who in His Son Jesus Christ loves all His children, in His children all men, and in men His whole creation. . . . All His perfections are the perfections of His love."[218] God's perfection is rendered appropriately in the perfection of God's love towards the entire humanity. In other words, God's essentialities are eternally in relation *ad extra*; it is in this orientation

210. Hunsinger, *How to Read Karl Barth*, 30.

211. *CD* II/1, 301.

212. *CD* II/1, 343. Italics mine.

213. *CD* II/1, 345.

214. *CD* II/1, 345.

215. *CD* II/1, 345.

216. *CD* II/1, 347.

217. *CD* II/1, 346.

218. *CD* II/1, 351.

wherein God is said to be truly divine, in and of himself.[219] Suitably, love is no less divine than freedom and vice-versa.

Nonetheless with Barth, love is first, because God is "first of all the One who loves"; then freedom follows because God is also the "One who is free."[220] This perhaps explains why Christopher Holmes, I presume, wrestles with the complexity of Barth's thought vis-à-vis Barth's prioritization of divine love over divine freedom. Holmes critiques that with this recalibrated vista, Barth "compromises, to an extent, the *clarity* of God's freedom."[221] But I worry this is not the case, because for Barth, divine freedom is clearly understood only in solid affiliation with God's everlasting love. It does not mean that with God, love is over freedom. Barth merely wishes to ensure that divine freedom must not outweigh divine love because it leads to misconceiving God as impersonal.[222] Barth holds God to be truly personal, so personal that God does not choose to live outside the covenant.

3.1 God's Sacrifice in Love and Freedom

What is truly outstanding with the personal God, according to Barth, is God's love; but this love is always partnered with freedom. In fact, God uses his freedom to sacrifice himself in Jesus Christ. Surprisingly, such self-sacrifice, in its truest sense, is the "deprivation of the freedom of God."[223] So how do we make sense of this? The clue lies in the formulation: God is the One who loves at the expense of his divinity. Barth claims:

> He [God] did not think His divinity too precious to disguise and eclipse it, even to cast it in the mire, by Himself taking on humanity and becoming one among men. . . . He brought this *offering* and presented this *sacrifice* (Eph. 5.2); the offering of His freedom to His love. So great is His love that He regarded it as worthy of this offering.[224]

Divine freedom in its highest degree is a freedom to love. Freedom without sacrifice is not the freedom God has in the covenant. This is the context of Barth's assertion in which God sacrifices his divinity to effect solidarity with humanity. God is said to have valued humans more than he values

219. *CD* II/1, 351.

220. *CD* II/1, 351.

221. Holmes, *Revisiting the Doctrine of the Divine Attributes*, 223.

222. Stratis, *God's Being Towards Fellowship*, 121–22.

223. *CD* II/2, 492.

224. *CD* II/2, 491. Italics mine.

himself. God does this by being human in Jesus Christ in order to reconcile humankind to himself. God delivers himself up to remove the "obstacle" to the covenant.[225] This obstacle is the being itself of humans; a being unworthy of the covenant.[226] That is why the *human being* of Christ represents the being of the entire humanity inasmuch as the divine being of Christ represents the triune being of God. In God's directing of the covenant, the unworthiness of humankind is replaced by the worthiness of Christ. Christ, therefore, is what makes the offering worthy.

God's directing in this fashion manifests a freedom driven by love. Yet in the offering of the divinity, Barth argues, God remains in himself since this act of delivery is done voluntarily.[227] The execution of the covenant is without detriment to the essentiality of the Executor because the execution is the enacting of the sovereignly free love. In a sense, as Barth sees it, the deprivation of God's freedom does not necessarily mean that God's sovereignty is deprived as well. God's sovereignty is best understood in God's freedom to love. It is un-Barthian to place divine freedom over divine love, but it is very Barthian to marry both, especially in election.

In election, God is indeed free in his outworking because God is absolutely free to love.[228] Here Barth treats the harmony and interdependence between freedom and love in view of the decree.[229] In the election of Jesus Christ, there is no divine love in itself, likewise, there is no divine freedom in itself; one consists in the other simultaneously. God's freedom, therefore, is *always* in love and God's love is *always* in freedom.[230] It is also in this backdrop wherein the freedom of the Electing God coincides with the love of the Elected God.[231] This is the foundation of Barth's developed doctrine of election.[232]

In the election of Jesus Christ, God has protracted his autonomous reality to the reality of human beings.[233] Barth construes, "God's freedom is essentially not freedom *from*, but freedom *to* and *for*. God is free for man, free to coexist with man and, as the Lord of the covenant, to participate in

225. *CD* II/2, 494.

226. *CD* II/2, 494.

227. *CD* II/2, 492.

228. *CD* II/2, 491.

229. *CD* II/2, 491.

230. *CD* II/2, 352.

231. *CD* II/2, 357, 443.

232. *CD* II/2, 443.

233. *CD* II/1, 443.

his history."[234] In other words, there is no naked freedom in God which stems from divine primacy. God's freedom has always been with being human; hence, this supposition is what I call the suffering freedom of God.[235] In Barth's mind, there is also no "naked sovereignty" which informs his understanding of divine freedom.[236] He elucidates:

> God's freedom is not merely unlimited possibility or formal majesty and omnipotence, that is to say empty, naked sovereignty. . . . In God's own freedom there is encounter and communion; there is order and, consequently, dominion and subordination; there is majesty and humility, absolute authority and absolute obedience; there is offer and response.[237]

God's freedom, in Barth's interpretation, is sovereign in completeness, not merely in terms of dialectic pairs, but especially in terms of the inherent intimacy in election. Subordination, humility, and obedience are worked out within the sphere of communion. Divine freedom exercised in communion with humanity *is* a suffering freedom. Jürgen Moltmann supports such suffering freedom in God being a "determining reality."[238] For Moltmann, it is in this self-determined freedom where God emanates his identity.[239]

Moltmann refers to God's self-identification with his chosen people as divine determining act—God is the God of Israel *before* Israel becomes his people.[240] This notion, Moltmann exposits, is Barth's vehicle of highlighting the divine freedom to love because it is God who determines his identity and the identity of Israel. This is the gospel, according to Moltmann, because the election bears witness to God's sacrificial ways and works in grace.[241] God in his freedom chooses to be with humans so that they will find meaning in God's identity; it is in this determining reality

234. Barth, *The Humanity of God*, 72. Italics original.

235. Palma, *Karl Barth's Theology of Culture*, 34.

236. For another view on divine freedom; cf. Pinnock, *Most Moved Mover*, 83–84. For more insight, see Hocking, *Freedom Unlimited*, 37n40.

237. Barth, *The Humanity of God*, 71.

238. Moltmann asserts, "The limitation of God's unending power is an act of God's power over Godself. Only God can limit God." Moltmann, *The Living God and the Fullness of Life*, 44.

239. Moltmann, "Predestination: Karl Barth's Doctrine of the Election of Grace," video, 11:25.

240. Moltmann cites God saying, "I will be your God and you will be my people." Moltmann, "Predestination," video, 11:25. Cf. Jer 7:23; 31:33. *CD* II/2, 691–92; IV/1, 22.

241. *CD* II/2, 3. Moltmann, "The Election of Grace: Barth on the Doctrine of Predestination," 6. *CD* II/2, 76.

where election is consummated.[242] The self-determined relativity of God's freedom is integral in understanding Barth's revision of election. God's freedom takes place in Jesus Christ—it is a freedom not without encountering the need of humanity.[243] In other words, the communal trajectory of God's sacrificial act is the *heartbeat* of all divine works.[244] In his reading of Barth, Moltmann amplifies God's freedom differently. Instead of seeking the sovereignty of God as in the Reformed tradition, i.e., to protect the divine life, Moltmann is rather attentive to God's communicable grace. Consequently, community instead of transcendency would be the focal point in advancing God's freedom in Barth's schema.[245] In this case, God's freedom targets humans who need grace. For Moltmann, therefore, the ultimate purpose of predestination in Barth is the communion of humanity with God, and crucially, for this to last forever.

Barth's concept of divine freedom, argues Moltmann, is a supreme type of freedom which "is not an attribute of a subject" but rather it is "a concept of relation."[246] Divine freedom is the freedom of choice *within* a relationship between Subject (God) and subject (humanity).[247] In this respect, Barth's understanding of God's freedom is likened to God's offer of friendship to rebellious humans.[248] In free love, God takes the initiative to commune with humans even before they see the need for such communion. In Jesus Christ, God shows his willingness to sacrifice in order to be one with humanity. When this concept is married to the notion of Christ the suffering intermediary, it is pregnant with the connotation of a restored friendship between God and humanity.[249]

Another issue Moltmann cites in Barth's doctrine of election is on the equilibrium between God's will and nature. Moltmann asks, "Is God's will absolutely free in the election of grace?"[250] He considers this question within Barth's treatment of God's will *ad intra* and *ad extra* by determining the

242. Moltmann, "The Election of Grace," 4.

243. Moltmann, "The Election," 4.

244. Moltmann, *Crucified God*, 129–30.

245. Although prevalent conceptions of God's sovereignty and God's grace underscore both unity and exclusivity, Barth conceives divine sovereignty and grace always in solidarity with humankind. Kleis, "God was in Christ."

246. Moltmann, "The Election," 6.

247. Moltmann, "The Election," 7.

248. *CD* II/2, 566–67. Also see Komline, "Friendship and Being," 2–3.

249. Komline, "Friendship," 3, 22. Hartwell, *The Theology of Barth*, 135. It is in this kind of friendship where sanctification blooms. See McSwain, *Simul Sanctification*, 24, 260.

250. Moltmann, "The Election," 7.

divine essence. In this way, God's will cannot be thought to be arbitrary in nature simply because God chooses to sacrifice himself. Moltmann is convinced that Barth's God is not only a loving God, but more importantly, loves by offering himself in substitution. God makes himself insufficient (by not willing to live alienated from humankind) when God decides to be sufficient for humanity (by willing to love unconditionally).[251]

Moltmann reiterates that for Barth, when God loves, it is a sacrificial dedication of "his whole being," and in it God elects.[252] God does what "corresponds" to his being.[253] In other words, God's will is always in conformity with God's essential nature, which is unconstrained reconciling love. So what does it mean for God to use his freedom? God uses his freedom, Moltmann asserts, only to love.[254] This thought reflects Barth's theology of the cross.[255] God's suffering freedom is eternal and finds its apex in the agony of the Father with the Son at Calvary.[256] Thus in the election of suffering, the Trinity is involved in ensuring humanity's return to God.[257]

Because Barth puts forward God's reality as the identifier of humanity's reality, so human freedom is appraised to have originated from God. In the spectrum of the substitutionary sacrifice, the God-given freedom of humanity entails subordination and obedience.[258] There is no *empty freedom* in the person who is within God's communion. Since God's freedom is a suffering freedom, therefore by interjection, human freedom has the

251. Moltmann, "The Election," 4.

252. Moltmann, "Predestination: Karl Barth's Doctrine of the Election of Grace," video, 23:30.

253. Moltmann, "Predestination," video, 28:22.

254. Moltmann, "Predestination," video, 23:50.

255. Moltmann, "The Election," 8. *CD* II/2, 123. In his own theology of the cross, Moltmann exemplifies God's selfless freedom in the agony of Christ. He alludes, "The God of freedom, the true God, is . . . not recognized by his power and glory in the history of the world, but through his helplessness and his death on the scandal of the cross of Jesus." Moltmann, *Crucified God*, 95. Moltmann firmly underscores God's sacrifice of his freedom is the evidence of God's true sovereignty. Accordingly, he also views God's selfless freedom in the context of God's history of suffering in election. Moltmann, "Predestination," video, 35:52.

256. *CD* II/1, 374. Also see Lewis, *Between Cross and Resurrection*, 211–12.

257. *CD* II/2, 122. Barth adopts Athanasius's conception of election by accepting that "Subject of this decision is the triune God—the Son of God no less than the Father and the Holy Spirit." *CD* II/2, 110. See also Loewe, "Two Theologians of the Cross," 536–37.

258. *CD* II/2, 106, 116.

feature of sacrifice.[259] This analogous type of freedom speaks of the friendship of humanity with God.[260]

Barth firmly situates the doctrine of election in the doctrine of God. God's essential nature speaks of God's decision *for* humanity. Similarly, it is final in the sense that God's decree is rooted in God's being; it is eternally binding because God's nature is everlasting—forever-lasting in himself in being free to love.[261] Surely, God is conceived as absolutely free to love in which God is said to have limited himself "to be this God and no other."[262] In other words, God is none other than the God who actively self-gives in Jesus Christ. Barth's concept of God's self-limitation for and with humanity is integral to his reconfigured Christology. Christ becomes the beginning and end of election since Christ is the expression of God's determination (to be in and of himself) for the good of humanity. Barth argues that God's eternal will cannot, and will not be a will other than to be human.[263] It is in such a being whereby God is said to be truly divine and truly eternal.

3.2 The Immovable Self-moved God

Barth treats divine suffering in election under God's free love. The election is the avenue which showcases God's determination to love humans freely—even to the point of disregarding God's legitimate right to punish or simply annihilate humanity. God instead takes the punishment; Jesus Christ is elected to be the Rejected to assume the rejection of all people. In God's liberty, humans are liberated from the shackles of evil. In divine self-limitation, the grace of God becomes uninhibited. In this manner, there is nothing that can stand in the way of seeing the God of election as truly the Lord of the covenant. God indeed directs the operation of the covenant, as well as its function in the final judgment.

Cognizant of the final execution of judgment, Barth posits that God, the Executor, loves humans so much by electing Jesus Christ "in place" of them; hence their penalty falls upon him.[264] In election, God even elects the people who will do evil, yet such evil is still within God's plan to bring about his purpose. For instance, the election of Judas as an apostle to betray

259. The "mark of the cross" will be dealt with in chapter 3 under §66 of *CD* on "The Call to Discipleship."

260. Cocksworth, *Karl Barth on Prayer*, 179.

261. *CD* II/1, 518.

262. *CD* II/1, 518.

263. *CD* II/1, 599.

264. *CD* II/2, 124; I/2, 92.

Christ; also, the election of Pilate's sentence of Christ "as a revelation of His judgment on the world."[265] Though it seems bewildering, but for Barth, God's election is the intention and application of love.[266] The intention is in readiness, and, the application is in grace. It is the readiness of grace for humanity which brings the election of Christ's self-sacrifice.[267] The epitome of divine suffering in light of the decree finds in God electing "the cross of Golgotha as His kingly throne."[268] Even the tomb, Barth continues, is elected as a testimony of how God loves the world.[269]

Despite the foreknowledge of the shortcoming of humans to decipher the divine will and to act according to it, God is still determined to love them. Barth asks:

> Did He [God] not foresee human unfaithfulness and ingratitude in this typical form when before the foundation of the world He directed His love towards man? Did it prevent Him even at the outset from purposing the supreme good of this very man?[270]

Barth contends here that even though God knows humans's tendency to act against the covenant, God nonetheless loves them in witness to the covenant. In this sense, God's preservation of liberty and humanity's abuse of liberty are both accounted in the covenant.[271] Thus it is in the knowing and willing that God is said to be self-moved, hence, self-changed in God's unchangeable determination to self-give. God, in the supreme exercise of his autonomous compassion, sacrificed God's prerogative to stay away from humanity. By being human, God is said to have sacrificed his divinity so humans can identify with Jesus Christ. This is how Barth conceives of divine suffering in the context of election.

The intrinsic nature of the electing God is clearly understood as free because it is free to love in suffering. Since Barth views God's love and freedom together, i.e., distinct in union, then he also sees the two with equal integrity in articulating divine suffering.[272] There is no such thing as enclosed self-indulgent affection in God; divine affection shows itself in affliction. However, affection is self-initiated, affliction is not. Affection in God is

265. *CD* II/2, 165.

266. *CD* II/2, 18, 26. te Velde, *The Doctrine of God in Reformed Orthodoxy, Karl Barth, and the Utrecht School*, 405.

267. *CD* II/1, 129–30. See also Hunsinger, *How to Read Karl Barth*, 93.

268. *CD* II/2, 165. Mozley, *The Impassibility of God*, 174–75.

269. *CD* II/2, 165.

270. *CD* II/2, 264.

271. *CD* II/1, 169.

272. *CD* II/1, 169.

borne out of decision. Barth stresses, "They [humans] experience His love as an election in which a final decision is reached."[273] This is how humans know God's final decision—"wholly and altogether as love."[274] God and the election itself are therefore known in the self-sacrifice of Jesus Christ.[275] This is the backdrop of God's self-movement as a sovereignly unaffected being; an idea that is critiqued by James Dolezal.

Dolezal attacks Barth's conception of a self-moved God from a Thomistic perspective. When God created the world, Dolezal argues, the world did not cause a change in God into a new relation or state of affairs.[276] One must deny God's immutability and God's pure actuality if one will deny God's impassibility. Dolezal views the creation in time as not being contingent to move God into a new state of affairs; to speak otherwise is to accept God as being of the same ontological order with the world itself. So God is not moved because, according to Thomas Aquinas, God is the "unmoved mover."[277] God does not coexist with something external of himself; God is unmoved by anything external of himself. Divine concern and care are authentic forms of affection inherent with God, thus identical to God's being. In other words, God does not need *to become* in his affection; but rather, being in himself is already pure affection due to it's eternal characteristic.[278]

Dolezal, I think, misses what Barth truly has in mind in seeing God as being self-moved in Jesus Christ. He confuses Barth's understanding of God's actuality with not being purely actual but rather purely historical.[279] Dolezal negates Barth by saying that in the divine pure act, God is love in the fullest sense without fluctuation or change, which is the human lot. Barth, on the other hand, argues God's affection in view of divine perfection—God's perfect love is the exercise of God's freedom. God makes his affection actual by consistently relating his love, not because it is not yet actual (or purely actual), but because God's free love is always relative with humanity. This is what makes God perfect in every respect. He remains perfectly unmoved with humankind, yet, simultaneously also, God is perfect in his self-movement in Jesus Christ.[280] We can therefore

273. *CD* II/1, 169.

274. *CD* II/1, 169.

275. *CD* II/1, 608.

276. Dolezal, *God without Parts*, 86.

277. Aquinas, *Summa Theologica*, 1.2.1. *CD* II/2, 78.

278. Dolezal, *God*, 87.

279. Dolezal, *God*, 86–87.

280. *CD* II/1, 518.

interject that the constancy and omnipotence of God is demonstrated in divine self-movement.[281]

Even if Dolezal cites Thomas's position that it is necessary to view God as the unmoved mover in order to understand God's nature and character, then consequently, I inquire: If God is in the business of moving, what hinders him from moving himself? Since Thomas's notion of God being the unmoved mover pertains to God's inner life, then Barth is right in viewing God to be truly dynamic—especially in being free to decide in God's self.[282] It includes God being moved, or even be changed without compromising God's constancy and omnipotence. Divine affection, as Barth conceives it, does not make God contingent to the world as to make him belong to the same ontological order with it. Because God pre-temporally chooses to suffer in the world, this suffering is deemed ontologically prior to creation.

When Barth speaks of God's sovereign affection, it is interpreted in relation to eternity and time because God's being in Jesus Christ is itself a "pure duration."[283] It means "God is simultaneous, i.e., beginning and middle as well as end, without separation, distance or contradiction" in self-giving.[284] God gives himself in the consistency of his power to be forever in the covenant. God is said to be constantly in God's self by being constantly in power to sustain the covenant.[285] Respectively, Barth does not have to deny immutability and pure actuality in God, he simply redefined it in his own terms. As a result, impassibility is considered in a fresh atmosphere; an atmosphere where God's incapability of being affected and self-movement thrive in systematic accord. It is possible in the context of the eternal free love.

God's love is demonstrated in God's constancy while God's freedom is demonstrated in his omnipotence.[286] Barth admits that this "does say the

281. Because Barth maintains divine potency and dynamism, he distances from Hegel on the ground of comprehensive philosophical reflection—something susceptible to viewing God as contingent upon creation. Barth, *Protestant Theology in the Nineteenth Century*, 420. Barth in this case cannot be considered to hold pantheistic tendency (God is identified with creaturely reality) because of his consistent differentiation or "diastasis" between Creator and creature. Hitchcock, *Karl Barth and the Resurrection of the Flesh*, 165.

282. *CD* II/2, 64–65, 106–7. Barth argues, "the Creator cannot be changed into a world-cause, a supreme or first cause or a principle of being. . . . We must give them a new significance, therefore, if we are to use them to describe God the Creator." *CD* III/1, 13.

283. *CD* II/1, 608–10.

284. *CD* II/1, 608.

285. *CD* II/1, 609, 658.

286. Barth treats God's constancy (in conjunction with unity, omnipresence, eternity and glory in the perfection of God's freedom in §31 of *CD*. Cf. Price, *Letters of the*

same thing differently."[287] In other words, he treats love and freedom in one category; these two are inseparable in his understanding of divine affection. In fact, Barth views God's constancy to be in God's omnipresence and vice-versa; thus God will always be "free to love."[288] This makes God the living eternal God so much so that in the simultaneous past and future, old and new, God continually repeats and affirms himself within the covenant.[289] So with Barth, a God who loves in freedom is also free to change (in suffering) in fulfillment of the covenant.

After examining how God is said to have been self-moved in Jesus Christ, we can now turn to discuss why Barth prefers the use of the term constancy over immutability.

3.3 Constancy and Immutability

When Barth states, "He [God] is not Himself subject to or capable of any alteration, and does not cease to be Himself," it does not mean that in God, there is no change or movement at all as understood in Western orthodoxy.[290] This alteration, in a sense, is coincident with God stepping out of the covenant. For Barth, God is incapable of doing so because the fullness of God's being is *in* the covenant. Again, it is easy to misconstrue what Barth means in such statement if the tone of the covenant is muted. Understanding Barth's talk of constancy, enables us to continue our exposition of the second text:

> His [God's] life is not only the origin of all created change, but is in itself the *fulness of difference, movement*, will, decision, action, degeneration and rejuvenation. . . . He does not do this of necessity but in freedom and love.[291]

Barth explicitly shows why God, in and of himself, highlights divine constancy, and not strictly, divine immutability. Being the *living* One, God is dynamic in himself that he is said to be "the source of all creaturely change" (*Ursprung aller geschöpflichen Veränderung*) as the Creator. God is, in fact, in being dynamic, the "fulness of difference and movement," (*Fülle des*

Divine Word, 171.

287. *CD* II/1, 490.

288. *CD* II/1, 491.

289. *CD* II/1, 492.

290. *CD* II/1, 491.

291. *CD* II/1, 492. Italics mine. Barth refers to Rom 8:35; Gal 2:20; and Eph 5:25.

Andersseins, der Bewegung) i.e., becoming old and new.[292] For instance, God is constant in himself even in the variableness of the Christ-event: from crucifixion (old) to resurrection (new).[293] In this case, God is said to be true to his determination for humanity. This is how God, as Barth proposes, repeats and affirms himself as the eternal within the covenant.

But how does the above text conform to Barth's subsequent proposition: "God is so faithful, so constant in the freedom of His love, that for the sake of it, while *remaining unchanged*, He could also become as unlike Himself as He did in the act of His delivery . . . ."[294] There seems to be a discrepancy between *CD* II/1 and II/2 whether God is changed or not; yet the context of the former likewise shows God to be unchanged, in and of himself, in the "unparalleled forfeiture of [his] freedom" (*Freiheits-beraubung sondergleichen*) upon God's own choice.[295] God remains unchanged in his boundless love; it is in this free love where God decides to offer his divinity in the being of Jesus Christ. As regards God's autonomy, Barth understands God to have "tied Himself to the universe," thus the "compromising of His freedom."[296] In other words, the fullness of God is not held hostage in God's self-delivery to the world. God remains the Lord of the world while being in it. The dialectical articulation of divine autonomy (to freely restraint oneself) is central to Barth's conception of constancy. God did change in taking the form of a human, hence the phrase "unlike Himself," yet this act is a free act in love which exhibits the unchangeable character of God. This is where the term "fulness of difference and movement" is viewed against. What is constant or unchangeable with God is his relational character.

Notice Barth's argument in the context of God's omnipotence; it is in such omnipotence wherein God is said to be capable of being who he is—in constancy. The fact that God is free in his power, and God's power is manifested in an uncompelled affection independent of any human conditioning or expectation. God is not the One who is necessarily but is the One who is unconditioned.[297] This is how Barth sees God to be truly alive; God is not altered or does not cease to be God in the covenant.[298] It is in this context where Barth advances his notion of God's *self*-change.

292. *KD* II/1, 553.

293. *CD* II/2, 678.

294. *CD* II/2, 492. Italics mine.

295. *KD* II/1, 546.

296. *CD* II/2, 166, 155.

297. *CD* II/1, 303.

298. *CD* II/1, 257–97. McCormack, "The Actuality of God," 231–32. Cf. *CD* II/1, 494, 496.

Barth argues for the predicate "immutable" as determined by the Subject (God of the covenant) and not otherwise.[299] Even if immutability is insisted, God has the final say how it is referred to himself. It is in this milieu wherein God's love is unshackled by divine essentiality.[300] Indeed, says Barth, what God cannot do, hence, cannot be, is to cease to love in freedom for the good of humanity.[301] This is where the suffering of God is to be understood and where the concept of immutability is to be viewed against.

Barth's definition of immutability, if this term is to be demanded, entails a consistent God in *every* change and in *every* movement.[302] Although God partakes freely in the alteration of creation, he does so as the Creator; God lords over that which causes him to change or move by God's own choosing. Barth thinks this act as proper to God. Barth uses the term "holy mutability" to refer to God being self-changed and self-moved, as opposed to the "unholy mutability of men" in which humans are forcibly subject to creaturely change and movement.[303] It is because of this sharp distinction that Barth prefers to rather use "constancy" (*Beständigkeit*) over "immutability" (*Unveränderlichkeit*).[304]

God's constancy in himself, Barth posits, does not mean "pure" immovability or "pure" incapability of being affected.[305] The term pure for Barth is meaningless if it is incongruent with his interpretation of divine perfection.[306] The pure-ness of God and in God is the "uninterrupted continuity" which is self-conditioned in the covenant; nowhere else.[307] Thus God is pure in his outworking if it is done in covenantal operation. Yet Barth cannot be regarded to have completely deviated from Thomas Aquinas in this regard. Stephen Webb attests, "Like Aquinas, Barth seeks to define God as purely actual and thus continually open, which suggests that God is never compelled to create the good or to love what is created."[308] So how can we make sense of Barth's position? The actuality of the election of Jesus Christ is so compelling that Barth's theology is heavily informed by his Christology. God can be said to be purely actual if this is *solely* seen in God's free love

299. *CD* II/1, 493.

300. *CD* II/1, 495.

301. *CD* II/1, 494.

302. *CD* II/1, 496.

303. *CD* II/1, 496, 500–5.

304. *KD* II/1, 552, 555. *KD* IV/1, 84, 86; IV/2, 92–93.

305. *CD* II/1, 494.

306. *CD* II/1, 324–25.

307. *CD* II/1, 493. Sumner, *Karl Barth and the Incarnation*, 126.

308. Webb, *Jesus Christ, Eternal God*, 210.

in Jesus Christ. Likewise, God is also purely actual in the everlasting self-repetition and self-affirmation in the Logos.

Thus the constancy in and of God is the purely actualized being of Jesus Christ. In him we can have a peek of the "inner life" of the Godhead because Jesus Christ is the manifestation of God's "eternal actuality."[309] So the God of Barth is not a prisoner of his own attributes; God's free love shapes the conception of what is purely perfect in God. In this way, God can be seen to be perfectly constant in suffering in Christ.[310] Divine immutability includes God's constant vitality, and not otherwise, since God is eternally free to sovereignly suffer; and it is in this divine expression where Barth sees God to have been confirming the God-self.[311] Thus, in this sense, God is said to have immutably suffered because in suffering, God remains true to his character.[312]

I do not believe Barth to have picked-up the Western traditional concept of immutability in discussing God's preeminence. God's character is enduring and dynamic in contrast to the prevalent notion of *immutabile*—God being immobile or immovable.[313] The insistence on immutability, more often than not, tends to be unproductive with Barth due to its metaphysical scope. To address such tension, I think Colin Gunton's synthesis is helpful: "What is immutability trinitarianly construed? Immanently speaking, God cannot but be love; economically speaking, God will not but see to it that his purposes for the perfection of the creation come to be fulfilled."[314] Rightly so, the suffering God who stays the same in suffering is taken in its proper meaning by considering God's faithfulness within the covenant. Barth has reservation in using the term "immutability" to avoid the usual abstract and sterile connotations that come with it. It explains why he instead favors the term "constancy" or "permanence" to stress the ontological resonance of the covenantal pattern in conceiving God. In this respect, it is helpful to attend to Paul Fiddes's definition of immutability in light of Barth's view of the suffering God.

Can we say that God truly suffers if God remains immutable in suffering? This is what Fiddes raises against Barth's theospaschite theology. Fiddes critiques, "Barth falls short of the true meaning of suffering when he thinks of God's suffering as being a matter of self-movement or self-change,

309. *CD* II/1, 494.

310. *CD* II/1, 494.

311. *CD* II/1, 495.

312. Leftow, "Immutability," para. 7.

313. *CD* II/1, 494.

314. Gunton, *The Christian Faith*, 189.

though he makes the essential point that God is free to suffer. Employing this latter insight of Barth, we should say that God is free to be changed."[315] Since Fiddes thinks of God as immutable in the sense that God remains perfect and constant even in change, thus God in this case cannot be seen to truly suffer.[316] Even if God risks something in going into the far country, Fiddes observes, the negative correlation of change is what Barth radically articulates positively for God's constancy—a God who suffers remains *in* himself.[317] According to Fiddes, Barth's attempt to reserve some kind of impassibility in God even in God's acts in the world undermines any talk about divine suffering because the discussion somehow moves from God's action in Jesus Christ to God's transcendent being.[318]

Fiddes continues that God's prerogative not to suffer is likewise counterproductive to the discussion on divine suffering.[319] Because God is ultimately free to decide to suffer or not, Barth runs into the quagmire of *what-might-have-been* speculations. God could not have decided to suffer but still God decided to suffer. In other words, God could have remained impassible instead he had chosen to suffer, hence God decided to be passible.[320] Yet in being passible, Barth contends that God remains impassible to stress that suffering is not necessary to the being of God.[321] This is where Fiddes argues that divine suffering is a choice not between possibilities, but it is rather a creative decision, i.e., God's act in Jesus Christ shapes the way God is conceived.[322]

Although Fiddes's argument is valid concerning Barth's attempt to uphold God's impassibility even in suffering, the concept of impassibility does not undermine the concept of divine suffering. Since Barth locates the suffering of God ontologically, namely, in God's primal decision to assume flesh in the person of Jesus Christ, so divine impassibility does not stand in the way in accommodating God's eternal immovability from outside actions and events.[323] Furthermore, Barth's rendition of God's freedom to choose for himself *in* himself stimulates the discussion on the reality of the suffering God. Barth finds that God's will to suffer does not counter

315. Fiddes, *The Creative Suffering of God*, 60.

316. Fiddes, *Creative Suffering*, 48.

317. Fiddes, *Creative Suffering*, 61–63.

318. Ward, *Rational Theology and the Creativity of God*, 122.

319. *CD* II/1, 303.

320. Ward, *Rational Theology*, 119.

321. *CD* II/2, 163.

322. Fiddes, *Creative Suffering*, 68.

323. More discussion on this topic in section 3.1 "The Twofold Attributes of God."

God's prerogative not to suffer because the Electing and the Elected God is always *for* humanity. Since Jesus Christ is central in understanding God's being, thus Barth does not dwell on the possibility of God not choosing to suffer. Barth rather devotes his effort to explaining what he means by God being a covenantal God.[324]

It is true that we cannot view God as conditioned other than by God's freedom to be changed because God cannot be forced to be other than himself. However in being a covenantal God, Barth says there is only one aspect God cannot do—to surrender his freedom *to* love.[325] Brian Asbill notes the coinherence of divine love and divine freedom in God's self-binding to humanity. Here love and freedom are taken in a "unified duality" in speaking of the covenantal God.[326] In other words, God is free to be the loving God in the covenant. We can see that Asbill puts into proper perspective what Barth means by a covenant founded on the non-contradistinction in God.[327] This is different from our previous discussion on God's surrender of his freedom *per se* vis-à-vis his divinity. God's surrender of his divinity is to sacrifice the exclusivity of God's inner life; whereas God's surrender of his freedom to love is to give up the covenant itself. What I think Barth endeavors to get across is that God chooses solidarity over solitude because he is a God of the covenant. There is no covenant-less God in election.[328] Since there is no *covenant-less* God in election, then there is no self-seeking, self-serving deity behind the election. The God of election is self-giving in uninterrupted continuity.

From Barth's standpoint, God is eternally consistent in himself, and it is in this constancy where God always repeats and affirms his self-sacrifice. God can be different from what humans perceive to him to be, i.e., aseity, simplicity, immutability, infinity, but the electing God cannot be different from One who sacrificially loves in freedom. In effect, God cannot impugn himself insofar as God's supreme love is concerned, albeit for the sake of God's love *per se* or in virtue of his freedom.[329] In other words, it cannot be said of God to not freely love because of God's freedom not to love. The key to Barth's understanding of the self-consistent suffering deity is in view of divine constant vitality. It is in God's potency to freely love where God

324. *CD* II/2, 8–13; 52–55.

325. *CD* II/1, 344–45. Asbill, *The Freedom of God for Us*, 120.

326. Asbill, *The Freedom*, 120.

327. Asbill, *The Freedom*, 183–84.

328. *CD* II/2, 9–10.

329. *CD* II/1, 495.

is seen to be flatly unalterable in his affection.[330] Similarly, this highlights the sovereignty and majesty of God. For Barth, God is said to be reliable by virtue of his sovereignty, and God is said to be consistent by virtue of his majesty.[331] Barth finds God's true simultaneity in himself in absolute freedom to love; it is an attribute exclusive only to God.[332] In this exclusive attribute, God does not will to be exclusive, but inclusive. As the One who lives under the covenant, God freely allows himself to sacrificially participate in the created order vis-à-vis time, of which the created order could participate in God's life.[333]

God participates in this way, Barth urges, not because God is compelled to or that he cannot be God if he does not will to sacrifice. Rather, God freely offers himself because he is this God, and, he does not will to be other than this God.[334] In essence, sacrifice is not foreign to God according to Barth. Self-offering is not something alien in God because God eternally chooses to subject himself to creaturely reality; but in this subjection, the order of creation itself follows after God's constant vitality. The fallen world becomes the covenanted world in the sovereign and majestic ordering of God.[335] Thus in subjecting to the created order, God is not ordered by it, but rather, he orders it. This is the meaning and efficacy of God acting and being acted upon in the world.

Evaluation

In my reading of *CD* II/1–2, I have discovered that when Barth firmly places the doctrine of election at the heart of the doctrine of God, the result is indeed unprecedented in dogmatics—the eternal act speaks of the eternal being. The subject-object theme accentuates God's being in subjective manner: acting; and objective manner: acted upon. This framework deepens Barth's christocentric conception of election. Also, this framework allows Barth to engage with impassibility in considering the omnipotence of God. The ontological/lexical study showing Jesus Christ as the Lord-Partner in and of the covenant sets the discussion on impassibility to an unusual route. Clearly, the play-out between eternity and time is critical. The discussion on impassibility is pulled back from temporality to pre-temporality. This is

330. *CD* II/1, 505.

331. *CD* II/1, 608.

332. *CD* II/1, 609.

333. *CD* II/1, 495–99, 501.

334. Hence, "God's Love is Volitional." Read Peckham, *The Love of God*, 90–93.

335. *CD* II/1, 492.

in view of God's committal to the covenant, and, in the renewed treatment of the Logos as *personal*. As the notion of the electing God is revisited, the actualistic, hence realistic treatment of election has appraised the being of God with the being of Jesus Christ.

Barth, in conversation with Western orthodoxy, ushers in fresh insights on impassibility. Barth not only challenges the implausibility of ascribing Christ's suffering to God, but also, solidify the balance of transcendence and immanence. Therefore, it is in this intensified argument where God is seen not merely in the Son of God, but critically, *in* Jesus Christ. Barth cannot speak of election apart from God's sacrifice. This sacrifice is considered in the self-movement of God in the world. The world becomes the venue where God is said to have been affected, still as a divine self-take.

In Barth's schema, God's immovability or being unaffected is interpreted against God's primal decision. The result could have been profitable to the rigid discussion on impassibility, yet again, Barth does not push in this direction. Moreover, the emphasis on *agape* over *apatheia* in discussing impassibility is somehow missing, even in the articulation of freedom and love as divine perfections. What he pushes in his argumentation is the connection of the personal Logos and the Word of the cross. This, I think, is key in developing a theopaschite theology in election. Likewise, Barth does not fully develop such connection. What he definitely develops is God's abrogation of incapability of being affected that is obviously a deviation from both Catholic and Protestant traditions.

What is not evident in the early Barth is the major role of the already-but-not-yet embodiment of the Logos. It creates a window, i.e., inclusion of a *quasi-anhypostatic essence*, to somehow apprehend the affected God of election. This window, as the term suggests, is not enough to concretely posit a theopaschite theology.[336] What is obviously concrete in Barth's evolved doctrine of election is the God who is self-obligated in the covenant. It has the following facets, namely, the divine will: God's sacrifice in himself (in which substitutional act is manifested); and the reference: the sinful and condemned humanity (by which divine substitutional act is accounted for).[337]

336. Barth's theopaschite expression is distinctly incompatible with Emil Brunner's rejection of timeless divine suffering or Wolfhart Pannenberg's emphasis on the suffering of the historical Jesus. This topic will be studied in depth in chapter 4. See Brunner, *The Christian Doctrine of God*. Volume I, 270–71. Pannenberg, *Jesus—God and Man*, 33–37.

337. Barth wonders, "If we would know what it was that God elected for Himself when He elected fellowship with man . . . ?" *CD* II/2, 164. Barth continues, "then we can answer only that He elected our rejection." *CD* II/2, 164.

So does Barth already have a doctrine of divine impassibility? I think he still does not have one, but, impassibility is directly engaged in this period. Though in one citation he explicitly says that God is "not impassible," Barth does not however explicitly say that God is passible. This implicit passibility inherent in Barth's thought is not tantamount to acknowledge a passible God in election. It is so because the suffering involved in Jesus Christ is concealed as it is disclosed in sovereignty. Although it appears that a passible God is more plausible with Barth's formulation of a God who loves eternally and unconditionally, yet he never sees God to be strictly passible. Even in the presentation of God as being "overwhelmed" by evil—though this assertion could effectually set the inflection for passibility, nevertheless what Barth underscores here is a *non-affectively self-affected* God in eternity.

It also dawns on me that the texts in *CD* II/1–2, in which Barth considers divine (im)passibility, are not categorical in substance, i.e., God is strictly impassible, or God is strictly passible, in election. Even though this form could be handled to mean *against* the traditional notion of immutability, Barth unfortunately does not elaborate the discourse on impassibility. Barth's use of the term "immutability," although relatively, is still not helpful in his over-all argument because it could lead to a misreading of his revitalized theology on divine suffering. Why not simply avoid the adjective immutable describing God and instead use the term "constancy" throughout his writings? The fact that he intends to underscore God's constant compassion in the covenant, which carefully involves self-change in self-movement, then immutability (as prevalently viewed) no longer fits Barth's theological program. What is consistently clear, in Barth's theology, is a God who is stable in terms of God's free love; but it is not invariable in terms of movement or "change." Here we can clearly derive Barth's doctrine of divine constancy.

Anyhow, whether or not God *had been affected* by the agony of Jesus Christ is something left hanging. Perhaps Barth wishes to be coherent with this view: God remains *known* yet simultaneously *unknown*. This God, is said to have willed something that is unnecessary. Notice that despite the elemental complication in articulating God in this manner, Barth's presentation of the reality of God and election are remarkably cohesive.

Another exhibit of coherence-in-complexity is found in Barth's cycle of dialectic and analogic methods in articulating God's will. For instance, in Jesus Christ being the Reconciler, God wills reconciliation, but God does not will the location of its actualization. Thus the relational-yet-resistant aspect of election is still evident. What is also apparent, at least to substantially inform my judgment, is the train of thought in support of the notion of divine suffering in Barth's mature doctrine of election: first, Barth's God is unambiguously *in* Jesus Christ in eternity; second, Barth's God therefore is absolutely free in self-revelation; and lastly, Barth's God suffers in himself as the ultimate expression of love to humanity.

The recurrent injunction in Barth's thought of negative and paradoxical terms, i.e., jeopardize, hazard, compromise, could not be mistaken as only unintentional or cursory in Barth's articulation.[338] The "ontic peculiarity" of evil, however, makes his account of divine suffering less satisfactory.[339] What is quite satisfactory is his advancement of the Godhood amidst the horrific conditions Jesus Christ subjects himself to. As a result, such negative terms are conceived positively because the involved paradox is made coherent under the covenantal theme.

Having already laid the groundwork on the divine freedom for humanity (in §13) and on how he understands the relationship between God's time and that of the creature (in §14), Barth is ready for an introductory discussion on impassibility in *CD* II/2. Nonetheless, it is far too early to make a clear statement on Barth's treatment of impassibility in revising predestination. His attention to the subject—mostly by way of passing references—serves his more basic concern to rethink the doctrine of election and so the doctrine of God.[340] Ultimately, the God of Barth is eternally in himself even in variableness or in assuming another form vis-à-vis being human. I think as long as we are conscious of how Barth understands God in this context, the less likely we will misread his thought on divine suffering.

There is one aspect which needs further investigation—Barth's treatment of impassibility in the pre-temporal humanity of the Son of God. The Son of God is referred to as a "man" in eternity past. In fact, "this human is Jesus Christ who was in the beginning with God."[341] Thus, in the next chapter, we have to resolve what Barth means by that especially against the Chalcedonian Formula. The issue at hand is treated substantially in *CD* IV/1–2.

338. As seen above, such terms are used in conjunction with evil.

339. *CD* III/3, 353. See Harrison, *The History of Evil in the Early Twentieth Century*. Volume 5, 107–8.

340. What Barth did not attempt to do is to engage head-on with the traditional conception of impassibility akin to other writers, e.g., Gavrilyuk in *The Suffering of the Impassible God* and Weinandy in *Does God Suffer?*

341. *CD* II/2, 162. Barth claims, "It is in this other person who is the person of God Himself in the flesh." *CD* II/2, 62.

Chapter III

Election and Divine (Im)passibility in Barth's Theology between 1951 and 1955

In chapter 2, I argued that Karl Barth has engaged directly with divine impassibility in *Church Dogmatics* II/2; that, to some extent, strengthens his argument on the electing God who suffers in solidarity with humanity. In this chapter, I shall argue that in suffering, God indeed upholds his sovereignty and lordship. To substantiate my point, I will shift my focus to *CD* IV/1–2 to ask what truly informs Barth's understanding of divine suffering with the following concerns: first, is God undeniably capable of suffering?; next, if God is capable of suffering, what precisely causes God's suffering?; and last, if God does suffer, how can he remain sovereignly God and Lord of all? In order to do so, I will consider one vital text, namely, *CD* IV/1, 187; here Barth has critically approached the issues of impassibility.

In what follows, I will begin with examining the relationship of God to outside actions and events by considering the ontology behind the proposed text. I will then turn to investigate how impassibility is handled against the *kenosis*. And finally, I will analyze what truly informs Barth's notion of divine suffering in view of his rendition of the atonement.

The first section of this study will inspect Barth's conception of God in "The Way of the Son into the Far Country," as the One who can be, and is moved by what is external.[1] It covers the conception of God as moved or touched *ad extra* by God's own will. It also considers certain German words to illuminate the ontological basis for God being the reconciling God. The second section will investigate Barth's articulation of the reconciling will of God to be both Servant and Lord in Jesus Christ. This explains why the impassible God suffers in temporal history as determined in the eternal decree.[2] The description of the Son of God (the Lord as Servant)

1. §59.1 of *CD*.

2. *CD* IV/1, 160–66, 180–82; IV/2, 51–64, 68–71.

who goes into the "Far Country" will be inspected in view of God's self-humility in the incarnation.[3] The third section will exposit God as the One who remains sovereignly God and Lord of all despite his suffering in "The Homecoming of the Son of Man."[4] Barth's notable depiction of the Son of Man (the Servant as Lord) who comes "Home" will be analyzed in light of God's victory over suffering.[5]

The three sections will unpack Barth's developed theopaschite theology; it will also assess why he allows the notion of a suffering God in his doctrine of reconciliation. Basically, this matter is heavily shaped by Barth's reconfigured Christology so we have to tackle his take on Jesus Christ's two natures in view of impassibility. To achieve this, the Chalcedonian Formula will be the platform for scrutiny since Barth engages with it substantially.[6]

We will now investigate why Barth thinks an impassible God suffers in reconciliation.

1. The Relation of God to Outside Events and Actions

Below is the key text which provides the framework for this chapter:

> He [God] is absolute, infinite, exalted, active, impassible, transcendent, but in all this He is the One who loves in freedom, the One who is free in His love, and therefore not His own prisoner. He is all this as the Lord, and in such a way that He embraces the opposites of these concepts even while He is superior to them.[7]

Barth approaches impassibility mainly in his doctrine of reconciliation.[8] For him, this topic should advance the discussion of the atonement in Jesus Christ, as well as foster a deeper appreciation of the implications derived

3. *CD* IV/1, 157. The interpretation of Melito of Sardis (c. 180) on the *forma servi* is significant here because this deals with the sacrifice of the Son in his service to the Father and to humanity. *CD* IV/1, 184–85. Although Barth also mentions Ignatius of Antioch, Irenaeus of Lyons and Caspar Olevian in the three texts considered in this study, nevertheless they are not major contributors to Barth's discussion on (im)passibility.

4. *CD* IV/2, 20–68.

5. *CD* IV/1, 160–66, 180–82; *CD* IV/2, 51–64, 68–71.

6. Kärkkäinen, *Christ and Reconciliation*, 187. Barth's Christology will then be examined in conversation with theologians who directly and indirectly contribute to the Chalcedonian Formula, namely, Cyril of Alexandria (c. 376–444); Nestorius of Constantinople (c. 386–450); Apollinarius of Laodicea (c. 390) and Eutyches of Alexandria (c. 380–456).

7. *CD* IV/1, 187.

8. Barth only explores the divine suffering in *CD* II/1–2. See *CD* II/1, 370, 371; II/2, 79, 163, 166.

from it.[9] In reconciliation, the perfection of God is in function in uniting humankind with God. In free love God becomes passible, etc.; yet God remains sovereignly unconstrained in himself. Barth also maintains the idea of the affected God by his very deliberate choice of particular words. These facets are discussed under Barth's ontological analysis of divine suffering.

1.1 The Ontological Basis of Divine Suffering

Barth's rendition of God's ontology addresses the concern whether God is truly affected *ad extra* or not. In the cited text, God is described as being both impassible and passible. The German word for impassible is *Unberührbar* which literally means "untouchable."[10] Barth utilizes a similar word (*Unberührbarkeit*) "immovability" to refer to God's quality too.[11] These key words are used in inclusive terms—God in and of himself, and not exclusively—God in and for himself. It indicates how Barth handles the question of divine suffering in light of God's relation to creation.[12]

Barth thinks of God as untouchable and immovable; God cannot be touched and moved by events and actions in creation. Nonetheless, he continues to say that the impassible God chooses to be passible in the being of Jesus Christ. How is it feasible for an impassible God to be moved?[13] Barth's answer is founded on God being "the Lord" due to God's superior freedom and love for the creatures. In this regard, God's impassibility is not, and will not be, a hindrance to God's all-powerful love; if God chooses to love wherein he is moved in the process, then God is free to do so. Barth articulates such autonomy in the context of the decree in which God determines himself to be human.[14] This decree is unchangeable because God ordains and affirms it in eternity.[15] What is unchangeable is God's self-determination towards humankind. Here Barth can argue for a God who suffers as

9. *CD* IV/1, 180–85.

10. *KD* IV/1, 204.

11. *KD* IV/2, 73. However in the ET of *CD* IV/1–2, both German words are simply translated as "impassible" akin to the Latin *impassibilis*. KD IV/1, 193. This translation does not reflect the nuances in Barth's thought in its specific context. McCormack, "Divine Impassibility," 158.

12. *CD* IV/1, 176–77, 186; IV/2, 68, 72.

13. For convenience onwards, I will only use the word "moved" as regards to the discussion on impassibility.

14. *CD* IV/1, 158–59, 195. Bender, *God's Time For Us*, 33.

15. *CD* IV/1, 131, 204.

human, yet in being so, God remains in himself. God is always in absolute control of himself even in being human.[16]

Moreover, Barth also considers God's other attributes, namely, infinity, exaltation, activeness, and transcendence in stressing the absoluteness of God even in being affected. God demonstrates he indeed is the Lord by embracing the opposites of these attributes in Jesus Christ. It is implied that aside from being passible, God suffers by being finite, lowly, passive, and immanent as human. It is in such a being where Barth logically views a self-determined God in this God-determined human. God is said to have been capable of pain and misery, hence, actually did suffer, by freely choosing to be in Jesus Christ.[17]

God's being in Jesus Christ, argues Barth, can be a statement about the divine inner being. Barth's understanding of the "inner being" of God is conceived within the divine relationship in divine history.[18] The inner being of God is viewed in terms of the *divine relationship* insofar as the obedience of the Son to the Father is concerned. Also, the inner being of God is manifest in *divine history* insofar as the outworking of a primal decision in time is considered. Despite the riddle inherent in the divine life, Barth infers, it is revealed in a way that is quite apprehensible; i.e., coincident in the life of Jesus Christ.[19] Since the obedience of the Son of God is treated as an "obedience of suffering," this act presupposes that God voluntarily submits himself to what inevitably befalls humanity.[20]

Having studied the ontological basis of divine suffering, we will now attend to the reason why Barth conceives God to have suffered in Jesus Christ in going into the far country.

2. The Relation of God's Suffering to Jesus Christ's Condescension

The background of our text shows the will of the Lord God to suffer as "the Servant" in Jesus Christ.[21] Barth makes this condescension poignant by

16. *CD* IV/1, 159–60.

17. *CD* IV/1, 188–89.

18. *CD* IV/1, 39; *CD* IV/2 105.

19. *CD* IV/1, 49–50.

20. *CD* IV/1, 177. See Levering, "Augustine and Aquinas on the Good Shepherd," 237.

21. *CD* IV/1, 163–65, 188, 193. Barth cites Phil 2:6–7 as the basis for Christ being "The Lord as Servant."

describing it as God's self-humility.[22] This notion is illustrated as "The Way of the Son into the Far Country."[23] We will have to critically analyze each element involved in this illustration to better appreciate the suffering God in Barth's doctrine of reconciliation.

2.1 The Far Country

In order to know the extent of divine suffering in the Son's obedience to the Father, we have to understand what Barth means by the far country. The far country, he asserts, is the "evil society," i.e., being human—"a being which is not God and against God."[24] Barth deploys the word "far" to highlight *who* humans are.[25] For him, even without sin, humans are considered *far* from God because they are very unlike God:

> The very fact that man was not God but a creature, even though he was a good creature, had meant already a certain jeopardising of the honour of God. . . . Man was in any case an extremely unreliable champion of this cause [i.e., honouring God], an extremely compromised servant of the divine will, compromising even God Himself.[26]

The full-blown product of Barth's development of the utter disconnect between God and humans is obvious.[27] Barth's reconception of the notion of the "infinite qualitative distinction" not only underpins God's self-revelation, but significantly, God's initiative to be the robust link between divine reality and creaturely reality. God in being the "wholly Other" is indeed like no other because God can be at the same time against Oneself without being other than himself.[28] Barth has managed to explain this under the proposition—the Lord God wills to become *and* has become a suffering servant.[29]

22. *CD* IV/1, 130, 177, 193–97.

23. In reference to Luke 15:11–24.

24. *CD* IV/1, 158.

25. *CD* II/2, 163–64.

26. *CD* II/2, 163. Brackets mine. Barth's anthropology in view of the election of Christ has advanced from arguing that God's will is only for *fallen* humanity (*CD* II/2) to simply positing that God's will is for human *beings* (*CD* IV/2).

27. Evidently at this junction, Barth's theology has not only undergone a complete turn-about from liberal theology, but also, is set to combat any modern appraisal of humanity.

28. Read Barth, "God, Grace and Gospel," 41.

29. *CD* IV/1, 157–59.

Furthermore, Barth also points out that the far country signifies the contradiction of humanity. Thus this place represents such twofold contradistinction. As stated in Barth's writing, humans contradict God by disobeying God's will to live in unity with him; and humans contradict themselves by obeying their own will to live apart from God because this will cause their peril.[30] Hence Barth calls this place an "evil society" because, to him, human beings are so corrupt that they do not only live contrary to God's will, but also, live contrary to their own existence.[31] Humanity likewise is accounted in its limitations in the flesh described as inherently weak and perverse.[32] In other words, the divine humiliation entails God's assumption of human contradiction and limitations as God's own.[33] The way of the Son into the far country is a symbolic portrayal of the incarnation. Barth claims that in the incarnation, God is terribly moved as a servant because God compromises or exposes (*kompromittiert*) himself to self-contradiction by owning what is not his.[34] This is the foundation of Barth's controversial idea: "God against God" in *kenosis*.[35] God is said to have been "against" himself when God humiliates himself, hence the Son's obedience is in actuality an "obedience of suffering" (*Leidensgehorsam*).[36] Ultimately, Jesus Christ is seen as the suffering servant.[37]

2.2 The Suffering Servant

For Barth, the actual assumption of human limitations and self-contradiction happens when the Lord Jesus comes in the form of a servant (*forma servi*). When Jesus Christ takes the form of a servant and voluntarily goes into the far country, it demonstrates God's total and decisive self-sacrifice.[38] This act, according to Barth, is the "history of the suffering of Jesus Christ"

30. *CD* IV/1, 11, 15.

31. Barth associates the "Far Country" with "human corruption and perdition." *CD* IV/2, 20.

32. *CD* IV/1, 158.

33. *CD* IV/1, 128, 130. Jüngel, *God as the Mystery of the World*, 185–87

34. *CD* IV/1, 158. *KD* IV/1, 173.

35. *CD* IV/1, 184. This idea does not sit well with the canonical interpretation of *kenosis*. *CD* IV/1, 180–81, 186. See Castelo, *The Apathetic God*, 114.

36. *CD* IV/1, 177; *KD* IV/1, 193–94.

37. Barth stresses this point by comparing Christ's suffering with the Apostle Paul's suffering. *CD* IV/1, 189; 1 Cor 15:31; 2 Cor 11:7; 12:9, 10.

38. *CD* IV/1, 176.

in God's reconciling event.[39] In other words, the Son as Lord humiliates himself by assuming the form of a servant.

I have argued that God's self-humility is central to Barth's conception of divine suffering. Our concern now is to analyze how the travail of Jesus Christ in *kenosis* involves his divine nature. Barth's view of this matter results from his handling of the insight below:

> [I]n Melito of Sardis (*fragm.* 13): Creation shudders and, astonished, says: "How, pray, can this new mystery be? The judge is judged and has been put to rest; the invisible is seen and does not blush; the incomprehensible is comprehended and does not consider it improper; the immeasurable is measured and does not resist; the impassible suffers, and does not take revenge; the immortal dies and says no word in reply."[40]

Melito of Sardis enigmatically presents God's response to creaturely reality. This presentation helps Barth in looking at Christ's divinity in *kenosis*. Melito provides substantial material helpful in understanding how the divinity is humbled via the concept of the *forma servi*.[41] Rightly so, Barth perceives God to have humbled himself in the form of a servant. This idea is expounded in Jesus Christ being the "Lord as Servant."[42] Here, the impassible Lord is also the passible Servant.

The suffering servant is the actual form of God in *kenosis*. Melito's concept of the *forma servi* gives a balanced view of Christ in the form of a servant, and, Christ in the form of God (*forma Dei*). Melito holds that when God takes the *forma servi*, God remains in the form of God.[43] So when God suffers in the form of a servant, such suffering is proper to God precisely because God's divine essence rests intact.[44] God's being is not diminished when he suffers; God remains fully God even in suffering. For Barth, Melito's formulation is the only alternative explanation of the *forma servi*; God indeed become

39. *CD* IV/1, 175. It is vital to understand what Barth means by "history" in this context. This is what grounds the human experience of the Son of God, and can be traced all the way back to Section 6 of the *Göttingen Dogmatics*.

40. *CD* IV/1, 176–77.

41. Although Irenaeus is also cited, Barth notes that Irenaeus's formulation of the "impassible passible" (C.o.h. III, 16,6) derives from "a kind of Modalism" which is later rejected by the Early Church, and also by Barth himself. *CD* IV/1, 197.

42. *CD* IV/1, 157.

43. Barth reformulates the *forma servi* as "Jesus Christ, the Lord as Servant" and the *forma Dei* as "Jesus Christ, the Servant as Lord." *CD* IV/1, 187 and broadly in §§59 and 64.

44. Thompson, *Christ in Perspective*, 56–58.

human without detriment to God's being.[45] In other words, when God takes the servant form, God is not deformed. There is no grotesque deity lurking behind Jesus Christ inconsistent with the eternal God.

However, Barth similarly observes that Melito's conception of Jesus Christ as God is not due to what Christ has done (act) but is due to his being the Son of God.[46] So Melito is not concerned with knowing God through God's action in human history. God can be known in his being alone, independent of God's action; a disposition Barth dismisses. What Barth puts forward is the idea that the work of atonement, as done in and by Jesus Christ, is an act of humility on the part of God himself, such that within the Godhead there is space for free and proper obedience. In this way too, we can better appreciate why in Barth's observation, the being of God parallels God's atoning act. Barth systematically articulates God's being in line with the atonement. God's being can be known in what was revealed in the Son of God being the Son of Man. In this context, the former is known in the incarnation, as the latter is known in Jesus Christ.[47] Barth thinks it is important to say that the Lord God suffers in the form of a servant, yet it is more important to say that God suffers out of his willingness to suffer in this manner.[48] In short, the impassible wills to be passible.

2.3 The Impassible Passibility

Apparently in Barth, the impassible Lord becomes the passible Servant only in the being of Jesus Christ. There can be no real *kenosis* without God assuming the form of a servant vis-à-vis the flesh. Although Barth and Melito differ in appraising the role of Jesus Christ in looking at the being of God, their consensus however on Christ's humanity in the form of a servant is integral to the issue of impassibility. Since both theologians see this human as also divine, they consent that God himself suffers in human form.[49] It was Melito's notion of "the impassible suffers" which might have influenced Barth's allowance for passibility.[50] God makes himself vulnerable to suffering in service to humanity.[51] Strictly speaking, in Barth's mindset, God

45. *CD* IV/1, 185.

46. Hall, *Melito of Sardis*, xliii–xliv. See also "The Christology of Melito," 155.

47. Barth insists on God's unambiguity, i.e., detached from metaphysical supposition, in view of Christ's experiences.

48. *CD* IV/1, 193.

49. Refer to the excursus in *CD* IV/1, 211.

50. McCormack, "Divine Impassibility," 162.

51. Jones, "The Riddle of Gethsemane," 153–54.

cannot be said to be rigidly impassible simply because God is capable of being passible at the same time.

In fact, when Barth says that God's will is "against Himself," this self-contradiction is consistent with who God is in eternity; i.e., the One who self-gives. God is viewed to have relinquished his autonomy on behalf of human beings by being among them. As a result, God is presumed to have become "limited in time and space," "impotent," "lowly," and "open to radical and total attack."[52] God takes all these creaturely realities upon himself according to Barth. It shows God's determination to be the Reconciler of the world; it demonstrates God's unity with humans in form and in substance. When God becomes human, in essence, this event is what Barth terms as "God against God" (*Gott wider Gott*) because in this way, God historically submits himself to the contradiction of humanity.[53] God abrogates his "supreme absolute non-worldly being," e.g. omnipresence, and rather assumes the human nature to be in *every respect* human.[54] Barth defends this formulation by seeing God as "supremely right to exercise His mercy in this way."[55] Even though this idea of God against God is contentious, Barth suggests that this formulation "has to be accepted."[56] We can see here Barth's strong and steady rendition of a suffering God in the atonement.

In the human nature, God puts into effect the liberty to determine Oneself. Even if God's immutability is to be maintained in this determination, Barth insists that immutability still does not stand in the way of God's empathy for humanity.[57] Immutability is reappraised within this formulation: God is impassible not without regard to his passibility. God can do this precisely because God is "not His own prisoner."[58] Thus divine sovereignty holds God to be preeminent to human conceptions of the divine. In absolute autonomy, God can be "absolute" in himself by being relative to time. For instance, argues Barth, God can be infinite as well as finite, exalted but also lowly, active yet also passive, transcendent and also immanent, divine as well as human. All these seemingly conflicting notions are made possible in Barth's exposition of the *forma servi* (Christ, the Lord as Servant) without repudiating the *forma Dei* (Christ, the Servant as Lord).

52. *CD* IV/1, 184.

53. *KD*, IV/1, 201.

54. *CD* IV/1, 184. This should be taken in tandem with Barth's view of God as the "incomparable perfect." *CD* III/1, 14.

55. *CD* IV/1, 184.

56. *CD* IV/1, 184.

57. *CD* IV/1, 187.

58. *CD* IV/1, 187. Lauber, *Barth on the Descent into Hell*, 124–25.

2.4 The Immutable Mutability

Barth sets no inhibition for God; God can be God, and is altogether God, without any contingency involved. Nevertheless, God has affirmed himself in being vulnerable under what is not God and against God. In this vulnerability, God is said to be truly in himself. James Haley observes that for Barth, "the Christ of the Scripture remains immutable *in His divine essence* . . . human essence also *becomes* the essence of God as He assumes and adopts it in Jesus Christ."[59] I do not agree that Barth, strictly speaking, holds to the idea of immutability *per se* especially in his late Christology. Also, Haley appears to convey a monophysite treatment of Christ's being, something which Barth resists.[60] If Barth simplistically aims to keep the notion of immutability, he would not have bothered to exhaustively articulate God's free choice cognizant of reconciliation. Of course, in Barth's view, God is immutable insofar as God's self-determination is upheld; God is also mutable insofar as the actuality of the flesh is considered. If it is to be insisted that Barth is committed to immutability (God being incapable of any addition or diminution, exaltation or abasement) then the emphasis on divine autonomy is eclipsed.[61] After all, to be absolutely sovereign in himself, God embraces the opposite realities, vis-à-vis immutability–mutability.

In Barth's assertion, God denies his immutability without alteration to God's self.[62] In this respect, God can be said to be mutably unchangeable as the Reconciler. Hence, Barth views God's mutability in his free act:

> He [God] has therefore done and revealed that which corresponds to His divine nature. His immutability does not stand in the way of this. It must be denied, but his possibility is included in His unalterable being.[63]

Here God is seen as mutable (in a qualified sense) under the notion "God against God." This mutability, nevertheless, does not mean God needs to complete something he lacks, but rather, God is already complete in himself in eternity.[64] In terms of praxis, Barth urges, "The recollection of the *immutabilitas Dei* had for them [Lutherans and Reformed] the same effect as a Soviet veto, and completely stifled any further thinking."[65] The strict commitment

59. Haley, *The Humanity of Christ*, 229. Italics mine.
60. This matter will be discussed in the section "Christology and Impassibility."
61. *CD* IV/2, 77–78.
62. *CD* IV/1, 184.
63. *CD* IV/1, 187.
64. *CD* IV/2, 53.
65. *CD* IV/2, 85.

to immutability fosters a static God; a precursor to stagnation in knowledge, especially in conceiving God in Jesus Christ.[66] Thus God is none other than the God who is active in Jesus Christ. Barth attests that "all earlier" Christology departs from what is truly a Christian belief by presuming an atoning yet unaffected deity. This, for Barth, connotes an absurd deity.[67] Yet in God's act of unity, the Godhead is not disunited in itself.

The demarcation between God's unchangeableness and changeableness is unclear in Barth's argumentation. The ambiguity, in this circumstance, is not so much on which attribute God is said to possess, but rather, on God's decision to become human. So the posturing of God is the point of contention among scholars on this issue. On the one hand, Barth is often associated with the Western orthodox commitment to immutability due to his firm stance on divine sovereignty. For instance, Hans Vium Mikkelsen thinks that Barth disallows the idea of changeability in God by not integrating the incarnation into the being of God.[68] For Mikkelsen, Barth does not connect the incarnation "back to God's original essence."[69] This places Barth on the side of orthodoxy. On the other hand, he is also susceptible to a sympathetically postmodern reading. For example, Graham Ward sees in Barth the potential "to present a radically orthodox voice that is genuinely postmodern and, therefore, post-secular."[70] One reason for this is due to Barth's theological language concerning eternity and time. Ward observes that Barth views eternity as the eternal "Now" which conveys the God-event as completed yet "changeable and self-changing."[71] It implies that in the axis of eternity and time, God is seen to have been unchanged inwardly yet God is also seen to have self-changed outwardly. Accordingly, the evaluations of Mikkelsen and Ward prove the binary concepts inherent in Barth's theological system.

Based on this study, Ward is more accurate than Mikkelsen in assessing Barth as a dogmatician. As it shores up in revisiting the atonement, Barth seeks a "kind of immutability" that does not prevent the divine humiliation.[72] Suitably, what he has in mind is like a "tolerable" mutability (God is constant in himself even in change) as opposed to the crude sense of mutability. This

66. *CD* IV/1, 549.

67. *CD* IV/2, 85.

68. Mikkelsen, *Reconciled Humanity*, 211n15.

69. Mikkelsen, *Reconciled Humanity*, 260–61.

70. Ward, "Barth, Modernity, and Postmodernity," 293.

71. Ward, *Barth, Derrida and the Language of Theology*, 167.

72. Ward, *Barth*, 167.

"new phraseology" fits Barth's restructured christological category.[73] As a "continual learner," he navigates through unexplored terrains without losing sight of his starting point.[74] One exhibit of this is his renewed treatment of the Logos in conceiving the unchanging-changed God.

In Barth's late Christology, the Logos has been essentially constant in eternity in view of the decree. Yet the Logos is seen to be capable of change, i.e., *Logos asarkos* (the Word without flesh) to *Logos ensarkos* (the enfleshed Word).[75] Although Barth treats the essence of the Logos in a single-event in divine history, yet he is clear that the Son had assumed humanness in pre-temporality.[76] God's actuality is said to have been changed into human form, yet God retains his deity. More importantly, since the Logos is eternally the *Logos incarnandus* in Barth's conception, so in Jesus Christ, God can be viewed to be eternally changed in self-change. The self-changed God is the constantly changed God in *kenosis*. It means that while the incarnation as such, and thus the assumption of flesh occurs in time, this is not a change in God's eternal being *per se*, because God never willed not to be without the creature.

But what is the actual nature of Jesus Christ in *kenosis*? Both divine and human natures of Jesus Christ are actually involved in *kenosis* according to Barth. When he intentionally uses the Son of God as the subject of humiliation, this subjectivity carries with it the servanthood of the Lord.[77] In other words, Barth does not intend to treat the two natures separately as in independently "two states," but rather, the two natures are treated in one-person—Jesus Christ.[78] Also, the Logos is seen synonymously with the Son of God in the act of condescension. So Barth does not draw a line between the pre-temporal and the temporal deity in conceiving the election. Since he sees the Electing God and the Elected Man as one, therefore, this one-person subject is carried over in articulating the divine suffering.

73. In the "Editor's Preface," *CD* IV/2, vii. See Hunsinger, *Reading Barth*, 167.

74. In the "Preface," *CD* IV/2, xi.

75. It is likely that Barth adopts the Athanasian Formula which states, "there was no time in which the *Logos* was not." See Grillmeier, *Christ in the Christian Tradition*. Volume 1, 326–28. Also read Webb, *Jesus Christ, Eternal God*, 238–40.

76. *CD* IV/2, 43. McGinnis, *The Son of God Beyond the Flesh*, 151. McCormack, "Grace and Being," 95–97. Note that in McCormack's reading, he observes that Barth never denies the propriety of the distinction between *Logos asarkos* and *Logos ensarkos*. What Barth does deny is that there was ever a *Logos asarkos* independent of the determination to be this person, Jesus.

77. *CD* IV/2, 21.

78. *CD* IV/1, 133–34.

The one-subject Christ is pivotal in understanding Barth's insistence of an eternal God who suffers. Since God chooses to be in the flesh to ensure reconciliation, Barth explores how Christ's humanity can be a statement about God.[79] The actual suffering of Jesus Christ takes place in divine history, also conceived as a historic event. Because the divine-human natures are indivisible, then divine history includes both pre-temporal and temporal realities. In other words, in Barth's talk of the suffering of God, he only refers to a singular pattern inherent within the Son of God being the Son of Man. There can be no suffering Son of God apart from the Son of Man and vice-versa.

Since the Son of Man is always the Son of God, so the suffering of Jesus Christ corresponds to the suffering of God. For Barth, there is only one subject of suffering in election, i.e., the Subject of the eternal decree. Thus the indivisibility involved in the two natures speaks of the indivisibility in the God who suffers. There is no deity behind or above the suffering of Jesus Christ. It emerges here how Barth equates God's suffering to Christ's condescension; and, how Christ's humanity can be a statement about God. We will understand this further as we consider the reconciling will and act of God.

2.5 God's Reconciling Will and Act

What has been laid out exhibits that divine suffering is *physically* enacted in the incarnation. The underlying reason behind God's self-limitation and self-contradiction is to atone for humanity. For Barth, God freely chooses to be in this world of evil to redeem humanity from the evil of self-destruction. Humans (with their liabilities) cannot redeem themselves; only Jesus Christ can redeem them. In this regard, reconciliation is contingent upon God, but suffering itself is not necessary to God.[80] God nonetheless uses his unfettered choice to be the reconciling God—the God who becomes human in order to be one with humanity.[81]

The "reconciling will of God" is the basis upon which Barth explicates how and why God is "capable, willing, and ready" to be human.[82] It is consummated in time in the "reconciling act of God."[83] In this way, humanity is thoroughly reconciled because in Jesus Christ, God is the One

79. Barth writes, "If we put the accent on "flesh," we make it a statement about God." *CD* IV/2, 20.

80. *CD* IV/1, 74.

81 *CD* IV/1, 193–94. Johnson, *T. & T. Clark Companion to Atonement*, 647.

82. *CD* IV/1, 159; *KD* IV/1, 174.

83. *CD* IV/1, 347.

who initiates, executes and completes the atonement. It is in God's own will and terms that humanity is atoned; hence in Barth's theology, God is not only the reconciling God, but also more significantly, he is the Lord of the atonement.[84] Being the Lord of the atonement is congruent with the inner being of the Godhead.[85]

In the process of the atonement, Scott Kirkland seems to argue that the Father is somewhat separated from the Son. Kirkland claims that the far country, as Barth sees it, is "the Son's descent into the experience of 'dazzling darkness,' a sublation of the *distance* between the Father and the Son."[86] In this regard, I partly agree with Kirkland insofar as the far country is a form of negation to God; but I have reservation about the distance suggested between the Father and the Son in this journey.[87] Although Kirkland thinks that the distance between the Father and the Son is never one that ontologically separates the two, it is nonetheless a distance which is a product of the human agents who have turned on Christ.[88] Such view still presupposes that the Son travels *without* the Father (though with the ministration of the Holy Spirit), infers a lacuna in the Godhead; an idea foreign in Barth's theology.[89]

Concerning the far country, Barth states that "the Son who complies" with the commission is the same as "the Father who disposes" it.[90] Barth does not simply say that the two Persons are equal in authority and attitude (in reconciliation), but what he truly conveys is the inseparability of the Father and Son—the two are *together* in this journey. Barth puts it, "The Father as the origin is never apart from Him as the consequence, the obedient One. . . . The One who eternally begets is never apart from the One who is eternally begotten. Nor is the latter apart from the former."[91] Thus, in view of the commission, it is implied that there is no distance or

84. *CD* IV/1, 158.

85. *CD* IV/1, 215. Read Kettler, *The Breadth and Depth of the Atonement*, 9.

86. Kirkland, *Into the Far Country: Karl Barth and the Modern Subject*, xxiv. Italics mine.

87. *CD* IV/1, 253; "*in der grenzenlosen Qual der Gottesferne*" *KD* IV/1, 278. Barth emphasizes here "the boundless agony" of having oneself "remote from God yet God is still at hand." The distance construed does not mean separation but a mere portrayal of extreme inner struggle. Hence, there is no breaking up of the triune God in *kenosis*. For a different perspective on this matter; cf. Johnson, *God's Being in Reconciliation*, 100–102.

88. Email correspondence with Scott Kirkland, January 11, 2019. Kirkland however says that "what takes place in the cross is an event that is always internal to the life of God because God is never three distinct centers of action."

89. *CD* IV/1, 129, 204–9. Harasta and Brock, *Evoking Lament*, 91.

90. *CD* IV/1, 209.

91. *CD* IV/1, 209.

gap generated between the Disposer and the Complier.[92] In other words, if the Holy Spirit is in the Son, then the Father is with the Son as well, so the eternal unity of the Godhead is upheld.[93] Such eternal unity is not confounded by the formulation of the one-and-the-same subject who commands and also obeys. Instead, Barth clarifies his position on this matter against subordinationalism and modalism.[94]

The title, "The Way of the Son into the Far Country" is not misleading if it is viewed under Barth's dialectical construct of the atonement. In this figurative portrait, where the Son journeys *into*, is also where the Father *is* in trinitarian perspective.[95] However Barth is explicit that the Subject of the incarnation is the "mode of being as the Son" that is "in unity with the Father and the Holy Ghost."[96] Barth has no intention of collapsing the Godhead in this formulation because the commission is dependent on the will and purpose of the triune God.[97] The *joint* decision-in-act of the Son and the Father is paramount in Barth's conception of the interaction between divine reality and creaturely reality. I therefore posit that in Barth's mind, the imminent danger that the Son experiences in going into the "dazzling darkness" is *in solidarity* with the experience of the Father.[98] Although God (the Son) terribly suffers, God (the Father)

92. Yet Barth also points out that in speaking of the divine suffering, the greater stress is laid upon the Son; it is due to the fact that it is the Son who assumes flesh. Read *CD* IV/2, 43–49.

93. *CD* IV/2, 129.

94. *CD* IV/2, 185–86. For Barth, God in Christ is the One who commands as well as the One who follows.

95. *CD* IV/2, 357. In a 1956 lecture at the Swiss Reformed Ministerial Fraternal conference in Aarau, Switzerland, Barth asks, "How could God's deity exclude his humanity, since it is God's freedom for love and thus his capacity to be not only in the heights *but also in the depths*, . . . not only in and for himself but also with another distinct from him, and to offer himself to him? . . . Why should God not also be able, as eternal Love, to be sufficient unto Himself? *In His life as Father, Son, and Holy Spirit* He would in truth be no lonesome, no egotistical God even without man, yes, even without the whole created universe." Barth, *The Humanity of God*, 49–50. Italics mine.

96. *CD* IV/2, 44. Nevertheless, Barth reiterates, "We must maintain the true deity of Christ *as identical* with the Godhead of the Father, but only in such a way that no hurt is done to His deity by His humiliation, lowliness and obedience." Excursus in *CD* IV/1, 197. Italics mine. Also see Johnson, *The Mystery of God*, 104–5.

97. *CD* IV/1, 204. Barth explicates the unity of the Son with the Father and Spirit is "in the deepest harmony of the whole Holy Trinity of the one God." *CD* IV/2, 44.

98. For Barth, Christ's death is found in the presence and solidarity with the Father. Chung, *Karl Barth: God's Word in Action*, 204. Barth's interpretation of "My God, my God, why hast thou forsaken me?" (Mark 15:34) centers on God "giving Himself up to the contradiction of man against Him." *CD* IV/1, 185.

is painfully pleased with the selfless act of the Son and what this act has decisively delivered, i.e., redemption and reconciliation.

What is the sense of the Son's compliance with the commission, if, in the process, the purpose of the commission is nullified? In other words, it would be futile for Jesus Christ to humble himself in this way if the atonement would not be achieved anyway, because he does not represent the fullness of the Godhead.[99] Barth asks, "What would be the value to us of His way into the far country if in the course of it He lost Himself?"[100] It is imperative for Barth that Jesus Christ's true deity, a deity "identical with the Godhead of the Father," must be maintained in *kenosis* because there is no reconciliation if Christ "surrenders His deity."[101]

There seems to be a lingering quasi-Nestorian agenda which threatens the eternal unity of the Father with the Son in suffering.[102] Despite having good intentions to protect the integrity of the Godhead against any form of diminution or harm to the divine inner life, such an agenda actually imperils the Godhead; and also the atonement itself. Thus Barth insists that the *fullness* of the Godhead is the acting subject who goes into the far country.[103] We can now see how Barth connects Jesus Christ's condescension with God, and how the divine self-giving is played out in Christ's extreme struggle. The condescension undoubtedly conveys the pain of Christ because of the actual risk and the real compromise which have transpired in divine history. So what causes the suffering of God? In analyzing Barth's arguments, it exhibits God to have deliberately and qualitatively humiliated himself in Jesus Christ. This act causes the divine suffering in the created time and world. In being human, therefore, God "essentially and necessarily suffers."[104]

Having probed how God suffers in his reconciling will and act, we will now examine Barth's reason behind Jesus Christ being the Reconciler *and* the Reconciled. This will explain why God remains sovereignly God and Lord of all in suffering.

99. *CD* IV/1, 159, 193.

100. *CD* IV/1, 185.

101. *CD* IV/1, 187, 197.

102. *CD* IV/1, 182.

103. *CD* IV/1, 202.

104. *CD* IV/1, 166.

3. The Relation of Jesus Christ's Suffering to the God-self

Jesus Christ's suffering, explains Barth, is properly assessed in the inner life of God.[105] Notably, Barth's reconfigured Christology expresses Christ's dialectic identity in the atonement; and also, Christ's dialectic identification with humanity.[106] Based on our principal text, the major argument centers on God being absolute as the Eternal One. Barth qualifies that in God's movement, God remains superior over that which causes him to move. God suffers without detriment to himself because God only *reiterates* his sovereign independence in eternity.[107]

Barth observes that the reconciling God is absolutely perpetual in time by being simultaneous with creation. This God chooses to be temporal in the world without ceasing to be eternal.[108] The Eternal being in time, is the being of Jesus Christ; the one-person, one-subject "author and finisher" of the atonement.[109] Thus the one-subject Christ gives credence to the preeminence of God in the atonement.[110] It is also in the one-subject Christ where Barth resolves the dispute about Christ's suffering. Here, the participation of the Logos and Jesus Christ is important in understanding how God is seen to have embraced these seemingly irreconcilable attributes: infinite yet finite; exalted yet lowly; active yet passive; transcendent yet immanent; and impassible yet passible.[111] Though Barth is not specific on this matter, he however presents some examples, which potentially befit the criteria for each twofold attribute.

3.1 The Twofold Attributes of God

For Barth, God is absolutely infinite as the Creator by simultaneously being finite as a creature. The Creator wills to be in solidarity with the world as a creature; not any creature, but the human Jesus.[112] But in Jesus Christ, God exists as altogether God.[113] Accordingly, Barth understands the *divine ownership*

105. *CD* IV/1, 195, 201.

106. *CD* IV/1, 128–37.

107. *CD* IV/1, 193, 197. Jüngel, *God's Being is in Becoming*, 63, 69.

108. *CD* IV/1, 188.

109. *CD* IV/1, 197. Rutledge, *The Crucifixion*, 511.

110. *CD* IV/1, 201–2.

111. *CD* IV/1, 201–2. Torrance, *Incarnation: Person and Life of Christ*, 204.

112. *CD* IV/1, 187; IV/2, 68.

113. *CD* IV/1, 131, 181.

of the form and cause of humanity whereby God is said to have become "worldly."[114] When the Logos and Jesus Christ are appropriated in reference to Christ as the Lord and Servant, the Alexandrian and Antiochene concerns have to be addressed.[115] Does it mean the Logos is the Lord and the Servant is Jesus Christ? Since the two are equal in union, so, Christ is both the Creator Lord, and the created Servant. The union between the Logos and Jesus Christ, Barth reasons, would not necessarily imply that one becomes subordinate, confined, or dissolved in the other.[116] Thus, the one-subject Christ in *kenosis* allows Barth to counter any sense of kenoticism.[117]

Barth finds that God is absolutely exalted as the Savior by simultaneously being lowly as the heavy-burdened. In this regard, Barth conceives of the Son's going into the far country in a soteriological sense. Christ the Savior redeems humans from self-destruction by carrying their burdens (contradiction and limitations); in this manner, Christ becomes lowly.[118] Christ's voluntary act of *divine redemption* is an act of sacrifice as the Burden-bearer.[119] In Barth's theological vision, God in Christ is exalted, yet at the same time lowly; in this way, God is able to promise rest to humanity.[120] Appropriately, it is strange to think that the Logos is the Savior and the One in need of redemption is Jesus Christ. Barth effectively magnifies the inseparable union of the two in Christ being the Savior and the One burdened. God's glory is similarly highlighted here; a glory which shines through in concealment.[121]

For Barth, God is absolutely active as the Judge by simultaneously being passive as the judged. In the *divine judgment*, the righteous God actively decides to be passively accused to pay the penalties of humankind.[122] This presumed the idea of exchange in which the Judge is the One judged, thus taking upon himself the condemnation of humanity. Consequently, humans are no longer condemned, but are, in fact, accounted righteous.[123] It is pivotal in this line of thinking that the one-subject Christ fulfills the Judge as judged

114. *CD* IV/1, 187.

115. McGrath, *The Christian Theology Reader*, 239.

116. *CD* IV/1, 180.

117. Calvinism here refers to the notion of the *extra-Calvinisticum*. Sirvent, *Embracing Vulnerability*, 24–25

118. *CD* IV/1, 160; 179.

119. Excursus in *CD* IV/1, 179. Busch, *The Great Passion*, 21.

120. *CD* IV/1, 179. Read Morrison, "Karl Barth on God's Self-humiliation and Political Preference for the Poor," para. 5.

121. *CD* IV/1, 188.

122. *CD* IV/1, 188. Lauber, *Barth on the Descent*, 16.

123. *CD* IV/2, 93.

on behalf of humanity. Barth exclaims, "the Holy One stands in the place and under the accusation of a sinner with other sinners"; "the One who lives forever has fallen a prey to death."[124] In this way, Barth is able to see God to have truly and freely suffered as a direct result of God's decision.[125]

In Barth's reasoning, God is absolutely transcendent as Spirit by simultaneously being immanent in the flesh. God is absolutely transcendent as Spirit, yet Barth affirms, God is also immanent in the *divine assumption* of flesh.[126] The one-subject Christ speaks of the one and the same person of Jesus Christ—a unique humanity.[127] Barth's impulse, in this case, is framed by the fact that despite the assumption of flesh, Jesus Christ remains distinct from humankind because he is the embodiment of God in the flesh; Christ does not cease to be God in and of himself.[128] Correspondingly, the flesh in enmity with God is the same flesh God takes to overcome human contradiction and constraints.[129] The one-subject Christ is not a being contrary to God but *it is for and with* God. It is so because Christ's humanity (in the human Jesus) is always in union with his divinity (in the Logos).[130] This is evident in the action of the one-subject Christ. Though the Logos is axiomatically ascribed to as the transcendent Spirit, Barth however devotes his attention to the *Logos incarnatus* and definitely not to the *Logos asarkos* in his doctrine of reconciliation.[131]

Barth grants that God is absolutely impassible as the Commander by simultaneously being passible as a follower. Since Barth denotes that the *divine commission* presupposes a Commander who is also a follower, so it infers the idea of suffering in deference.[132] The impassible God chooses to be passible to show he can do this, and that he alone can do this as the Commander and follower.[133] How can the one and the same God command and obey? Would this not threaten the being of God because it necessitates disunity in God, one which suggests subordinationism? Barth is cautious and yet candid in his allegation by conceiving God as "above and below,"

124. *CD* IV/1, 176

125. *CD* IV/1, 157.

126. *CD* IV/1, 205–6.

127. *CD* IV/1, 205–6.

128. *CD* IV/1, 179, 208. Burgess, *The Ascension in Karl Barth*, 30.

129. *CD* IV/1, 171. Jesus Christ does this by being the Mediator between God and humanity. *CD* IV/1, 123, 208.

130. *CD* IV/1, 208.

131. *CD* IV/1, 124, 127–28, 181; IV/2, 64–68. Cf. McGinnis, *The Son of God Beyond the Flesh*, 152.

132. *CD* IV/1, 177.

133. *CD* IV/1, 185–86, 201.

thus the "superior and the subordinate"; and this principle applies to the Logos and Jesus in the one-subject Christ.[134] In other words, Barth is neither positing a subordinationist view because the Commander-Follower are treated equally in essence, nor favoring a modalist view because he asserts the Father-Son relationship in travelling afar.[135]

Concerning impassibility, Darren Sumner however observes that in Barth's post-metaphysical ontology, impassibility is dispensed with "almost entirely."[136] Sumner concludes, "God does not remain impassible in and for Himself because God *does not remain in and for Himself*."[137] Although this argument considers God's covenant, Sumner still falls short of seeing the underlying principle in Barth's God being (im)passible in the act of reconciliation. God in his inner life, Barth contends, is always the reconciling God, eternally including humankind in himself without losing the God-self.[138] Sumner's failure to appraise the nuance of the decree, I think, is corollary of a misreading of Barth about the common actualization of the Logos and Jesus Christ.[139] So I made it apparent that Barth thoroughly identifies the two in the one-subject Christ; a formulation which guarantees Christ to be the Reconciler, *and*, the Reconciled.[140] Christ's idiosyncratic identity results from the mutual relationship between the Logos and Jesus.[141] In this manner, God's being is reiterated or "activated" (as he intends to be) in eternity; the actualization involving the two essences is not new to the Godhead.[142] Nevertheless, Sumner is right that such actualization is *special* because it refers specifically to the incarnation.[143]

The incarnation indeed speaks of the relation of Christ's suffering to God. Christ's suffering, argues Barth, is constitutive of *divine history* because the divine ownership, redemption, judgment, assumption, and commission are viewed to have happened as a single event.[144] Since this is called divine history, God is the Lord of this history. In other words, in spite of the

134. *CD* IV/1, 193, 195.

135. *CD* IV/1, 196, 198. Migliore, "The Journey of God's Son," 93.

136. Sumner, *Karl Barth and the Incarnation*, 219. The word "dispenses" means Barth's borderline rejection of impassibility. Sumner, *Karl Barth*, 220.

137. Sumner, *Karl Barth*, 219.

138. *CD* IV/1, 204–5.

139. Sumner, *Karl Barth*, 221–22.

140. *CD* IV/2, 64, 70; IV/1, 126–27, 140. Allen, *Karl Barth's Church Dogmatics*, 152.

141. Barth understands this relationship to be the "communion of natures." *CD* IV/1, 158–59; IV/2, 64, 69.

142. *CD* IV/1, 204, 216. McCormack, "The Doctrine of the Trinity," 108.

143. Sumner, *Karl Barth*, 138. *CD* IV/2, 114.

144. *CD* IV/2, 64–65.

servanthood of God in this event, the fact remains that the Servant *is* Lord because God prevails over what has beset Christ.

3.2 God's Unalterability in Suffering

Barth's one-subject Christ is critical in understanding why Christ is the Lord in suffering, and why his humanity is superior from the rest of humankind. Although the Son suffers in the far country, he nonetheless remains sovereignly God and Lord of all as discussed in "The Homecoming of the Son of Man." *The home* in this context is where God is; where the Son of Man belongs, "to His place as true man, to fellowship with God," and also, "to relationship with His fellows."[145] This place of abode symbolizes the Son's reinstatement. Barth intentionally uses the subject "Son of Man" instead of the "Son of God" because he intends to make a statement about humankind, which the Son of Man embodies.[146] Thus "the home," in Barth's thought, again, is not a location but rather it represents what humans ought *to be*—to be with the Father, not away from him. In other words, the home also signifies God's restoration and glorification of humankind.

The act of coming home, according to Barth, exemplifies God's lordship.[147] The fact that the Son has not been lost or trapped along the way, but rather returns home, indicates divine sovereignty. Here the Son is shown to be the true Reconciler of humankind, in essence, by reuniting with the Father. Despite becoming human, the Son nonetheless bridges the chasm between God and humanity. Similarly, only when the Son goes to where humans are, signifies that humans are able to be where God is.[148] In addition, the Reconciler is also the Reconciled since Christ represents the restituted who have once been away from God.[149] It is because of the Son's obedience that the lost humans are found. As a result, humans are reunited with God.

Being with God, in Barth's mind, demonstrates the bond between God and humankind. In this bond, Jesus Christ is said to be the true Representative of God and humanity. Barth articulates that when the *Son of God* goes into the far country, he comes home as the *Son of Man*.[150] This representation is key

145. *CD* IV/2, 20. "The home," Barth adds, is "the presence and enjoyment of the salvation" of the Son of Man. *CD* IV/2, 20–21.

146. Barth writes, "But if we put the accent on 'the Word,' we make it a statement about man." *CD* IV/2, 20.

147. *CD* IV/1, 185.

148. *CD* III/4, 685.

149. Refer to §69 in *CD* IV/3.

150. *CD* IV/2, 21.

to Barth's theopaschite theology because the God who suffers never ceases to be God; and simultaneously never ceases to be human. This divine-human characterization points not only to reconciliation *per se*, but also, to the relation of Christ's suffering to God. The imagery of Christ going to and from the far country depicts the sovereignly suffering of God in the atonement.[151] The formulation of the suffering Son of God and the victorious Son of Man has initiated Barth's reconsideration of impassibility.[152]

The one-subject Christ challenges the notion of impassibility which isolates suffering to Christ's humanity.[153] Since Barth sees suffering in the two natures (without separation or distinction), he then corrects the usual connotation on impassibility. For him, it is a "common misunderstanding" to use the distinction between the two natures to promote an unqualified impassibilist view of God.[154] Barth inquires:

> Why is it that the protest was made: the creator wills in eternity to remain distinct from all his creatures, even from that matter which he assumed (Olevian, quoted from Heppe², 326)? It is a complete—if common—misunderstanding to attribute this protest to a barren intellectual zeal for the axiom: the finite cannot hold the infinite, and therefore for the impassibility of the divine essence.[155]

Such "protest" should be treated with fresh eyes according to Barth. This can be done by viewing "the presence of the divine in the humanity of Jesus Christ."[156] Barth continues that such protest is devised to insist on the insusceptibility of what is infinite in assuming what is finite. The Creator God remains sovereignly free in this *specific creature*—Jesus of Nazareth. The firm statement on the union-in-distinction of the two natures

151. Barth states, "The atonement as it took place in Jesus Christ is the one inclusive event of this going out of the Son of God and coming in of the Son of Man." *CD* IV/2, 21.

152. This formulation is certainly at variance with Irenaeus's concept of "the impassible passible" which borders between Sabellianism and Patripassianism—a conception Barth objects to. *CD* IV/1, 197. However, Barth posits the participation of the Father in suffering as cited by the early Patripassians. See *CD* IV/2, 357.

153. The Church Fathers teach, "God is by nature immutable and impassible." They argue that God remains in his aseity even in the incarnation of Jesus Christ. To them, the Incarnation took place in the person of the Son; hence the proper character of both natures was preserved. In effect, this articulation implies that "the divine nature did not lose its impassibility." Thus in the midst of Christ's suffering at Calvary, they insist that God "knows no suffering." St. Leo the Great, *Letter to Flavian, in Decrees*. Volume 1, 78–79; Athanasius, *Epistola ad Epictetum*, 6.

154. *CD* IV/2, 68–69.

155. *CD* IV/2, 68.

156. *CD* IV/2, 68.

addresses the issue of impassibility. In fact, the protest here aids Barth's theopaschite theology since God is seen to be in every respect free in the suffering Jesus Christ. Divine suffering is not out of compulsion in the confinement of flesh, but rather, it remains God's choice. Thus the one-subject Christ accounts the divine liberty as distinct from any attempts to create God after human imaginings.[157]

The one-subject Christ highlights divine sovereignty *in* the union of the two natures. In Jesus Christ, the infinite divinity is not above the finite humanity, or the former dissolved in the latter: the integrity of both is kept in its union.[158] In this way, Barth precludes the futile emphasis on the Creator's transcendence over the assumed creature. Noticeably, Barth endeavors to offer a productive consensus between the older Lutheran theology (with special attention to the human nature in Christ's divinity) and the older Reformed Christology (with special attention to the divine nature in Christ's humanity).[159] He speaks of the protest above with new emphasis by arguing that the infinite God can be, and is, and remains, in a finite human in the one-subject Christ. The Creator *can* assume creaturely reality, but only in the reality of Jesus Christ. In other words, Barth's interest (as opposed to the Reformed concern) is to capture the continuing union of the dual natures most especially in suffering.

Since Barth conceives of the suffering of God in Jesus Christ's two natures (without separation *in* distinction), then the formulation of a one-subject Christ is indispensable in dealing with christological disputes. This formula is the solution to the dangers of the Reformed tendency to de-divinize Christ's divinity in suffering, and, the Lutheran tendency to divinize Christ's humanity in suffering. Though Barth does not favor one camp over the other, he however points out that the one-subject Christ finds more support within the Lutheran interest in the communion of natures.[160] Barth approaches the communion of the two natures by considering the Christologies of Alexandria and Antioch.

157. Klempa, *A Unique Time of God*, 111–15.

158. Thus Barth's one-subject Christ is the defence against monophysite and Nestorian rejection of divine passibility.

159. Barth comments that the older Reformed dogmaticians failed to provide a vibrant picture of Christ because of their preservation of the "continuing distinctiveness of the divine essence of the Logos" in the human Jesus. *CD* IV/2, 68.

160. *CD* IV/2, 69.

3.3 Christology and Divine Suffering

Alexandria and Antioch differ in Christology in terms of the interaction between the divine and the human. Alexandria is committed to the union of Christ's two natures with a *real interpenetration* of the two.[161] Antioch, by contrast, preferred the amicable co-existence of such divinity and humanity without any interpenetration of the two.[162] In order to appreciate these differing views, we have to trace the Alexandrian and Antiochene schools of thought on the relationship between the dual natures in the being of Jesus Christ.

The Alexandrian School has a different perspective from the Antiochene School in looking at the being of Jesus Christ. The Alexandrian School has its emphasis laid on the *ontological oneness* of Jesus Christ. It means that as the soul of Jesus is united to the his body, so Jesus's divinity is united to his humanity.[163] Jesus Christ is conceived as having a single entity in the union of Godhood and humanhood, hence the term *miaphysis* (two natures united without blending).[164] This conception is known as the "Word/Flesh model" in which the Logos inhabits the body of Jesus Christ without the former being entangled with the latter.[165] In other words, Jesus of Nazareth is also the Son of God.[166] The great chasm between divine and human is bridged in the being of Christ. Whereas the Antiochene School has its emphasis laid on the *historical twoness* of Christ. It means that the

161. This is the model of *henosis kata physin* (union of natures). See McGrath, *The Christian*, 239.

162. This is the model of *henosis kat' eudokian* (union according to good pleasure). McGrath, *The Christian*, 239. Ryan Reeves however dismisses the christological split or distinction between Antioch and Alexandria. "Disputes on Christ: Nestorian and Cyril," video, 12:10. In fact, Michael Reeves points out that Adolf von Harnack invents such distinction that in a way "crippled" Barth's Christology. "An Evangelical Assessment of Barth," video, 23:55.

163. Weinandy, "Cyril and the Mystery of the Incarnation," 33n28.

164. Parry, *The Blackwell Companion to Eastern Christianity*, 88.

165. It is also called the "Logos/Sarx Christology"; it has the tendency toward the middle-Platonic metaphysical approach which builds on the argument: what is seen is not truly real. Jesus is conceived to have a body without soul, which explains the an-enhypostasia. This conception exemplifies the divinity of Jesus because his humanity is somewhat seen as incomplete apart from the Logos. Grillmeier, *Christ in Christian Tradition*, 133. The dominant text in the Alexandrian School is Colossians 2:9 which proclaims, "For in Him dwells the fulness of the Godhead bodily." This suggests the idea of miaphysis whereby Christ's two natures are in one being. Eckman, *Exploring Church History*, 33–34.

166. This connotes Mary to be the mother of God or the God-bearer (*theotokos*). See Pelikan, *The Emergence of the Catholic Tradition (100–600)*. Volume 1, 230–32.

Logos inhabits the body of Jesus, so the divinity simultaneously exists with the humanity.[167] Jesus Christ is viewed as having dual entities in the indwelling of the Godhood in humanhood, hence the term *dyophyses* (two natures in one person). This view is known as the "Word/Man model" in which the Logos replaces the soul of Jesus.[168] In other words, Jesus Christ is the Son of God *and* the son of Mary.[169] Here the great chasm between the divine and human is unbridged even in the being of Christ.

In spite of the Antiochene School's emphasis on the distinction between Christ's two natures, it somehow accommodates the union of the two *only* as a moral union, not an ontological one as proposed in the Alexandrian School.[170] The reason for Antioch's emphasis is to avoid attributing Jesus's human weakness to his divinity. However, such emphasis runs the risk of having two subjects in the being of Jesus Christ, namely, the Logos and the human Jesus. The two hypostases implies two beings as well. To better understand how these schools of thought come about, we have to consider the leading figures behind it.[171]

Cyril of Alexandria insists upon the one incarnate nature of the Word because he believes that there is a real unification of Christ's divinity and humanity despite its differences. The Logos is united to Jesus Christ, and in effect, the Logos assumed the human nature of Jesus. Jesus Christ therefore is not an independent being because he has no essence without

167. Weinandy, "Cyril and the Mystery of the Incarnation," 34.

168. It is also called the "Logos/Anthropos Christology"; it is inclined toward the Aristotelian metaphysical approach which centers on the presupposition: what is seen is concretely real. Jesus is conceived to have a body with soul, which is why the Logos knocks out the soul from Jesus's body before inhabiting it. In this case, the humanity of Christ is exemplified since Christ's humanity is treated as complete apart from the Logos. Cf. van Loon, *The Dyophysite Christology of Cyril of Alexandria*, 550–54. The dominant text in the Antiochene School is John 1:14 which states, "And the Word became flesh." This promotes dyophysitism which clearly distinguishes the person of Christ from his two natures. Quasten, *Patrology*, Volume 3, 136–40.

169. This implies that Mary could bear only a human child being human herself.

170. Despite the differences of the two schools, they agreed on many points, namely, the confirmation of the non-confusion of natures between the divine and human; the attestation that the Godhead did not suffer, let alone die; the assertion of the humanhood of Christ; the confession of salvation in and through Christ; the affirmation of the integrity of both natures. Fairbairn, *Grace and Christology in the Early Church*, 62–64.

171. The main theologians associated with the Alexandrian Christology are Cyril of Alexandria and Athanasius the Confessor (c. 296–373) while with the Antiochene Christology are Nestorius of Constantinople, Diodorus of Tarsus (died c. 390), and Theodore of Mopsuestia (c. 350–428). Fairbairn, "Patristic Exegesis and Theology," 12–15.

the Logos.[172] On the same note, Athanasius posits the taking on of flesh by the Logos. He argues that "the Logos has become man, and has not entered into a man" otherwise Jesus Christ is like any other prophets if the Logos "merely entered into a holy man."[173] This means that Christ is truly divine in human form; and also, the existence of such a being shows that the union of the two natures can never be undone. In contrast, Nestorius (who is associated with the teachings in Antioch) asserts Christ's humanhood by affirming his real and perfect being as human. The two natures are separate and independent from each other since what is divine can never be united with what is human.[174]

Diodorus concurs with Nestorius by maintaining the true divinity of Jesus Christ. True divinity, according to Diodorus, is a divinity untouched by humanity, even by the humanity of Jesus. The union of the two natures appears to be a mixture of the Logos and flesh; something that is impossible to happen.[175] This strict distinction between the two natures has led to the search of the real human Jesus. Here Theodore becomes a significant character as he advances the exegetical interest in the historical Jesus. Theodore challenges the allegorist interpreters of Scripture by insisting on the primacy of the plain sense of biblical texts over any symbolic meaning of it.[176] In this way, he wishes to avoid the interpretation of figurative language or metaphorical expressions to represent concrete reality about Jesus Christ. Theodore is also said to be responsible for the developed argument on the real, complete, and independent humanity of Jesus.[177]

In the progressive Christology of the Early Church, the advancement of the one substance of Christ's divinity and humanity, to some extent, allows for the unchangeable Person to become capable of change.[178] This is true in the conceptions of Cyril and Athanasius; something that puts the notion of divine impassibility into reconsideration. However, the persistent

172. Kelly, *Early Christian Doctrines*, 319–20.

173. Kelly, *Early Christian Doctrines*, 284–87.

174. Chadwick, *Henry Chadwick: Selected Writings*, 104–6.

175. Lohse, *A Short History of Christian Doctrine*, 85–86. Diodorus argues that Jesus is like any other prophets insofar as the indwelling of the divine (Holy Spirit) is concerned, but Jesus is also unlike the prophets because the divine (Logos) permanently dwells in him. Lohse, *A Short History*, 86.

176. The Antiochene School favors a literal translation of Scripture with special attention to the importance of the historical Jesus; whereas the Alexandrian School favors an allegorical translation of Scripture in search of the real meaning of biblical passages about Jesus. Fairbairn, "Patristic Exegesis and Theology," 14–15.

177. McKim, *Theological Turning Points*, 36.

178. O'Keefe, "Impassible Suffering?" 41, 51.

articulation of Nestorius, Diodorus, and Theodore concerning the actual separation of the two natures in the person of Christ disallows any notion of an affected God.[179] Barth's handling of these opposing views is key to finding out how the suffering of Jesus Christ implies the suffering of God. Barth's thought does not parallel either Alexandrian or Antiochene positions on the relationship between the dual natures.[180] The focus is not on the human or on the divine in his theopaschite thinking, but on the union of the two.[181] Jesus Christ suffers not merely in his humanity but also in his divinity.[182] There is no isolated suffering insofar as Christ is concerned; Christ's suffering is a *suffering in union*—a suffering which refers to the communion of natures.[183] Christ's human nature is in full possession of divine glory.[184] Barth affirms this by saying, "God cannot be considered without His humanity."[185] When God reveals himself as divine and human in earthly history, God is precisely acting out his reconciling will:

> Already in the eternal counsel of God, and especially in its execution, the divine humanity of Christ is not a relationship between two equal or even similar partners, but the work of the mercy of God turning in inconceivable condescension to very dissimilar man.[186]

The idea of God's self-disclosure in hiddenness in Jesus Christ is here preserved. God has humbled himself in this one-of-a-kind human. Barth's usage of the term "divine humanity" (*Gottmenscheit*) supports such idea; also,

179. O'Keefe, "Impassible Suffering?" 52, 54, 56. Nestorius and Theodore object to the compromise of God's impassibility as a result of the "concretely realized union" of the eternal Logos and the human Jesus. Daley, *God Visible*, 188.

180. Evidently, Barth avoids Nestorius's claim of different subjects in divine actions and human experiences. He also deviates from Lutheran Christology wherein Christ's humanity is somewhat diminished in favor of Christ's divinity. Barth rather conceives only the one-subject Christ in speaking of God, even in matters of being affected vis-à-vis human suffering.

181. *CD* IV/2, 63–64.

182. It is fair to say, however, that the Alexandrian and Antiochene schools have their deficiencies. Neither is entirely or fully right, and Chalcedon contains elements of both. Barth's Christology maintains that the two natures of Jesus Christ are united but not in union to avoid any Apollinarian or Eutychian tendencies. Barth treats the union of the divine and human in strict balance to avoid also the weight of distinction of the two natures prominent in the Reformed Christology.

183. *CD* IV/2, 64.

184. *CD* IV/1, 182; IV/2, 77–78, 82–83.

185. *CD* IV/2, 102.

186. *CD* IV/2, 52.

advances God's glory in humility.[187] This term is significant in analyzing how Barth treats Christ's suffering in view of the decree. Hence, the one-subject Christ and the divine humanity work hand in hand in Barth's formulation of an "inconceivable condescension"—a herald of (im)passibility.

The (im)passible God is the product of Barth's renewed insight on the communion of natures. Jesus Christ's suffering is a suffering in union because of the two-sided communion of natures.[188] When Christ's divinity suffers by humiliation in the incarnation, Christ's humanity suffers as well; also, when his humanity suffers in the events following the incarnation, his divinity likewise suffers. Barth takes God's condescension as double-sided, in much the same way when he applies it to God's majesty.[189] In a sense, God is said to have impassibly suffered. Barth's notion of the one-subject Christ further allows him to take God *also* as passible since the divinity is not independently conceived from the humanity. So, accurately speaking, the actual Person that suffers in *kenosis* is the divine humanity.

This suffering in the divine humanity, for Barth, results from the conception of the single Subject in and of suffering.[190] In such divine humanity, Barth thinks that God has not become a stranger to suffering.[191] God remains the self-same God of eternity even in his limitation in the flesh.[192] This is in conflict with the idea of the *extra-Calvinisticum* wherein the divinity of Jesus Christ extends beyond his humanity, which hits the core of Barth's inquiry.[193] When God self-limits in Jesus Christ, this involves his deity as well.[194] Barth has no problem in involving the divine in God's self-limitation:

187. *KD* IV/2, 56, 60–61, 128.

188. *CD* IV/2, 70.

189. *CD* IV/2, 71.

190. *CD* IV/2, 70.

191. *CD* IV/1, 183.

192. *CD* III/1, 50–56. In Barth's circumspect approach, "the doctrine of the *Logos asarkos* can only describe the manner of God's self-movement in eternally becoming the *Logos incarnandus*." Asbill, *The Freedom of God*, 198. This as such is the "being of Christ in the beginning with God." *CD* II/2, 107.

193. *Extra-Calvinisticum* is the notion that the divine nature of Jesus Christ cannot be enclosed or imprisoned within his human nature, but continues beyond it. The divine remains trans-finite despite being in union with a finite body. Hoogsteen, "Vere Deus, Vere Homo," 84–89. Barth's inquiry on Caspar Olevian. *CD* IV/2, 68.

194. *CD* IV/1, 158–59. Such notion is considered radical in the post-Kantian manner which "confines God in himself to a formally known and uncharacterisable source." Milbank et al., *Radical Orthodoxy: A New Theology*, 33.

> There is no element of human essence which is *unaffected by*, or excluded from, its existence in and with the Son of God. . . . Similarly, there is no element of His divine essence which the Son of God, existing in human essence, *withdraws from* union with it and participation in it.[195]

What Barth postulates by the "element" in relation to Christ's humanity is the "moment" or particular time of existence of Christ's human being (*Moment des menschlichen Wesens*).[196] Likewise, the "element" in relation to Christ's divinity means the particular time of existence of Christ's divine being (*Moment seines göttlichen Wesens*).[197] The humanity has been with divinity at all moments that make the interaction of the two natures proper to God. Even if Barth conceives Christ's suffering to be God's suffering, this conception is articulated with caution due to the shared-time concept in the history of suffering. Because the union of the two natures does not mean the unity of the divine-human, argues Barth, so in divine suffering, there is no blending of God's distinct characteristics.[198] Though humanity participates in divinity through the communication of its distinctive features, this communication is still "without change and admixture, cleavage and separation" between the two.[199] The strict union-in-distinction between the dual natures is strong in the Chalcedonian Definition, which also upholds the true divinity in the true humanity of Jesus Christ.[200] Barth's use of the christological definition of Chalcedon is important in how he articulates God's agony and victory in the divine humanity. The Chalcedonian Formula, in a sense, conveys the Son's condescension and glorification.[201] Though the Fathers concentrate somewhat on the preservation of God's majesty as they read this formula, Barth reads it to focus on the exalted God as a result of the divine humiliation.[202]

After investigating how Christology and divine suffering are interconnected in Barth's conception, we will now turn to analyze how he reconsiders impassibility as he engages with Chalcedon.

195. *CD* IV/2, 64. Italics mine.

196. *KD* IV/2, 69.

197. *KD* IV/2, 69.

198. *CD* IV/2, 63. Thus Barth uses the term "unity" to refer to the event of reconciliation, i.e., the unity of God and humanity, not to the nature of Christ. *CD* IV/2, 64, 113.

199. *CD* IV/2, 51.

200. Kärkkäinen, *Christ and Reconciliation*, 127.

201. Pelikan, *The Emergence of the Catholic Tradition*, 266.

202. *CD* IV/1, 68–71.

The notion of an "indissolubly one Christ" is easily accommodated in this formula.[203] Obviously, however, Barth's idea of "God against God" does not sit well with the position of Chalcedon.[204] It states:

> THEREFORE, following the holy fathers, we all with one accord teach men to acknowledge one and the same Son, our Lord Jesus Christ, at once complete in Godhead and complete in manhood, truly God and truly man consisting also of a reasonable soul and body; of one substance with the Father as regards his Godhead, and at the same time of one substance with us as regards his manhood . . . recognized in two natures, *without confusion, without change, without division, without separation*; the distinction of natures being in no way annulled by the union, but rather the characteristics of each nature being preserved and coming together to form one person and subsistence, not as parted or separated into two persons, but one and the same Son and Only-begotten God the Word, Lord Jesus Christ.[205]

There is no concept in Chalcedon whereby God limits and contradicts himself in the flesh. But there is more that must be said concerning the language of Chalcedon. The preferred language governing the thought of the theologians put forward the "sameness and the diversity" in the nature of Jesus Christ.[206] What the Chalcedonian Council endeavors to do: (1) affirm the union of divine and human natures in Christ; (2) confirm the two distinct natures in Christ; and (3) reject the notion that Christ had only one nature.[207] Although these aims are in tune with Barth's one-subject Christ, they are nonetheless swayed more on the distinction between Christ's divinity (one substance with the Father as the Logos) and Christ's humanity (one

203. *CD* IV/2, 64.

204. Even though the Reformed and Lutheran construct their Christology within a fundamentally Chalcedonian framework of Jesus Christ's being one person in two natures, each has its own reservation. The Reformed dissent of Chalcedon is due to the notion of the *extra-Calvinisticum* (viewed by Lutherans as partly Nestorian) while the Lutheran dissent of Chalcedon is due to the notion of *communicatio idiomatum* (viewed by the Reformed as partly Eutychian). For Barth, he is neither purely Reformed nor purely Lutheran in his conception of the two natures in Jesus Christ.

205. Translation from Bettenson, *Documents of the Christian Church*, 73. Italics mine.

206. Ayres, *Nicaea and Its Legacy*, 41. The phrase "sameness and diversity" is originally applied to the relationship of person between the Father and Son.

207. accordingly, these aims arise from the letters of Cyril against Nestorius, the Tome of Pope Leo and the challenge brought about by the Monophysite doctrine. See *The Acts of the Council of Chalcedon*. Volume 1, 1–5.

substance with humankind by having soul and body). This distinction is defined explicitly and negatively as un-confused, un-changed, un-divided, and un-separated; hence, the divinity and the humanity are to be recognized in two distinct natures.

Although this formula talks about the "Lord Jesus Christ," it does not give weight on the particularity of the humanness of Jesus of Nazareth. In effect, there is no tenable way of seeing the Logos to have been constrained, much less impugned in the person of Jesus Christ. In Chalcedon's perspective, the integrity of the Logos is unconfused and unchanged in this person yet at the same time, both are undivided and unseparated in God's condescension. The Logos and Jesus Christ remain distinct in their natures in terms of suffering. The emphasis on the preserved eternal being of the Logos, even in the suffering of Christ, makes Barth's idea of God against God implausible. Barth does not attend to the human (in an Antiochene manner) or to the divine (in an Alexandrian manner) in his theopaschite thinking, but to the union of the dual natures. In other words, the suffering in union refers to Jesus Christ as well as to the Logos *as one person*; hence, the suffering of the divine humanity.[208]

So the divine humanity is Barth's reaction to the Chalcedonian tendency to isolate the Logos from Jesus Christ in view of divine suffering.[209] The divine humanity indeed speaks of God's condescension in the indissolubly one-person Christ. Although Chalcedon makes a statement about God's condescension, it is only indirectly, i.e., as a means to make God known to the world.[210] This is due to its formulation which is hospitable to the continuing distinction of the two natures. The variance between how the Fathers use the Chalcedonian Formula as opposed to how Barth uses this formula becomes apparent. The stark difference lies in whether it is true or not, that what the humanity of Christ experiences can also be predicated to his divinity. Barth sees this formula helpful in his theopaschite conception of God. The Chalcedonian pattern is utilized to speak of Jesus Christ without compromising either his humanity or his divinity as it coexists with another (especially in suffering).[211] The key here is how Barth handles the Chalcedonian

208. The divine humanity is the very being of the person of Jesus Christ. *CD* IV/1, 52–53.

209. See *CD* IV/1, 127, 133; IV/2, 26. Barth is *not* correcting Chalcedon in these passages, but distinguishing between Lutheran and Reformed Christologies.

210. McGuckin, *St. Cyril of Alexandria*, 240.

211. "The identity of the Son was at the heart of the two major phases of conciliar deliberations in the early church. . . . From these conciliar achievements, the church developed a grammar or way of speaking that tried to attend to the divinity and humanity of Christ." Castelo, *The Apathetic God*, 112.

conception of the person of Christ as without confusion, change, division, and separation within his doctrine of reconciliation. This has substantial impact on how he is able to magnify the exalted God in humiliation. Inasmuch as Barth considers this formula positively, he takes the excesses of Alexandria and Antioch seriously.[212] When the accent is on the two natures being unconfused and unchanged, he stresses the participation between the divinity and humanity without duress on its distinction.

When the accent is on the two natures being undivided and unseparated, Barth concentrates on the totality and definiteness of the union. He is circumspect in this reformulation so as not to fall within the Alexandrian excess. Barth does this by viewing the "indestructible union" of the two natures as speaking powerfully of Christ's humanity, that indeed the God-self is reiterated in Jesus.[213] This hypostatic union, Barth reasons, must be "understood only in terms of itself" (*sui generis*), so the suffering and majesty of God must be taken to mean as a double-sided restatement of God in eternity.[214] Moreover, and equally important, Christ's humanity is exalted not at the expense of his divinity, or, Christ's divinity is humiliated not at the expense of his humanity.

Barth sees the indestructible union of the two natures as protection against Antiochene excess. The concept of divine humanity guarantees the union to be "not merely partially but totally," and "not merely temporarily but definitely."[215] It means that the humiliation of the divine and the exaltation of the human are also to be taken inseparably as an event in one being.[216] In other words, such an event happens simultaneously in the indissolubly one Christ. Furthermore, this one event happens totally and definitely in the divine humanity. Similarly, it implies singularity of the humiliation and exaltation in being an event. So Barth, in turn, cannot find wisdom in the Logos not being limited and contradicted in the person of Jesus Christ. Contrary to Chalcedon, the notion of divine humanity is the tenable way of conceiving God to have been the "God against God" in Christ's event. But, of course, Barth qualifies that the Logos is un-confused, un-changed, un-divided, and un-separated in Christ's humiliation and exaltation. In fact, Barth cannot consider the Logos without Jesus Christ, and, vice-versa simply because of the indestructible union of the two in the atonement.

212. *CD* IV/2, 63–64.

213. *CD* IV/2, 64. Anderson, *Reclaiming Participation*, 96.

214. *CD* IV/2, 52. This qualification eschews any Nestorianism-Eutychianism amidst such communication of distinctive properties between the Logos and the flesh.

215. *CD* IV/2, 64.

216. *CD* IV/2, 64–65.

Respectively, God is who he *is* in history, i.e., the atonement history. God is constant insofar as his self-determination is concerned, but God is also variable—in a qualitative different sense insofar as his freedom to love is concerned.[217] God's aseity, at some length, is terminated yet God remains true to being sovereign. Barth posits, "God's divine nature is in a way discontinued with Himself yet there is still no alteration of Himself and such discontinuity is not foreign to Himself."[218] That is why the Chalcedonian Formula supports Barth's notion of suffering in the indissolubly one Christ; yet also, the same formula frustrates Barth's idea of self-contradiction in the divine humanity of Christ.[219]

To examine how exactly the Chalcedonian Formula, in a way, coincides and conflicts with Barth's theology, we need to account his conversation with Cyril, Nestorius, Apollinarius, and Eutyches in modifying Christology.[220] We will explore the Chalcedonian definitions of Jesus Christ's being, and what these theologians intend to say, and not say, about impassibility.[221]

3.4 Christology and Impassibility

Cyril's proposal of the union of Jesus Christ's dual natures is adopted in the Chalcedonian creed.[222] Cyril speaks of the *one-person* hypostatic being of Christ wherein the two natures cannot be viewed alongside each other; Christ is fully God and fully human in a single *person* (a conscious acting Subject). Whereas Nestorius stresses the unhypostatic treatment of the being of Jesus Christ which somewhat infers a *dual-subject* Christology. The two natures in the one-person Christ are simultaneously distinct without regard to its union. The Council at Chalcedon discards such a claim.[223]

217. God being the Creator into being Creator-creature and being divine into being divine-human in Jesus Christ out of his divine perfection, e.g. mercy, grace, et al.

218. *CD* IV/1, 184.

219. *CD* IV/2, 64–65. As defined in Chalcedon, God—the eternal Logos, does not obliterate, but rather preserve, all traces of the humanness of Jesus. Daley, *Visible God*, 230.

220. These I think are the principal interlocutors in search of Barth's consideration of the notion of impassibility in the Chalcedonian Christology. See excursus in *CD* IV/1, 181; *CD* IV/2, 67 also *CD* III/2, 355.

221. Cyril, Nestorius, Apollinarius, and Eutyches not only impacted the Christology of Chalcedon but also furthered the discussion on impassibility.

222. Torrance, *Incarnation*, 204.

223. Torrance, *Incarnation*, 199.

The Council likewise dismisses the propositions of Apollinarius and Eutyches because they also deny the complete union of the two natures.[224] They cannot see Jesus Christ as totally human.[225] Jesus Christ is *more of God* and less human (or Jesus only appears to be human). [226] Apollinarius's proposal centers on the *one-subject* "monophysite" treatment of Christ's being wherein Christ has only one nature.[227] Eutyches's proposal centers on the lopsided treatment of Christ's being wherein the divine overshadowed the human. Despite the differences on their emphases, they both claim that Jesus Christ has eventually become fully God in person.

On the one hand, Barth partly accepts Cyril's presupposition in reconfiguring Christology, yet the result is quite variant in terms of the treatment of impassibility.[228] On the other hand, Barth has no use, even in part, of the Christologies of Nestorius, Apollinarius, and Eutyches because their formulations are incongruent with his single-subject Christology. Thus the contrast between them in treating impassibility is obvious. In other words, what Barth accepts or discards (wholly or partly) in each christological position informs his thought on impassibility. Because Cyril views the two natures in unity, so the distinction between the two is only understood theoretically. Conversely, Nestorius denies the convoluting of Christ's dual natures simply because he refuses any form of union between the human and the divine. Even though Cyril, Nestorius, Apollinarius, and Eutyches have contending positions, they all agree, but with nuances, that the eternal God is impassible. It is so due to their conception of God as not, and will not be causally dependent on what is external; hence, God is altogether eternally immutable. Here, the travail of Jesus Christ in the incarnation cannot be wholly or partly applied to God.[229]

224. Torrance, *Incarnation*, 197. Eutyches believes that in Jesus Christ, the divine had swallowed up the human. Since Apollinarius denies that Jesus has human soul, thus Jesus is not completely human.

225. *The Letter to the Bishops in Diocaesarea*, 4.1, 4.4, 4.5.

226. Monophysite Christology is the combination of the two natures but the remaining nature is divine, no more human, hence having only one "changed" nature (*monophysis*). This type of Christology is associated with Apollinarianism and Eutychianism.

227. Jesus uniquely has a divine mind instead of a regular human soul. Meredith, *Christian Philosophy in the Early Church*, 107.

228. Note that Barth's Christology has a juxtaposition of Alexandria and Antioch.

229. Sirvent, *Embracing Vulnerability*, 24–25. In Cyril's own words: "We do not mean that God the word suffered in his Deity . . . for the deity is impassible because it is incorporeal. But the body which had become his own body suffered these things, and therefore he himself is said to have suffered them for us. The impassible [God] was in the body which suffered." Bettenson, *Documents of the Christian Church*, 47.

Cyril, however, thinks of the Logos to have "suffered impassibly" because there is *a real union* of humanity with divinity.[230] When Jesus Christ suffers, the Logos, in essence, also suffers yet distinctively. When the Logos suffered impassibly, in Cyril's thought, God himself is said to have been affected and involved in the human conditions of Christ.[231] In this case, however, God remains uniquely affected and involved. Thus Cyril takes the Creator-creature contrast to underline the distinction of the suffering of the Logos from that of Jesus Christ. Because the Logos is infinite so it cannot, in any way, be affected by what is finite.

For example, Cyril argues that in the crucifixion of Jesus Christ, the Logos is said to have "both suffered and did not suffer" because the disposition of the Logos is unique.[232] The capability, as well as the incapability, to suffer has something to deal with the union-in-distinction of Christ's two natures. Though Cyril has a point worthy of consideration, Barth nevertheless points out the flaw of such an argument. When the Logos and Jesus Christ are distinctively treated in suffering, it unintentionally breaks the *real union* of Christ's humanity and divinity. In this circumstance, Cyril ends up becoming semi-Nestorian. Barth has no intention to sustain the "Creator-creature distinction" in this way because it does not serve his argument on impassibility. Certainly, in Barth's own words, "the Creator became a creature."[233]

In addition, Barth has no superfluous statement on divine suffering in pre-temporality. Cyril's predication of divine suffering solely on temporal grounds overlooks the eternal determination of God towards humanity; this is an idea central to Barth's rendition of the atonement.[234] The God-self truly suffers as this assertion finds meaning in his doctrine of reconciliation. What Barth intends to say clearly is that it is the reconciling will of God to suffer. God is said to have been tormented, bled, and even died in the Jesus Christ. This is God's reconciling act—a temporal act which originates in eternity.[235]

230. *The Second Letter of Cyril to Nestorius*, 4.8, 4.9, 4.10. Gavrilyuk, *The Suffering of the Impassible God*, 147–48. Castelo, *The Apathetic God*, 114.

231. Gavrilyuk, *The Suffering of the Impassible God*, 159.

232. Sumner, *Karl Barth*, 57.

233. *CD* IV/2, 58; IV/1, 186.

234. "Cyril recognized that the predication of suffering to the divine alone would render the assumption of humanity superfluous, whereas the opposite extreme, the attribution of suffering to the human nature alone would jeopardize divine involvement." Gavrilyuk, *The Suffering of the Impassible God*, 174.

235. *CD* IV/1, 176–88.

The reconciling will-and-act in Jesus Christ is key to Barth's christological revision. Despite his refutation of the Apollinarian and Eutychian Christologies, yet Barth prefigures an interaction of essences between the dual natures. The divinity and humanity are both affected equally and simultaneously.[236] It is so since there is always a union with and participation which transpires between the two in its existence. In other words, when this union-in-participation is seen within the all-time sharing of the two essences, the interaction between the dual natures becomes viable. It does not imply God to have changed by being conjoined with Jesus Christ, hence the term distinction-in-participation. Even in the inseparable moments of the divinity and humanity, Barth insists on the two to have retained each other's integrity. Likewise, such interaction does not denote God to have lost causal independency on what is external.

Thus Barth agrees with Cyril, Nestorius, Apollinarius, and Eutyches concerning God's causal independence; albeit Barth rebuts the use of aseity to discard divine potency for adversity.[237] He has no interest in the metaphysical injunctions of impassibility for the sake of protecting immutability in its crude sense.[238] Barth's strong disagreement with them emerges from his firm position on the suffering in union in the divine humanity. Although, to some degree, Cyril influences Barth in reconfiguring Christology, the former however fails to convince the latter in formulating a formidable version of theopaschism. In effect, Barth formulates his own argument for divine suffering which underpins the exalted suffering deity in the person of Jesus Christ.[239]

When Barth rethinks his Christology, he is able to give attention to the uniqueness of divine suffering in the *an-enhypostasia*.[240] The dialectic pairing of this dual formula gives depth to what it means for God to be in the very existence of Jesus Christ.[241] This suffering is only analogous to

236. Neder, "History in Harmony," 174.

237. Indeed, Barth's concern with God's aseity never wavers. For Barth, God—as the acting Subject—remains God and thus sovereign over himself and all of God's acts with and for humanity.

238. Barth puts it, "If ever there was a miserable anthropomorphism, it is the hallucination of a divine immutability which rules out the possibility that God can let himself be conditioned in this or that way by his creature. God is certainly immutable. But he is immutable as the living God and in the mercy in which he espouses the cause of the creature." *CD* III/4, 109. Cf. Gavrilyuk's comments on the Patristic's marking of God's unlikeness to everything in the created order. Gavrilyuk, "God's Impassible Suffering," 139.

239. *CD* IV/2, 53.

240. *CD* IV/2, 58.

241. *CD* IV/2, 49.

the inseparable one event in one being, understood only in terms of the self-humility of God in Jesus Christ. In other words, the suffering of God is characteristic only to the divine humanity; it is distinct from the suffering of humankind. Even in Christ's humanity, Barth suggests, the suffering is dissimilar from what people experience. Christ's suffering, therefore, is treated dialectically: like human but unlike human. Though the pain is incurred in human flesh, yet this humanity is always in communion with the divine essence.[242] This conception is pertinent in Barth's treatment of Jesus Christ's ordeal being a category of its own.

Christ's suffering, says Barth, is unique because it takes place *only* in Jesus. It is in this facet that Ian McFarland wishes to articulate the Chalcedonian Definition constructively so as not to blur the distinction between Christ's divinity and humanity. McFarland retains the boundaries between nature and hypostasis.[243] He views the divine nature as always hidden to human perception, thus distinct from the life of Jesus Christ. What we can observe empirically is the divine person which manifests itself in Christ. Notably, McFarland makes a distinction between divine nature and divine person.[244] For him, what we see in the divine person does not necessarily reflect the divine nature. As a result, what Christ experiences cannot be said of God. Thus in the context of impassibility, the suffering of Jesus is made distinct from God.[245] But my contention is: What kind of nature does this divine person have? As Barth alludes, Jesus Christ has human-divine natures; divine nature, strictly speaking, cannot be separated from the divine person.

So the Chalcedonian Formula, in its truest sense, does not preclude that Jesus of Nazareth could be referred to as *altogether God*. This is the case in Barth's *Dogmatics* as well. The person of Jesus Christ is also in every respect divine. Because the Chalcedonian Council asserted the unity of divine and human natures in Christ, so the Council consistently considers Christ as fully God and fully man. But in terms of speaking of divine suffering, it is apparent that Chalcedon is extra careful in rendering Christ's suffering in connection with the inner life of God. Chalcedon affirms that the *incarnate God* experienced temporal suffering. The Father did suffer but it is distinct

242. *CD* IV/2, 33–34.

243. McFarland, "Spirit and Incarnation," 144. Habets, *Third Article Theology*, 227–28.

244. McFarland, "Challenges in Christology," video, 42:42. McFarland further argues that the "what" in Christ is the flesh and blood, whereas the "who" in Christ is the God-self. McFarland, "Challenges," video, 42:42. Also see Lawrenz, *The Christology of John Chrysostom*, 63–65.

245. This formulation finds companion with Kathryn Tanner's proposal that God is "beyond suffering." *The Gift of Theology*," 6.

from Jesus Christ's suffering, it does not follow that Christ's suffering can be located in the inner life of God.[246]

Correspondingly, the theologians in Chalcedon intended to preserve such a theopaschite formula, as propounded by their predecessors.[247] The Church Fathers teach that "God is by nature immutable and impassible."[248] Although these Fathers were open to further conversations on the nature of God, they were more inclined to be in line with their predecessors. Thus from Constantinople to Chalcedon, the "desire to accommodate" still does not imply "willingness to compromise."[249] The Chalcedonian Fathers strongly argued in favor of God's aseity even in the incarnation.[250] To them, the incarnation took place in the *person* of the Son; hence the proper character of both natures was preserved. In effect, this articulation implies that "the divine nature did not lose its impassibility."[251] Thus in the midst of Christ's anguish on Calvary, they see God to have known no suffering.[252] Substantially, this theological instinct is imbedded in the formula of the Council of Chalcedon.[253] Though this formula acknowledges the "divine-human paradox of the Christ event," it still retains an unaffected God in the divine person.[254] But Barth does not thoroughly pursue this line of thinking especially in *CD* IV.

246. Swinburne, "The Coherence of the Chalcedonian Definition of the Incarnation," 167n26.

247. Note: The language of the Chalcedon is purely christologic, thus, it is not concerned with formulating a "new creed" but in affirming the previous creeds. Chalcedonian Creed is not in its exact sense a creed but merely a statement of faith to unify the church.

248. St. Leo the Great, Letter to Flavian, in *Decrees*, vol. 1, 78–79.

249. Ayres, *Nicaea and Its Legacy*, 258.

250. For instance, Athanasius of Alexandria remarks about God, "He it was Who suffered and yet suffered not. Suffered, because His own Body suffered, and He was in it, which thus suffered; suffered not, because the Word, being by Nature God, is impassible." Athanasius, *Epistola ad Epictetum*, 6. In elaborating this notion, Paul Gavrilyuk states, "The appropriation of the flesh meant that in the incarnation God acted and suffered in and through the flesh, and did nothing apart from the flesh." Gavrilyuk, *The Suffering*, 162.

251. Gavrilyuk, *The Suffering*, 162.

252. This notion in Latin is "*impassibilis Deus*." Yet the Tome to Flavian of St Leo the Great also states that God "did not despise becoming a suffering man (*homo passibilis*)." Emery, "The Immutability of the God of Love," 30.

253. Emery, "The Immutability of the God of Love," 30.

254. It shows that "while the council at Chalcedon was willing to tackle the divine-human paradox of the Christ event—and admit the difficulty of reconciling the two natures—it was unwilling to compromise on the doctrine of divine impassibility." See commentary by Leo the Great, bishop of Rome (400–461), in *Sermons*, Tract. 28.4,

What Barth accommodates is an absolutely free God who wills to compromise whatever stands in the way of God's love; an eternal love which surely brings eternal solidarity. That is why the suffering of the "divine person" is the basis of humanity's assurance of God's solidarity, and also, the victory over human contradiction. Notwithstanding the assumption of the constraints and contradiction of humanity, Jesus Christ overcomes it instead of being overcome by it.[255] Christ in the flesh triumphs over the flesh; Christ's humanity is not a being detached from God, but rather the opposite. In fact, since Barth insists on the indissolubly one Christ, so Christ's human nature is always and totally *with God and for God*.[256] Gary Deddo calls such existence a wellspring of "covenantal content" of humanity's being.[257] It is so when the Son obeys the Father (as opposed to humanity's disobedience to God). In other words, Christ is like humanity because he assumes the flesh; yet Christ is also unlike humanity because he never disobeys the Father even in the flesh. In the Son's obedience to the Father, Jesus Christ triumphs over what overcomes humanity. For Barth, such triumph is also accounted for humanity, which translates to the atonement.

3.5 The Lord of Suffering

Based on Barth's assertions just explained, we can deduce that God (in the indissolubly one Christ) remains in himself despite suffering because: first, although God humbles himself in the form of a servant, he remains Lord, hence the title "The Servant as Lord"; second, God is glorified in his suffering; and last, the humanity God assumes is superior to all humankind because God dominates over suffering in Jesus Christ. God remains sovereignly in himself because God accomplishes his mission as Lord. God remains the Lord in his mission because it is here where the Son of Man truly represents humankind.[258] In this representation, Barth presupposes, is where the Son demonstrates his lordship.[259] In other words, it is when God suffers that humankind comes into the fullness of its being—under the lordship of God.

138.141. Grillmeier, *Christ in Christian Tradition*, 537.

255. *CD* IV/2, 30. "He [God] overcomes the flesh in becoming a flesh." IV/1, 185.

256. *CD* IV/2, 28–29.

257. Deddo, *Karl Barth's Theology of Relations*. Volume 1, 82.

258. *CD* IV/2, 20–21; also in III/2, 209.

259. *CD* IV/2, 20.

The lordship in Jesus Christ is where people find their existential grounding by sharing in God's glory.[260] Without the suffering of God, humans are eternally lost; and if humans are eternally lost, the glory of God loses its true meaning.[261] It is only through humiliation that Christ is exalted; and the exaltation of Christ is likewise the exaltation of humankind.[262] Barth sees Jesus Christ as superior to all humankind (as thoroughly man, not as a "superman") as this man is subjected to the harsh conditions of the far country, and indeed, he actually suffered.[263] Thus Christ is preeminent not in terms of his human substance *per se*, i.e., the exceptional nature of his flesh (or that he is only partly human and more divine), but because Christ succeeds where humans in general fail.[264] It is Jesus Christ who suffers but does not become subservient to suffering; though he is subjected to suffering, he is not subjugated by it. For example, despite his death, he does not decay but rather resurrects from the dead. No other human can compare to how Jesus Christ conquers death itself.[265]

God indeed dictates the outcome of his suffering; not the other way around. God's self-binding therefore, cannot be accounted as "self-blinding" as Brandon Gallaher infers.[266] I do not read in Barth that in *kenosis*, God makes himself blinded, i.e., be unaware of what happens afterwards. In Barth's view, God remains sovereignly cognizant of creaturely reality especially in the suffering flesh. Suffering, as such, becomes God's instrument for self-attestation through self-affirmation. How? It is because suffering *per se* is dispensed by God and not otherwise. God, in this case, is not reduced to being restricted or inferior against suffering itself. In fact, God demonstrates his sovereignty by suffering in the divine humanity, and in it, wins for humankind. In the victory of the Jesus Christ, humankind is *home with*

260. *CD* IV/1, 294. This thought might have been shaped by what Barth had experienced during and after the two world wars.

261. *CD* IV/1, 217–19.

262. *CD* IV/1, 203.

263. *CD* I/1, 513.

264. *CD* IV/1, 135.

265. *CD* IV/2, 147–48. For Barth, God's supremacy is established by restoring humans unto himself and exalting them with himself. God in Christ is not destroyed by death but rather is the One who has destroyed it. IV/1, 481.

266. ". . . God eternally binds Himself to creation in Christ through His own self-blinding—the self-binding is a self-blinding." Gallaher, *Freedom and Necessity In Modern Trinitarian Theology*, 241.

God. This is, for Barth, the *raison d'être* of all human beings.[267] The coming home is achieved by Christ being the Royal Man.[268]

The Royal Man is the epitome of Barth's correction of the traditional view of impassibility because the royalty of this Man is gained from lording over suffering.[269] The Royal Man, therefore, signifies the kingdom of God where true reconciliation has happened.[270] By extrapolation, the Royal Man is the impassible-passible being because in the execution of the atonement, his substitutionary sacrifice has sufficed without himself being substituted.[271]

In Jesus Christ's substitutionary act, the true Lord God is revealed, yet still, in a dialectic fashion. Barth puts it,

> The Almighty exists and acts and speaks here in the form of One who is weak and impotent, the eternal as One who is temporal and perishing, the Most High in the deepest humility. The Holy One stands in the place and under the accusation of a sinner with other sinners. The glorious One is covered with shame. The One who lives forever has fallen a prey to death. The Creator is subjected to and overcome by the onslaught of that which is not.[272]

All of these are manifested in the Royal Man—the Lord of suffering.[273] Thus for Barth, God's capability to suffer (*Leidensfähigkeit*) as the Royal Man undoubtedly speaks of divine glory.[274] Impassibility is not a push back for this Man; also, passibility does not prevent this Man from being the King. It is in impassibility that suffering does not defeat the Royal Man whereas it is in passibility that the Royal Man defeats suffering. So in Barth's theology, the *locus in quo* of divine suffering is that it happened in and through Jesus Christ.[275] Ascribing suffering to God does not dishonor what is eternally divine, but rather the effect is otherwise. The true honor of God comes from his will-act

267. Kaltwasser, "Karl Barth on What Makes Us Human," para. 5.

268. *CD* IV/2, 155.

269. This is in line with Barth's conception of Christ as the "second Adam." *CD* IV/2, 155. Also read Barth, *Christ and Adam*, 60.

270. Excursus in *CD* IV/2, 155. Barth reasons that God's kingdom is to be understood as "the end of the whole present order and the advent of the new order of existence." Barth, *Prayer and Preaching*, 40

271. *CD* IV/2, 157–58, 164.

272. *CD* IV/1, 176.

273. *CD* IV/2, 167–69. Naudé, *Pathways in Theology*, 275.

274. *CD* IV/2, 86. *KD* IV/2, 94.

275. *CD* IV/2, 43. Jüngel alludes to a modified form of Patripassianism imbedded in Barth's theology. *God's Being is in Becoming*, 99–102.

to suffer and still be Lord. The fact that the *kenosis* happens in God's history, therefore, God wills the events and actions which cause his suffering because all of these are under God's discretion—in his kingdom.[276]

The same could be said about Barth's stand on the issue of impassibility. I have argued that, in his schema, impassibility is taken alongside passibility in light of the Royal Man. If Barth is ready to conceive God in opposite categories, e.g., impassible and passible, the same dialectic principle could be true for his understanding of redemption. T. F. Torrance says something to this effect if (im)passibility is treated soteriologically.[277] We will better understand this by examining what Barth means that Jesus Christ "stands in the place and under the accusation of a sinner?"

3.6 Divine Suffering and Reconciliation

When Barth posits that Jesus Christ is the Lord of suffering, it is taken in view of judgment:

> That Jesus Christ is very God is shown in His way into the far country in which He the Lord became a servant. For in the majesty of the true God it happened that the eternal Son of the eternal Father became obedient by offering and humbling Himself to be the brother of man, to take His place with the transgressors, to judge him by judging Himself and dying in his place.[278]

Barth here articulates how God's suffering is related to soteriology. Jesus Christ's substitution, in soteriological sense, makes the judgment good for humanity. In judgment, God's affliction is accounted for humans so they do not have to suffer in judgment. The vicarious sacrifice is the righteousness of God's judgment.[279] It is in this righteous judgment that Barth articulates his view on justification.[280] God takes the accusation and condemnation unto himself to pardon the sinner. Barth adds: "By suffering death—our death—for us, He did for us that which is the basis of our life from the dead."[281] In

276. *CD* IV/1, 134, 208–9.

277. Torrance's view, although more centred on the doctrine of the Trinity rather than on Christology, is indeed helpful in this regard. He writes, "Thus we may say of God in Christ that he both suffered and did not suffer, for through the eternal tranquility of his divine impassibility he took upon himself our passibility and redeemed it." Torrance, *The Trinitarian Faith*, 185.

278. *CD* IV/1, 157.

279. *CD* IV/1, 516.

280. See "The Justification of Man" in §61 of *CD*.

281. *CD* IV/1, 514.

this sense, the sinner lives as a result of Christ's death. It is the efficacy of God's suffering love acting freely in judgment. Thus the guilty is justified by the sacrifice of the innocent Justifier.

Justification, says Barth, is not merely about the proclamation of what Jesus Christ has done for humanity, but pertinently, about the confession of what humans were and what humans have become because of Christ's sacrifice.[282] Humans are now "truly" and "actually" reconciled by God's righteous act. Accordingly, the reconciled have a new life; a justified life with Jesus Christ.

Reconciliation, as the execution of God's judgment is played out as the "event of the death of Jesus Christ."[283] Why does Barth regard justification as a sacrificial event? It is because the justified life of the reconciled comes as a result of God's shared history with humanity:

> It takes place as the history of God with man. That which is twofold but one in it is the righteousness and grace of the one God above, condemning and pardoning, killing and making alive; and corresponding to this divine activity the dark Whence and the bright Whither of the one man below, experiencing His judgment.[284]

The shared history is the history of suffering.[285] In this history, the "pardoning" and the "making alive" of humans is the product of the "condemning" and the "killing" of Jesus Christ. The "Whence" is not the focus of judgment but the "Wither," yet the meaning of the latter is derived from the former. The present state of the sinner is confronted by the past and future states in judgment.[286] Judgment therefore is an established event which has a pivotal effect. Barth qualifies:

> [H]is [human's] transition and progress from that yesterday to this to-morrow, his coming out of the wrong which is removed and destroyed, his coming, therefore, out of his own death, and in that coming—this is his present—his going forward to his new right and therefore to his new life.[287]

282. *CD* IV/1, 515. Küng, *Justification,* xix–xxii.

283. *CD* IV/1, 514.

284. *CD* IV/1, 545.

285. *CD* IV/1, 558. "What He has done for us as the eternal Son of God He has done rightly." *CD* IV/1, 558. Here Barth pertains to what Christ has done "in His death," of what Christ is as "the Crucified." *CD* IV/1, 558, top excursus.

286. Dawson, *The Resurrection in Karl Barth*, 176–77.

287. *CD* IV/1, 545.

This relates to Jesus Christ's resurrection which has effected the justification of humanity. The word "transition" especially the word "progress" are not helpful in this context because the idea of development or improvement of human state, or having the possibility of reverting to the former state is definitely unreflective of what Barth has in mind. It is due to the fact that the old life can neither be developed nor improved, but rather, it should be *replaced* by a new life. Also, once the new life has taken over, the old life is gone—no longer retrievable thus it cannot be relived.[288] What Barth appropriately conveys is the "passing and stepping out" (*Übergang und Schreiten aus*) of what humanity used to *be* prior to God's intervention.[289] That is why the concepts of death and resurrection are applied to explain what it truly means to be justified. The life that Jesus Christ has lived is the exact life which has been granted to replace that of humankind's.[290] In other words, the reality of the new life originates from the triumphant life of Jesus Christ. Without death, there is no resurrection; without resurrection, there is no new life. This is what Barth calls "the unity of the transition" in judgment.[291] Such an event is key in understanding how God's suffering is important in Barth's soteriology.[292]

Even though absolute reconciliation is futuristic, Barth however clarifies that God's pardon is once, and, for all vis-à-vis the history of humankind. The future, in this respect, is seen as a "realised eschatology."[293] In God's end-time judgment, the set direction for humanity comes to light by stepping onwards with God. In reconciliation, humanity becomes the true and actual co-traveller with God. In this journey, Barth argues, justification leads to sanctification; then eventually ends in redemption (God's ultimate purpose for humanity).[294] This enlightens what it means to have a new life completed in succession; the reconciling act of God effects the transformation of the reconciled. So in

288. *CD* IV/1, 549, 552. In Barth's assertion, the forgiven sin "is now the old thing . . . something which is past and has no future." Excursus in *CD* IV/1, 256. The new being lives and abides forever. *CD* IV/1, 749. Barth refers to 2 Cor 5:17.

289. See *KD* IV/1, 608.

290. *CD* IV/1, 552–53.

291. *CD* IV/1, 558.

292. Barth's soteriology is deeply connected with his ecclesiology. Lindsay, "Barth, Berkovits, Birkenau," 4.

293. *CD* IV/1, 598. Barth posits, "Where and when the promise is given to him, it is true and reliable; it cannot fail in anything of its content. As eschatology it is "realised eschatology." In and with it, its whole content enters the present of man." *CD* IV/1, 598–99. Here Barth's soteriology is inseparable with his eschatology.

294. *CD* IV/2, 530. In this study, the term "redemption" is preferred over "salvation"; redemption exactly fits Barth's concept of reconciliation wherein the idea of restoration or coming back to God is propounded.

order to get into Barth's soterio-eschatological framework, we have to examine how the sacrifice of God correlates with sanctification.

The ongoing effect of God's sacrifice can be further deduced from Barth's articulation of sanctification.[295] Sanctification is described within his doctrine of reconciliation:

> The action of God in His reconciliation of the world with Himself in Jesus Christ is unitary. It consists of different "moments" with a different bearing. It accomplishes both the justification and the sanctification of man. . . . The one is done wholly and immediately with the other.[296]

Sanctification is married with justification in Barth's formulation of God's reconciling act.[297] God is active in humility as well as in glory; the former is the corollary to justification while the latter is the corollary to sanctification.[298] God is the "active Subject" in the conversion experience of a person.[299] In it, though having different experiences, yet it has one indivisible character in its unanimous outcome, i.e., to be with God and stay with God.

Rightly so, for Barth, the two moments of justification and sanctification happen in the "one event" of reconciliation.[300] In reconciliation, the person is said to have been united and continue in unity with God. It is therefore in justification that a person is sanctified inasmuch as this one event points to God's one event with humanity. As regards God's resignation to death, Barth argues, humans are now enriched with a sanctified life.[301] Barth continues, "His [Jesus Christ's] resurrection from the dead, is a moment and aspect of the mighty reconciling action of God which has taken place in Him."[302] Barth seeks to indicate that though sanctification is an ongoing moment, the person under it is already deemed as sanctified.[303] This is true to Barth's conception of the "not yet" in human history (temporal)

295. See the "Sanctification of Man" in §66 of *CD*.

296. *CD* IV/2, 501–2.

297. Justification, for Barth, is God's "turning in free grace to sinful man"; while sanctification is God's "converting of man" to himself in the same free grace. *CD* IV/2, 503. Teleologically speaking, sanctification can be seen to have priority over justification in view of God's intention. See Haley, *The Humanity of Christ*, 319.

298. *CD* IV/2, 503.

299. *CD* IV/2, 500.

300. *CD* IV/2, 500.

301. *CD* IV/2, 511, 516. Barth quotes John 3:16.

302. *CD* IV/2, 516.

303. *CD* IV/2, 517, 583.

and the "already so" in divine history (eternal).[304] That is why he treats the not yet and already so collectively and positively as the new reality.[305] The new reality is not static, but rather a dynamic movement coincident with redemption in Barth's soterio-eschatological understanding.[306] In this respect, we can interject that reconciliation anticipates redemption.[307]

Christ's death is the way to reconciliation as Christ's resurrection is the testament to redemption. Barth states:

> But God the Father raised Him [Jesus Christ] from the dead, and in so doing recognised and gave effect to His death and passion as a satisfaction made for us, as our conversion to God, and therefore as our redemption from death to life.[308]

There are three points in this passage that need explanation. First, how does the Father give effect to the Son's passion and death? Second, how satisfaction is made in the reconciliation of humankind? And last, how does conversion take place?

The resurrection signifies the Father's recognition of the Son's passion and death. Barth alludes that the Father acknowledged and put into effect (*anerkannt und in Kraft gesetzt*) the substitutionary work of the Son by raising him.[309] In other words, though the Son fulfills the requirement for reconciliation, the Father is the One who executes and consummates it. The divine fulfillment, execution, and consummation are the precursors to the satisfaction made for humanity. The term "satisfaction" literally means an accomplished legal act (*vollbrachte Rechtstat*), hence, the functions of the Father and Son in reconciliation are already performed.[310] As a result, the "conversion" of humans showing their "redemption" is attained.

In connection with what I have discussed about the relation of suffering to reconciliation, the need for justice is met through justification (satisfaction) that initiates sanctification (conversion) which indicates new life (redemption). Therefore the conversion takes place right after a person is

304. *CD* IV/1, 661.

305. Busch, *Barth in Conversation*, 129. Cf. 1 John 3:2. Compare how this new frame of mind contrasts with Barth's early pessimistic view. See McCormack, "Longing for a new world," 135

306. *CD* IV/1, 646, 661. Redemption is complete as long as it is understood as an accomplished fact; yet also an event because of its eschatological finale. See Haley, *The Humanity of Christ*, 127n142.

307. *CD* IV/2, 516.

308. *CD* IV/1, 157.

309. *KD* IV/1, 171.

310. *KD* IV/1, 171.

made right with God through the merit of Jesus Christ. The experience of satisfaction and conversion describes what it means to be redeemed. All of these compose what Barth means by reconciliation in and through Jesus Christ. More importantly, the reconciliation unto redemption is the telos of God's suffering.

Furthermore, Barth speaks of conversion in effect of reconciliation as "our redemption from death to life."[311] Jesus Christ, being the Subject of judgment, represents humankind being its object. Here the election of Jesus Christ typifies the election to redemption.[312] Thus in reconciliation, the person is thought to have been redeemed in the divine sacrificial act. Barth finds the converted person to be a redeemed person.[313] God, as the active Subject in the redemption of humanity is likewise the active Subject in suffering. That is why in Christ's death, humans live in sanctity.[314]

In this respect, reconciliation unto redemption is God's own act.[315] The "new actuality" of those who are in Jesus Christ is something inherited, not acquired.[316] Barth continues, "His [Jesus Christ's] resurrection from the dead, is a moment and aspect of the mighty reconciling action of God which has taken place in Him."[317] In Christ, being one with God is not yet to be achieved, but rather, it is already achieved.[318] It is only in Christ where humanity's conversion is said to be real.[319] Pertaining to those who see themselves positively within the covenant, Barth attests, "The captivity is behind them, freedom before them" in and with Jesus Christ.[320] The reconciled are therefore freed to live with the hope of redemption.[321] It is in this context where God's suffering is understood as impetus for redemption. What remains for humans, Barth thinks, is to accept their new actuality with gratitude; and it should translate

311. *CD* IV/1, 157.

312. *CD* IV/1, 157.

313. *CD* IV/2, 509.

314. *CD* IV/2, 511, 516. Barth quotes John 3:16.

315. *CD* IV/2, 516.

316. *CD* IV/1, 249; IV/2, 531. Goroncy, "Sanctification," 3.

317. *CD* IV/2, 516.

318. Barth points out that "if one addresses him [a believer] concerning God's eternal election and concerning its consequence that Jesus Christ died and rose again for him and concerning the citizenship he received at his baptism, then one presupposes that the promise holds good for him and continues sure." Barth, *The Teaching of the Church Regarding Baptism*, 64.

319. *CD* IV/2, 517, 583.

320. *CD* IV/2, 533.

321. *CD* IV/2, 532. Barth cites Gal 5:1.

into action.[322] The reconciled therefore are summoned to live like Christ.[323] In this way, humans participate in the community of the redeemed and in the suffering of God.[324] Barth notes that in suffering, Jesus Christ stands as the Brother of the reconciled.[325]

It is part of the mission of God to call out his people to also suffer. For Barth, Jesus Christ's representation signals a subsequent action, i.e., the reconciled are to follow their Lord. Those represented by Christ are elected to suffer as they are elected to conversion. Barth asserts, "He [Jesus Christ] has already found them to the extent that He has elected them. . . . He thus establishes His particular relationship to them by commanding them."[326] In other words, Jesus Christ commands those who already belong to him, those who treat him as Lord.[327] The command is to follow Christ, not according to when and how they want to do so, but to follow Christ in full submission.

It is also in this backdrop where the exaltation of the reconciled is properly viewed. In weakness and humility, the reconciled affirms the power of God in them. It is the power which overcomes their suffering, and also, the power which transforms them. The Holy Spirit draws the people who are being sanctified into an active decision to live with and in Christ.[328] It is in this framework, explains Barth, where the reconciled experience the fullness of reconciliation.[329] That is why the reconciled are sanctified as the disciples of Christ.[330] Here Barth contends for the "mark of the cross" laid upon those whom God has sanctified.[331]

322. CD IV/2, 516.

323. *CD* IV/2, 516.

324. *CD* IV/2, 517. See Dreyer, "Barth on election and the Canons of Dort," 8.

325. *CD* IV/1, 157.

326. *CD* IV/2, 535.

327. *CD* IV/2, 535.

328. *CD* I/2, 203, 278. This in turn translates to a Christian life which "allows space for joyful reception and projection of God's loving freedom." Capper, "Karl Barth's Theology of Joy," 177. Contrary to Reinhold Niebuhr's allegation that cynicism and despair are somewhat inherent in Barth's theology. Elgendy, "Hope, Cynicism, and Complicity," 182–98.

329. *CD* IV/2, 535. Yocum, *Ecclesial Mediation in Karl Barth*, 93–94.

330. *CD* IV/2, 533. For Barth's thought on "The Call of Discipleship," see §66.3 of *CD*.

331. *CD* IV/2, 499.

3.7 The Cross Revisited

In following Jesus Christ, the disciples are called upon to imitate the love God has for humanity.[332] It is therefore in sacrificial love whereby the mark of the cross is made evident.[333] In eschatological terms, the disciples follow the Lamb in self-denial:[334]

> Self-denial in the context of following Jesus involves a step into the open, into the freedom of a definite decision and act, in which it is with a real commitment that man takes leave of himself, of the man of yesterday . . . in which he gives up the previous form of his existence, *hazarding* and totally *compromising* himself.[335]

Unexpectedly, Barth uses the same self-degrading words he employs in describing the self-humbling of God. The mark of the cross is upon the disciples who undergo distress and discomfort by "hazarding and compromising" themselves for their love of God and fellowmen.[336] This is how they exercise self-denial—a personal attack upon self.[337] It is in such self-denial wherein Barth sees the Spirit to be at work.[338] The Spirit facilitates the mark of the cross upon the reconciled by helping them to commit to a life of discipleship.[339] Being a disciple is to live within the covenant of God. A disciple no longer lives in opposition to true human existence by being obedient to God akin to the Son's obedience to the Father.[340] Having the mark of the cross is being against self by being *with* God; in continued opposition to self, the disciple is no longer rebellious to God.[341] Respectively, the mark signifies the ceasing of the contradiction of humanity: obeying God's will instead of obeying one's will. In this way, humans no longer live contrary to their own existence. Here we can deduce Barth's articulation on self-compromise: the notion "God against God" is indeed a controversial idea, however, the command to the disciples to go against self is non-controversial, but rather

332. *CD* IV/2, 535, 584.

333. *CD* IV/2, 535.

334. *CD* IV/2, 537. Barth refers to John 8:12 and Rev 14:1.

335. *CD* IV/2, 539–40. Italics mine.

336. Swann, "Discipleship on the Level of Thought," 168–70.

337. *CD* IV/2, 543.

338. *CD* IV/2, 556–57.

339. *CD* IV/2, 539.

340. *CD* IV/2, 540.

341. In suffering, humans become "bound" to Jesus; not become *like* Jesus. *CD* IV/2, 546. See McCormack, "Participation in God, Yes, Deification, No," 372–73.

proper (in the standpoint of the church). So the mark of the cross in each disciple is seen in the obedience of suffering. In this sense, the disciples are also suffering servants like their Lord.

In other words, a disciple is one who lives out the conversion experience; it is in sharp contrast to the person who stays in the far country. A disciple does exactly what the Lord commands, i.e., to come out of the far country and be with God.[342] In "willingness and readiness," a disciple is to obey God at all cost, even in losing one's life in the process.[343] There can be no obedience of suffering without being willing and ready to compromise oneself in following Christ. To think and act otherwise, Barth contends, is an evidence of non-conversion.[344] The disciple is no longer the old person.[345] Thus the reconciled is truly one with God in light of the eschatological reality in Jesus Christ.[346] In this scenario, we can better appreciate how the *now* is linked with the *not yet*.[347] This simultaneity is strengthened not only by the mark of the cross, but more crucially, in the "dignity of the cross."[348] For Barth, the dignity of the cross speaks of true sanctification, hence, true reconciliation.[349] Barth states, "We refer to the cross which everyone who is sanctified in Jesus Christ, and therefore every Christian, has to bear as such, the people of God in the world being ordained to bear it."[350] In other words, the dignity of the cross points to the ordination to suffering of those who are in Christ. It is in carrying the cross (*tolerantia crucis*) of self denial that the sanctified people embody hope for their future redemption.[351] As the

342. *CD* IV/2, 541.

343. *CD* IV/2, 541.

344. *CD* IV/2, 540.

345. *CD* IV/2, 573.

346. *CD* IV/2, 574.

347. *CD* IV/2, 574. Barth in this sense reformulates Luther's notion of *simul iustus et peccator*. Barth argues, "as he who is still wholly the old and already wholly the new man—he has not fallen out with himself partially but totally, in the sense that the end and goal of the dispute is that he can no longer be the one he was and can be only the one he will be." *CD* IV/2, 574. Cf. Neder, *Participation in Christ*, 48–49. McDowell, "Learning Where to Place One's Hope," 337. Also, McDowell, *Hope in Barth's Eschatology*, 6–7.

348. Barth expounds the "Dignity of the Cross" in §66.6 of *CD*. Barth's own version of the theology of the cross is influenced by Luther's presupposition that a God who loves is a God who suffers. Bradbury, *Cross Theology*, 51–52.

349. *CD* IV/2, 598.

350. *CD* IV/2, 599. Barth, in this regard, cites Dietrich Bonhoeffer. For insights on Bonhoeffer's position on true discipleship, read Bonhoeffer, *Letters and Papers from Prison*. Also see Puffer, "Dietrich Bonhoeffer in the Theology of Karl Barth," 46–61.

351. *CD* IV/1, 253; IV/2, 599.

reconciled deny themselves, they in turn are not denied of hope in Christ. Indeed, God's command comes with a promise.

Concomitantly, the reconciled are to be "disciples of the Rejected and Crucified," and in being so, they proclaim their allegiance with the Suffering Reconciler.[352] The bearing of the disciples's cross, in Barth's mind, resonates with the suffering love of God and its effect on the world:

> [H]is [believer's] cross, not in identity but in similarity with the cross of Jesus. His cross points to the fulness and truth of that which he expects, and to which he hastens, as one who is sanctified in Jesus Christ. It points to God Himself, to His will for the world, to the future revelation of His majesty, to the glory in which his Lord already lives and reigns.[353]

The mark and the dignity of the cross is Barth's supplemental way of accentuating God's sacrifice and triumph. Here we can appreciate the manner by which (im)passibility can be treated soteriologically. The mark of the cross symbolizes Christ's humiliation reflected in the present life of the reconciled; while the dignity of the cross signifies Christ's exaltation reflected in the future life of the redeemed. This is what I conceive as the discipleship of suffering and blessing. The cross of Christ is the glory of God wherein the disciples find comfort and hope.[354]

That is why Barth puts forward God's history of suffering as a springboard for the actualization of redemption.[355] Hence, in this argumentation, the history of suffering is the impetus for redemption history:

> His [Jesus Christ's] self-proclamation documented in the Gospel, the nerve of the history between God and man which took place in it, the history of redemption, is essentially the history of the passion.[356]

On this account, the redemption history is the passion history. Though the passion happens in the created time, its essence originates in the eternal decree. Thus for Barth, the being of Jesus Christ is the "nerve" of the shared history because his existence is succeeded by the history of humanity.[357] Barth sees this simultaneous history as the "history of the covenant of salvation."[358]

352. *CD* IV/2, 600.
353. *CD* IV/2, 606.
354. *CD* IV/2, 605.
355. Graham, *Representation and Substitution in the Atonement Theologies*, 350.
356. *CD* IV/1, 167.
357. *CD* III/2, 162.
358. *CD* III/2, 160.

This is the "concrete truth"—the history of suffering demonstrates God's adoption and transition of creaturely reality.[359] Barth even stresses that people's "agony and pain" are no longer theirs but God's.[360] The decisive factor that turns the scale is that the fate of humanity is already "enacted" in Christ.[361] In the decree, God covenants with humanity in the person of Jesus Christ.[362] Christ is not only the physical manifestation of God's covenant, but also, Christ is "the true Covenant-partner of God."[363] The Son, in fellowship and cooperation with the Father, makes Christ the Bearer and the Fulfiller of the covenant.[364] In being the Covenant-partner, Jesus Christ has assumed the negative dimension of the covenant so humans can be seen positively within it.[365] Here, the unreconciled becomes reconciled; in Christ, a person as "covenant-breaker" now becomes a "covenant-partner."[366]

For Barth, therefore, the eternal covenant speaks of the unitary act of God. The Father's acknowledgment of the Son's sacrifice, says Barth, is opposed to the notion of a *transactional agreement* between him and the Son.[367] There is no negotiation involved in the fulfillment, execution, and consummation of reconciliation. The satisfaction made for humanity is a triune decision in eternity; there is neither prior nor conciliatory covenant. When Barth writes: "His [God's] promise, in which He binds and pledges Himself to man, and His command by which He pledges and binds man to

359. *CD* IV/1, 168.

360. *CD* I/2, 113.

361. *CD* III/2, 161.

362. *CD* II/2, 7–8.

363. *CD* IV/2, 527. For a more nuanced interpretation of covenant-partnership; cf. Fiddes, *The Creative Suffering*, 15, 67.

364. *CD* IV/2, 527.

365. McKenny, ""Freed by God for God," 136.

366. *CD* IV/2, 525. For Barth, God's covenant-partners are freed to love God and others. Clough, *Ethics in Crisis*, 108.

367. This in reaction to Johannes Coccejus's formulation of "*pactus salutis*." Read *CD* IV/1, 59–66. This formulation permeates the Reformed view of the covenant. "In Reformed theology, the *pactum salutis* has been defined as a pretemporal, intratrinitarian agreement between the Father and Son in which the Father promises to redeem an elect people. In turn the Son volunteers to earn the salvation of his people by becoming incarnate . . . by acting as surety of the covenant of grace for and as mediator of the covenant of grace to the elect. In his active and passive obedience, Christ fulfills the conditions of the *pactum salutis* . . . ratifying the Father's promise, because of which the Father rewards the Son's obedience with the salvation of the elect. And because of this the Holy Spirit applies the Son's work to his people through the means of grace." Clark, *Covenant, Justification and Pastoral Ministry*, 168. For the implications of *pactum salutis*, see Fesko, *Beyond Calvin*, 288.

Himself," there is only one Subject in mind—the triune God.[368] The one-subject covenant is absolutely christocentric because it is in Jesus Christ where the whole content of the will of God is revealed.[369] The content speaks of the being of humanity because Christ is the "concrete reality and actuality of the promise and command of God, the fulfilment of both."[370] This is the foundation for Christ being the true fellow-human evident in the covenant of redemption.[371]

In other words, there is no plurality of decrees, but rather, there is only one eternal decree. Likewise, there is no temporal covenant, only an eternal covenant (comprising the old and new covenants).[372] This eternal covenant is fully contained in Jesus Christ and God administers this covenant solely in Christ.[373] But another question arises: What is the *physis* or nature of Jesus Christ under the covenant of redemption?

Jesus Christ being the eschatological identity of humanity is suspected to suggest a sort of "divine-human uniphysism" in the Son, in which the Son is said to be the redeeming God and also, fallen-and-redeemed human.[374] This language of uniphysism emerges from God and humans participating together in common being. I would argue that Barth's objection to the use of the term "God-man" is quite reflective of his view against any synthesis of divine/human natures or monophysitism.[375] Using the term God-man, says Barth, causes confusion, if not dissimulation in the minds of readers; it also hints a "middle being" which "obliterates the historicity" of Jesus Christ being the Subject.[376] This is the reason behind Barth's adoption of the phrase divine humanity.

If there is any hint of uniphysism arising from Barth's idea of the common participation between God and humans, it is a participation in *common history*, not in common being. The uniphycal problem suspected

368. *CD* IV/1, 53. Darren Sumner is right in his conclusion: "The story of God the Father and God the Son negotiating a mutually acceptable arrangement for the accomplishment of redemption requires unacceptable alterations to the doctrine of God." See "The Pactum Salutis, Divine Agreement, and Karl Barth."

369. *CD* IV/1, 53.

370. *CD* IV/1, 53.

371. *CD* IV/1, 64.

372. *CD* IV/1, 65–66.

373. More on this in chapter 4 as we consider how Barth unpacks the eternal covenant in view of the Trinity.

374. Bucey, "Previewing Karl Barth and Thomas Aquinas on Analogy," video, 51:40.

375. *CD* IV/2, 115.

376. *CD* IV/2, 115. Barth, referring to the word "God-man" says that "except in quotations, we ourselves have preferred to avoid it." *CD* IV/2, 115.

in Barth's thought is a consequence of his concept of *Geschichte* as a place of God's active redemption. Here, time and eternity meet in fulfillment of God's will, plan, and purpose in election. Jesus Christ is the common event of God and humanity; Jesus Christ is the only being in which God reaches out compassionately to all humankind. There is no excluded middle in Barth's Christology, even in relation to onto-soteriology, simply because the conception of the Son of God/Son of Man is rigidly and symmetrically dyophysitic all throughout the *Church Dogmatics*.[377] Hence, the divine humanity of the Son (without the idea of polar opposite natures or hybrid of natures) is the Subject of soteriological identification.

Evaluation

Barth's reconfigured Christology is pivotal in formulating his own schema on divine suffering. The metonymic Eutychian and Nestorian attack on Chalcedon are seriously addressed in finding a way to speak of God's suffering in the very existence of Jesus Christ. The following are Barth's christological views on impassibility, namely, first, the being of the Son of God is determined in the decree; second, the Son of God has no being apart from the being of Jesus Christ; third, the human essence exists with the Son of God prior to creation (*Logos incarnandus*); fourth, the Logos exists without flesh but Jesus Christ cannot exist without the Logos; fifth, the Logos and Jesus Christ are both mutually affected by the other in their union; sixth, the experience of Christ can also be the experience of God. In sum, Barth accommodates God's capacity to suffer in God's voluntary and victorious act. Correspondingly, we can derive what Barth has in mind about the suffering being of the indissolubly one Christ; an outcome of a continued dialogue with Lutheran and Reformed Christologies.

The immediate and outer contexts of our text depict God's suffering in relation to God's active will.[378] Thus the literary design of Barth's doctrine of reconciliation advocates an absolute God who is determined to be *actively* suffering. This shows Barth's functional association of divine suffering with God's autonomous decision (or sovereignty); a method designed to display God's capacity and willingness to embrace "the opposites" or dialectical

377. For the ontological relevance of symmetrical dyophysitism, see Gallaher, *Freedom and Necessity*, 106. Also see John Meyendorff's qualification of symmetrical and asymmetrical dyophysitism in "Chalcedonians and Monophysites after Chalcedon," 16–30.

378. See *CD* IV/1, 35, 49, 51, 80, 93, 128, 166, 175, 176–77, 179, 183, 184, 185, 186, 188, 193, 294–95.

pairs.[379] Such a method does not equate divine suffering with God's insusceptibility to change (or immutability) in order to eschew any irrelevant speculation of its ramifications.[380] Barth, therefore, fundamentally disassociates divine suffering from the notion of impassibility *per se*; or more accurately, God being "absolutely untouchable in contrast to all contestation" to strongly highlight the activeness of the reconciling God in suffering.[381] In this manner, any mechanistic theories of the atonement are shunned.

The implication of this schema is vital in Barth's treatment of (im)passibility. Because Barth ingeniously accounts suffering (*Leiden*) in terms of God's decision, and not on God's non-reaction, he is able to view the atonement within the decree. Likewise, he finds a common ground with the traditional conception of God, especially with the Reformed view.[382] In this circumstance, Barth can speak of a suffering God without abandoning God's impassibility. Likewise, he can also say that God freely takes suffering in God's inner life without ceasing to be unaffected. In other words, the actively affecting God can be, at the same time, the passively suffering God.[383] This schema is beneficial in advancing Barth's doctrine of reconciliation. When he intentionally defines the reconciling God in its dialectic identification with humanity, he is obliged to argue extensively in this framework; which helps modify his late Christology. In effect, Barth has managed to safeguard the solid union of the Logos and the human Jesus in the one-subject Christ against the Alexandrian/Reformed tendency (de-divinize Christ's divinity in suffering), or the Antiochene/Lutheran tendency (divinize Christ's humanity in suffering).

However, Barth is not consistent with his schema throughout his train of thought due to his habitual change of category in speaking of divine suffering. He randomly transitions from God's active decision to God's description, i.e., movability in suffering, then shifts back later as he progresses in his argument. It is so because he also considers the divine suffering comprehensively with God's other attributes. Barth nonetheless is cautious throughout his writing to "not to lose track" of his overarching theme—God's being is

379. Barth never really revised his view on this matter since the Göttingen period.

380. *CD* IV/1, 181–83, 193, 203.

381. "*Durchaus nur unberührt im Gegensatz zu aller Anfechtung*." *KD* IV/1, 203. In the ET: "inviolable in contrast to all temptation" is quite incompatible with the usual notion of impassibility.

382. *KD* IV/1, 203. *CD* IV/1, 133, 160–61.

383. If Barth rigidly accounts suffering with untouchability, he will have to infer God's abandonment of his impassibility in favor of his passibility. For a more nuanced interpretation concerning God's suffering on the cross; cf. Hunsinger, *Reading Barth*, 122.

in God's act.[384] This literary style is problematic because it is indicative of a lack of specificity in Barth's articulation that inevitably results in disputation on his exact position on impassibility.[385]

Why is this so? Obviously, it is because Barth chiefly treats divine suffering within his doctrine of reconciliation. In it, God is in what he does, hence, the *is* (being) takes center stage rather than the *does* (act).[386] This is the "pervasive" conception (reminiscent of Melito's concept) in Barth's mature thought on God.[387] The effect is disadvantageous to his argument. The divine quality takes precedence, or worse, somehow dims the divine action wherein the latter is key in this doctrine (God does *because* God is). The substantiality of God's suffering, therefore, is essentially relegated as a modifier to and of divine quality. It carries a sense of inactivity instead of denoting an action. Here God's choice to be the One and also the Other is critical in understanding Barth's formulation of God against God. But since the notion of divine perpetuity is sustained in suffering, Barth's God cannot be exactly referred to as God against God. Rather, the suffering One can be taken accurately as *God dialectically in God* as actualized in the divine humanity of Christ. Because God's self-unveiling in the Christ's veiling is upheld, the *an-enhypostatic* language has served Barth well.

So does Barth finally have a doctrine of divine impassibility? My answer at this stage is still negative. What he has is a doctrine of divine suffering; his engagement with the issue of impassibility is under this doctrine.

384. Foreword of *CD* IV/1, ix.

385. Cf. *CD* IV/1, 157–58 and 160, 162; 185 and 187–88; IV/2, 64–70 and 92–94. Bruce McCormack sees Barth's consistent view that divine suffering is out of God's freedom. McCormack, "Divine Impassibility," 161. Paul Dafydd Jones supports McCormack's conclusion by saying that since Barth believes that Christ is both the "electing God and elected human," the necessary consequence is that the Father and the Spirit also share in the suffering. Jones, *The Humanity of Christ*, 148. In contrast, George Hunsinger posits that Barth maintains the orthodox notion of the "perfect being" of God in discussing impassibility. As such, God is perfect in himself even in change. Hunsinger, *Reading Barth*, 167. Paul Molnar compliments Hunsinger's position when he speaks of God's condescension, "Thus, it disclosed the nature of God as one who can suffer on our behalf while remaining one who does not suffer by nature." Divine Freedom, 128. McCormack and Jones are arguing from the perspective of God's active decision (freedom and election) while Hunsinger and Molnar are arguing from the perspective of God's description (being or nature). That is why "there is no shortage of disagreement" when it comes to Barth's accommodation or rejection of impassibility. Keating and White, *Divine Impassibility*, 26.

386. Although God's active decision in suffering is prominently rendered in §59.2 "The Judge Judged in our Place," however in §64.2 "The Homecoming of the Son of Man" the emphasis somewhat reverts to God's being when Barth engages with Chalcedon about the issue of divine suffering.

387. Johnson, *God's Being in Reconciliation*, 26.

Does Barth advocate impassibility? My answer would still be yes and no. He advocates an impassible-passible God of reconciliation. A reconciling God truly effects the conversion of the reconciled. What informs his understanding of divine suffering? My reply would have been God's active decision to be passive in Jesus Christ, if Barth would have argued consistently in this schema. But since he is not, then I argue that God's dialectic qualities generally inform his view on divine suffering.

What is also axiomatic up to this point is that Barth situates the doctrine of divine suffering at the heart of the doctrine of God. In the next chapter, we will scrutinize the implications of Barth's dialectic theology for the doctrine of God proper in view of impassibility, election, and Trinity.

Chapter IV

Implications for the Doctrine of God Proper: Impassibility, Election, and Trinity

In chapter 3, I argued that God's choice to be in Jesus Christ fundamentally informs Karl Barth's understanding of divine suffering. In his doctrine of reconciliation, God is impassible yet at the same time passible. God's qualities, as Barth describes it dialectically, are positive expressions of the divine nature; they do not undermine the God-self.

In this chapter, I shall argue that in Barth's renewed doctrine of God, (im)passibility speaks of a consistent deity; and also, that divine suffering is a statement about the Trinity. It means the Father, Son, and Holy Spirit can be said to have suffered in the suffering of Jesus Christ.[1] To support my point, I will investigate the impact of Barth's conception of divine suffering on his doctrines of God, election, and the Trinity. In order to do so, we have to inspect the following: first, Barth's focus on God's faithfulness in light of divine suffering; second, Barth's trinitarian motif in conceiving God's perfection; last, Barth's understanding of *kenosis* in view of God's selflessness. The themes of faithfulness, perfection and selflessness function as interrelated indicators in appreciating God's commitment to humankind.

In committing to humankind, God demonstrates how faithful he is to the eternal decree. This notion is comprehended in the continuation of our exposition of the text in *CD* IV/1, 157. The *perichoresis* between the Father, Son, and Holy Spirit will be considered in view of the suffering of Jesus Christ. In addition, Jesus's cry of dereliction will be examined in relation to the supposed participation of the three divine persons in the event at Calvary.

We will now examine why Barth thinks that in suffering, God manifests his faithfulness.

1. Refer to *CD* IV/3, 414.

1. The Faithfulness of the Suffering God

Barth strengthens his conception of divine suffering in the theme of God's faithfulness as shown in our main text for this chapter:

> That Jesus Christ is very God is shown in His way into the far country. . . . For in the majesty of the true God it happened that the eternal Son of the eternal Father became obedient by offering and humbling Himself. . . . But God the Father raised Him from the dead.[2]

The faithfulness of God is demonstrated in the relationship between the Father and Son. The Son obeys what the Father commands "in the glory of the true God" (*Denn es geschah in der Herrlichkeit des wahren Gottes*).[3] This shows not only the stark contrast of Jesus Christ's attitude towards the Father from that of the rest of humanity, but more importantly, the uniqueness of the obedience of Jesus itself. According to Barth, Christ's obedience is utterly distinct from any human obedience because He does it as the majestic God. No one else is *capable* of such obedience except the Son of God. That is why in obedience, Jesus Christ acts according to his glorious nature being the true God.

In addition, Barth also points out that no one is also *ready* for such condescension and sacrifice except Jesus Christ.[4] In the "otherworldliness" of beings other than God, pride and self-gratification are the traits available.[5] This is the reason for Barth's repugnance for the obedience of human beings who only bring ridicule to God instead of honor.[6] Jesus Christ is solely the One who is "capable and willing and ready" for this sacrificial act because only the true God can faithfully obey what the Father commands.[7] Moreover, since Barth articulates our main text within his doctrine of reconciliation, it is also pertinent to say that the reason behind God's sacrificial act is to atone for sins. In this respect, it is clear in Barth that only the true God can carry out the atonement.[8]

2. *CD* IV/1, 157.

3. *KD* IV/1, 171.

4. *CD* IV/1, 159.

5. For Barth, there can only be "false gods" who can be inferred in this regard who only reflect "human pride." *CD* IV/1, 159. Rather, acts of "theft, murder and adultery," etc. are what humans naturally do. Excursus in *CD* IV/1, 160–61.

6. Barth says of the human being, "It is he who does despite to God, who offends and disturbs Him." *CD* IV/1, 485.

7. *CD* IV/1, 159.

8. *CD* IV/1, 158.

Another worthy point here concerns the inseparability between the One who obeys from the One who is obeyed. At a first glance, it seems that the Son who obeys is treated separately from the Father who commands. Although Barth does account for the distinction between the two Persons in going into the far country, he nonetheless underlines the oneness of the two in understanding the "offering and humbling" involved in *kenosis*.[9] Barth states that in *kenosis*, the Son "gave himself to himself" (*er sich selbst dazu hergab*) which denotes that the Son's self-offering and humbling is done unto himself in the mode of the Father.[10] This notion reinforces Barth's radical conception of the divine sacrifice wherein the Follower and the Commander are conceived in one being but in *distinct ways* of being (*Seinsweise*).[11] Barth sees God as one in three ways of being—Father, Son, and Spirit (*Gott ist Einer in drei Seinsweisen, Vater, Sohn und Heiliger Geist*).[12] It magnifies the coincidentality of the persons of the Godhead in eternity.[13] This conception will be discussed further as we critically analyze how Barth articulates the divine suffering in trinitarian perspective. But for now, the focus of the text above is on God's self-offering.

The Father's offering of the Son, in a sense, shows how the Godhead (considering the Spirit too) is determined to mend its conflict with humankind.[14] Being true to its determination, the Godhead suffers (in Jesus Christ) so that humans do not have to suffer eternally.[15] So Barth accentuates here the unity of the divine persons in determining themselves for humankind. Since such unity is eternal, so the trinitarian view of self-giving represents God's unending faithfulness to his redemptive work.[16]

Barth resists the idea that humans can obey God willingly.[17] Humans are in need of redemption from themselves because in disobedience to God, humans act contrary to their nature.[18] Concomitantly, sufferings in the world would never cease; however God, in solidarity with humanity, chooses to suffer in order to disrupt the natural consequence of

9. Barth stresses, "Jesus was 'sent' but He also 'came'. As He is in the Father, the Father is also in Him." This is in reference to John 14:10. Excursus in *CD* II/2, 106.

10. *CD* IV/1, 159.

11. Excursus in *CD* I/1, 413–14; cf. *KD* I/1, 379–80.

12. My translation of this excerpt in *KD* I/1, 379. See how Barth uses the German *Existenzweise* and *Seinsweise*. *CD* IV/1, 221–22; IV/2, 47, 55.

13. Oh, *Karl Barth's Trinitarian Theology*, 165.

14. *CD* IV/1, 158.

15. *CD* IV/1, 254; II/2, 450.

16. *CD* IV/1, 161; II/2, 164.

17. *CD* IV/1, 175, 398.

18. *CD* IV/1, 164.

disobedience.[19] God does this by taking "the place of the former sufferers and allows the bitterness of their suffering to fall upon Himself."[20] Before the divine intervention in Jesus Christ, humans suffer without hope of redemption from suffering.

This redemption from suffering comes from Jesus Christ's faithful obedience leading to the event at the cross.[21] At the cross, Jesus suffers "the wrath and judgment of God" on behalf of humankind.[22] For Barth, this substitutionary act is intentional because Jesus cannot will "anything other in the obedience."[23] By being judged, Jesus Christ affirms the divine sentence on humankind by assuming it on himself. This line of thinking augments Barth's thought on "God against God." It is congruent with the concept of God giving himself to himself. It means that when the Father offers the Son, in its truest sense, the Son offers himself because the offering is viewed to be one divine act. Thus there can be no offering of the Father apart from the self-offering of the Son.[24] This formulation exemplifies God's glory-in-oneness in the divine self-giving.

In keeping up with the theme of "God against God" in view of the divine self-giving, we need to consider Barth's conversation with Anselm of Canterbury because of its relevance to our main text.[25] Barth engages with Anselm on the "aseity of God" (*aseitas Dei*) and on "how great is the weight of sin" (*quanti ponderis sit peccatum*).[26]

Anselm's conception of aseity, Barth comments, is not about God's transcendence but about God being "free to exist in Himself."[27] Barth sees this approach as positive because instead of presenting God as untouchable (immune from all external conditions), God is rather presented as

19. *CD* IV/1, 220–21, 563. For more insights, see Hunsinger, *Disruptive Grace*, 16–17.

20. *CD* IV/1, 175.

21. Jesus Christ wills to suffer the event of the cross, and "suffered it to the very last." *CD* IV/1, 309

22. *CD* IV/1, 175.

23. *CD* IV/1, 164. In this respect, Barth says of Jesus as the "One who is qualitatively different and stands in an indissoluble antithesis to His disciples and all other men, indeed to the whole cosmos." *CD* IV/1, 161.

24. Barth reiterates, "His [Christ's] obedience consists in the fact that He commends or offers up His spirit, that is, Himself—He delivers up Himself." Excursus in *CD* IV/1, 306.

25. according to Barth, Anselm builds on the argument for the necessity of the incarnation. It is in this event where the heaviness of sin is, in a sense, borne, thus resolved. Excursus in *CD* IV/1, 253, 485–87.

26. Excursus in *CD* II/1, 302; IV/1, 407.

27. *CD* II/1, 302.

"independent" (at liberty to be what God desires to be).[28] What Barth endeavors to highlight is the manner by which God relates to humankind. It is in this active mode where God is said to have been aseitic in time. In other words, Barth's articulation of divine independence is always in the context of the Son of God being the Son of Man. In Jesus Christ, the Godhead demonstrates its freedom in its redemptive work. Barth's primary concern in engaging with Anselm's thought on aseity is to argue how divine independence could be a strong case for divine faithfulness.

But how does Barth conceive of divine faithfulness in light of the idea of "God against God?" Again, he turns to Anselm to expound what it means for the Son to bear the "extent of sin."[29] When Barth considers the extent or weight of sin, he does so in the context of what Jesus Christ has done, i.e., self-sacrifice so that humanity can be emancipated from sin. The potency of sin, argues Barth, is somewhat *subjected* to what is not desired by God. This is where Barth paradoxically speaks of God's action over and against what does not exist. How is this possible? According to him, God has judged the host of evil—the "man of sin."[30] This sinful human (or sinner), in a sense, is where evil finds its actuality.[31]

1.1 The Burdened God

Who is this sinner? For Barth, the sinful human is a figurative depiction of humanity—a being "controlled and burdened by sin."[32] It is so because the sinner is "at odds with God and his neighbour."[33] The focus here is not on what the sinner does or does not do, but rather on what the sinner *does not know*. Though the sinner knows he is "limited, deficient and imperfect" but he does not know the utter burden he carries, i.e., the "inner conflict of his existence."[34] Barth calls this ignorance as "negative determination."[35] The sinner is in self-negative determination because he does not realize

28. *CD* II/1, 302; IV/1, 482.

29. *CD* IV/1, 407.

30. *CD* IV/1, 390. The subject in whom evil exists by which that subject becomes the evil one.

31. *CD* IV/1, 360.

32. *CD* IV/1, 358.

33. *CD* IV/1, 360, 403.

34. *CD* IV/1, 360–61.

35. *CD* IV/1, 361.

that his life counters his very own existence; hence, in reality, this person is also at odds with himself.[36]

Moreover, the sinner can only see the negation of creaturely existence in the knowledge of the Son.[37] Barth describes, "It is again Jesus Christ in whose existence sin is revealed, not only in its actuality and sinfulness, but as the truth of all human being and activity."[38] By looking at Christ, the sinner will know what sin truly is and how bad is its consequence; here sin is unmasked. In this, Barth rightly asks, "What is the evil of evil?"[39] Despite the fact that humanity makes evil actual, it is only in Christ that the evil in and of humanity is properly comprehended. By extrapolation, God's dominion over evil comes as a result of Christ's affliction for the sinner. This is where the weight of sin is viewed with the destruction of evil.

For Barth, the destruction of evil is in effect the destruction of the sinner.[40] The manner whereby God destroys the sinner is key in understanding how heavy sin is. The sinner is destroyed in Christ's death and resurrection.[41] Christ had suffered and died in "solidarity" with the sinner.[42] This solidarity is not merely being one with the sinner; Barth avers that Christ himself takes the place of the sinner.[43] In other words, Jesus Christ makes the sinners's situation his own by taking to himself their sin.[44]

Though without sin, Jesus Christ takes to himself the "alien sin" which makes him heavy burdened.[45] In this way, Christ *bears* the sin of humanity.[46] Barth's employment of the word "carry" (*trägt*) or "bear" (*trüge*) emphasizes Christ's sacrifice at it relates to the weight of sin.[47] Barth posits that all sin

36. *CD* IV/1, 364. This echoes the thought of being "far" (in relation to God) we have discussed in chapter 3.

37. *CD* IV/1, 390. Esminger, *Karl Barth's Theology as a Resource for a Christian Theology of Religions*, 108.

38. *CD* IV/1, 403.

39. *CD* IV/1, 400.

40. Barth puts it, "*[I]ch bin als der dem Nichtigen Zugewendete im Tode Jesu Christi zunichte gemacht.*" *KD* IV/1, 575. "I am destroyed as the one who has turned into nothingness in the death of Jesus Christ." Cf. *CD* IV/1, 515. The term *dem Nichtigen* here is used in conjunction with *das Nichtige* which, according to Barth, is the evil. See also *KD* IV/1, 452, 454.

41. *CD* IV/1, 390.

42. *CD* IV/1, 391.

43. *CD* IV/1, 391.

44. *CD* IV/1, 404.

45. *CD* IV/1, 397.

46. *CD* IV/1, 405.

47. *KD* IV/1, 195, 448, 503.

"needs to be carried"; and since Christ has carried all sin, no one is condemned. But if Christ did not "bear all sin," everyone is damned.[48] In fact, in carrying all sin and bearing the penalty of humankind, the Son of God is deeply and utterly affected. Barth describes:

> We are all whom God Himself put an end in Jesus Christ; made past in Him. All of us are the bearers of the old garment that was stripped and destroyed because Jesus Christ becomes for us the old man Himself who has been overtaken, condemned and executed by God's wrath.[49]

God has put an end to the past status of humanity by Jesus Christ bearing it. The old person, as assumed by Christ, is the One "overtaken, condemned and executed by God's wrath." Such a description brings to mind the point I have raised in chapter 2 wherein the Son of God is "overwhelmed" by evil in taking the human essence. This essence, in Barth's articulation, is the evil in its "complete and comprehensive content" because it contains the entrapment of "evil deed and evil being."[50] God, however, decides to make human reality to become God's reality, hence the incarnation. In the being of Jesus Christ, God counters human acts of arrogance and disobedience.[51] This is the contingent being of humanity as opposed to the inherent being of Christ, i.e., humble and obedient.

In order to set humans free from evil entrapment, Barth claims, God sets himself up to face his own wrath.[52] Although Barth here does refer to God's two modes of being, he nonetheless stresses "in each the whole

48. See this in the original German text: "*Alle menschliche Sünde, ob groß oder klein, flagrant oder unbeachtlich, bedurfte und bedarf dessen, daß er sie getragen hat und trägt. . . Trüge er sie nicht, so wäre auch die kleinste Sünde groß genug, den Menschen gänzlich zu verdammen.*" *KD* IV/1, 448. Cf. *CD* IV/1, 405.

49. My own translation of: "*Wir Alle sind die, mit denen, und sind das, womit Gott selbst in Jesus Christus Schluß gemacht, was in Jesus Christus zur Vergangenheit gemacht ist. Wir Alle sind die Träger des alten Kleides, das dort ausgezogen und vertilgt wurde, mehr noch: der alte Mensch selbst, der dort, in Jesus Christus, von Gottes Zorn ereilt, verdammt und hingerichtet worden ist.*" *KD* IV/1, 432. Cf. *CD* IV/1, 391.

50. *CD* IV/1, 390.

51. *CD* IV/1, 390–91.

52. *CD* IV/1, 175. Barth writes, "For God is in the right against Him [the Son]." *CD* IV/1, 175. In reading Barth in this context, Adam Johnson says, "only by being the Triune God can God bear his own wrath 'creatively.'" Johnson, *God's Being in Reconciliation*, 74–75. On the same note, Jeremy Wynne refers to Barth's conception of God's wrath in view of God's perfection. In wrath, the triune God demonstrates the uncompromized freedom of the divine life and the "redemptive mode" of God's righteousness. See Wynne, *Wrath among the Perfections of God's Life*, 13, 110.

God" (*in jeder der ganze Gott*).[53] We cannot say, strictly speaking, that the incarnate Son had to face the angry Father because to infer this signals a failure to see each mode against the whole God.[54]

Furthermore, we do not have to overlook the other aspect of God's wrath. We have to principally understand that in Barth's view, the divine favor takes "the aspect of wrath."[55] It is to accentuate the immanentist interpretation of God's dealing with sin. Yet God decides to negate the negation of humanity by overriding anger with love. With this backdrop, argues Barth, "the grace of God is concealed under His sentence and judgment, His Yes under His No."[56] Here, the accountability of human beings is no longer in arrears because Jesus Christ has paid it, and paid it completely. Barth asserts that Christ "has removed us sinners and sin, negated us, cancelled us out: ourselves, our sin, and the accusation, condemnation and perdition which had overtaken us."[57] Christ has done what humans cannot do and are not willing to do. Christ has cancelled the sin which has overtaken humans by allowing himself instead to be overtaken by it.[58] Thus the so called "wrath of God," as Barth sees it, is God's "hidden good will" because it is in judgment where humans find vindication in and through Christ.[59] It is in sentencing sinners to death whereby God intervenes with grace; God, in his sovereignty, chooses to forgive.[60] It is not out of arbitrariness or caprice, but rather, of God's righteousness.

For this reason, Barth conceives of God's wrath as the necessary and complete "rule of righteousness."[61] It is necessary because in anger, God shows his sheer contempt and defiance of sin. The sinner is rejected and therefore "stands under the wrath and accusation of God."[62] It is complete because anger is paralleled with mercy, which makes the accusation of sinners become a

53. *CD* IV/1, 203; *KD* IV/1, 222.

54. Barth qualifies that, accurately speaking, it is to death (not to the Father) that Jesus Christ delivers himself to while hanging on the cross: "It is therefore to death that He bows His head and commits Himself. In and with the fulfilment there of the will of God it is nothingness which can triumph over Him and in and with Him over the whole of the human race represented by Him." Excursus in *CD* IV/1, 306. Barth alludes to Luke 23:46.

55. *CD* IV/1, 41.

56. *CD* IV/1, 173.

57. *CD* IV/1, 253–54.

58. *CD* IV/1, 254.

59. *CD* IV/1, 555.

60. *CD* IV/1, 563. Lindsay, *Covenanted Solidarity*, 297.

61. *CD* IV/1, 536.

62. *CD* IV/1, 173.

precursor to their forgiveness.[63] It is in this context where Barth interjects that in the wrath of God, something incredible has happened, i.e., "the inconceivable crowning of unrighteous man with grace and mercy."[64]

In absolute autonomy, God is free to be angry with sinners and God is also free to assume the consequence of such anger.[65] Divine wrath is an aspect of the depth of God's life; a part of God's constant and whole character. In anger, Barth also sees God to be repeating himself—One who is truly in an intimate relationship with humankind.[66] So divine wrath is a manifestation of God's free love. If the eternal God is truly *pro nobis*, the underlying purpose of God's wrath should be for the good of humanity, not otherwise.

In addition, anger is God's way of showing his lordship.[67] Because the Lord God is present with creation, his dealings correspond to creaturely reality. The concept of wrath is required only in creaturely time to showcase the Trinity's response to sin.[68] When God chooses to make human reality his reality, God communicates in a manner by which humans can relate. But in communion (covenant-relationship) with creatures, God does not abrogate his true being—God can embrace the contradictory possibilities between wrath and mercy without detriment to his free love.[69] Divine wrath as paralleled with divine mercy is a manifestation of being alive. For Barth, God is truly alive in this fashion because sinners who stand against God are "surrounded and maintained by His life."[70]

So Jesus Christ's suffering from the divine wrath is Barth's creative way of depicting how the God who suffers *is* the same God to whom wrath is attributed. For Barth, the triune God is always active in the suffering of Jesus Christ. In Christ, the Father, Son, and Spirit act as *the whole God* even in taking human reality as their reality. This formulation highlights not only the oneness of God in suffering but also the oneness of God in the affirmation of divine judgment.

In the affirmation of divine judgment, God in Jesus Christ has become the sinner by carrying the weight of sin.[71] In this way, the human essence

63. *CD* IV/1, 354. This is underscored in Christ's death being the precursor to Christ's resurrection.

64. *CD* IV/1, 563.

65. *CD* IV/1, 482.

66. *CD* IV/1, 175.

67. *CD* IV/1, 165.

68. *CD* IV/1, 175. Wynne, *Wrath among the Perfections of God's Life*, 136.

69. As Barth puts it, "The love of God burns where they are, but as the fire of His wrath which consumes and destroys them." *CD* IV/1, 220–21.

70. *CD* IV/1, 541.

71. *CD* IV/1, 390–91.

that had been taken by the Son in pre-temporality comes into fruition in assuming flesh in temporality. The actual reality God has assumed upon himself in order to demonstrate the new reality for humankind is here affirmed. The actual evil deed out of the evil being of humanity is what God bears in the person of Jesus Christ. The weight of sin that Jesus Christ has carried and the condemnation that he has borne are truly devastating that has resulted to his execution. According to Barth, the divine sacrificial act has to happen so that humanity can treat its reality as an old one.[72] In speaking of the old reality of being human, we may well expect that the question on "the evil of evil" brings to light the heaviness of sin.[73] We need to understand this clearly to better appreciate how Barth's notion of "God against God" effectively highlights God's faithfulness in suffering.

1.2 The Weight of Sin

Discussing the weight of sin expounds how the triune God takes unto itself (in the person of Jesus Christ) the bitterness of human suffering. Barth pictures Christ carrying the weight of sin in a horrific fashion. According to him, the weight of sin has caused Christ to tremble and shudder in fright (*sie schrecket ihn dermaßen, das er dafür anhebt zu zittern und zagen*).[74] The evil in and of humanity becomes almost unbearable for God in the mode of the Son. Evil, in this sense, has taken a violent toll on Jesus Christ. Under the weight of sin, this human did not only die, but he even died in great terror. In this way, Jesus Christ, the perfect Man, has become that which he is not—the Man of sin.[75] Basically, it is only in Christ humans know who they really are in the kind of existence they have.[76] On the one hand, Barth posits, Christ acts like a "mirror" where people can see that they are sinners.[77] On the other hand, in Christ, people can also see that they are in fact no longer sinners.[78] Hence, Jesus Christ has perished so

72. Barth proclaims, "As our wrong and death are our past in His [Christ's] name, in Him, so our righteousness and life are our future." *CD* IV/1, 555.

73. *CD* IV/1, 400.

74. *CD* IV/1, 397. *KD* IV/1, 439.

75. *CD* IV/1, 404.

76. Here Barth is indebted to Luther's insight on the reality of being a sinner. See excursus in *CD* IV/1, 415–16.

77. *CD* IV/1, 397.

78. *CD* IV/1, 407. Barth puts it, "Now that Jesus Christ has come, to represent the person of man in His own person, to restore and renew the person of man and therefore man himself in His own person, we are all of us disclosed as the man who in his own person is the man of sin." *CD* IV/1, 407.

sinners might not perish. This is the faithfulness of God which guarantees the destruction of evil.[79] Barth writes:

> But we can say it in the light of the fact that in Jesus Christ, in His death (the meaning of which is shown in His resurrection to be His victory and the liberation of man), we see evil overcome and indeed shattered and destroyed by the omnipotence of the love and wrath of God.[80]

The victory over sin, Barth alludes, is accomplished by God, not only in terms of assuming humanity *per se*, but more importantly, in overcoming sin through death. This is what it entails for God to be totally and utterly against who God is. Yet also, in dying, God has revealed who he is resolved to be (out of God's authentic autonomy)—the One who faithfully loves. Jesus Christ being the Overcomer of sin, and also, the Man of sin vividly displays how God is faithful in himself despite being against himself.

When God becomes human, God deals decisively with the sinfulness of humanity.[81] But, in doing so, God has solved evil and sin. That is why Barth conceives of sin as a masked "impotence" before Jesus Christ.[82] Barth continues, "The truth is that Anselm's question: *quanti ponderis sit peccatum*? is given an answer either from the cross of Christ or not at all. It is given an answer from the cross of Christ."[83] When Christ dies on the cross, God has shown the true measure of sin. Sin, with its devastating effect, is made ineffective. God's triumph over sin in such sacrificial fashion gives evidence to God's suffering faithfulness—in himself in three modes of being, and also in fellowship with humankind. In other words, Barth views God's self-offering as a dynamic way of confronting the weight of sin.[84] For this reason, Barth refers to the sinner as the "old man" because by virtue of what Christ has done, the sinner is now the "new man"—humans are no longer sinners in Jesus Christ.[85] The new man is the product of the Godhead's self-giving.[86]

Thus Anselm's pondering on the weightiness of sin is reconceived in terms of humanity's disobedience as opposed to Christ's obedience.[87] Barth

79. *CD* IV/1, 406.
80. *CD* IV/1, 408.
81. Barth, *Deliverance to the Captives*, 16–17.
82. *CD* IV/1, 408.
83. *CD* IV/1, 412.
84. *CD* IV/1, 413.
85. *CD* IV/1, 391.
86. *CD* IV/1, 407. Swain and Allen, "The Obedience of the Eternal Son," 117.
87. As portrayed in §60 of *CD*.

puts it, "The knowledge of Jesus Christ is finally the knowledge of the significance and extent of sin."[88] Although Barth recognizes the gravity of sin, he nonetheless shows its weakness under God's power. Sin, in Barth's conception, is the product of evil and "whatever evil is, God is its Lord."[89] No matter how heavy the toll of sin is, God nevertheless has overcome it. In Jesus Christ, therefore, God has made evil "an instrument of divine triumph."[90]

1.3 Divine Suffering in Trinitarian Perspective

Having inspected how Christ's suffering speaks of God's faithfulness, we can now probe why Christ's suffering can be a *true* statement about the Godhead. Since God's aseity is properly understood in terms of God's independence, such understanding resonates with Barth's rendition of the Trinity. Why point to the Trinity in considering Barth's thought on divine suffering? The Trinity is central to his conception of God being absolutely selfless, i.e., the decree to self-sacrifice.[91] Barth saw God as selfless when he reworked the doctrine of election within the doctrine of God. The true God is revealed in the election of Jesus Christ; a reprise of Barth's theme—God "reveals Himself through Himself."[92] The revealed God is the same God "in unimpaired unity," vis-à-vis the Father, Son, and Holy Spirit.[93] In other words, God *is* God in triunity; there is no deity before or after this God or an overriding deity over this God.[94]

The triune God is eternally one in itself for the sake of the creatures. Barth argues for the three selfless ways of the being of God. The Godhead, Barth construes, demonstrates its selflessness by being "something other and infinitely less than God," or to be "God outside of Himself" i.e., human—a being expressive of all conceivable misery.[95] On this account, Barth sums up

88. *CD* IV/1, 407.

89. *CD* IV/1, 408.

90. *CD* IV/1, 408.

91. Barth expounds on the triune God in §§8–12 of *CD* I/1. Although these sections do not directly deal with divine selflessness, they nonetheless show the Trinity's commitment to humanity. Jenson, "Karl Barth," 47. McCormack, "Divine Impassibility," 160, 172–74. *CD* IV/1, 168.

92. *CD* I/1, 296.

93. *CD* I/1, 299.

94. In his doctrine of the Trinity, Barth prefers to use the term "triunity" or "three-in-oneness" in place of "unity in trinity" and "trinity in unity." *Church Dogmatics* I/1, translated by G. W. Bromiley and T. F. Torrance, 368. Triunity is a conflated term which avoids any one-sided emphasis on unity or trinity. *CD* I/1, 423–24.

95. *CD* IV/1, 417.

his conception of the Trinity (or the meaning of his doctrine of the Trinity) as the revelation of the Godhead in Jesus Christ.[96] The essentiality (who God is) and the operation (what God does) of the Trinity are viewed as *one* in Christ simply because Barth argues for a God who *is* in what God does, and who acts out of who he is. Such consistency is prominent in understanding the existential relation of the Trinity whereby each Person exists interdependently with the other two; hence each Person is taken as a way of the being of God. So the essentiality of God is truly understood in the united selfless affinity to human beings by being human.[97] In a sense, God's altruistic act speaks of the triune being.[98]

We have just seen how Barth's focus on God's faithfulness announces a trinitarian perspective of divine suffering. We will learn more about the implication of God's elected suffering on the Trinity as we analyze Barth's view of divine perfection.

2. God's Perfection in Suffering

The perfection of God is shown in being the Lord and Servant.[99] Barth asserts that Jesus Christ "is very God" when "He the Lord became a servant."[100] It means that God's lordship is rightly understood in the divine outworking, i.e., in the incarnation. It is in humility where God is said to be perfect. When Barth says God is eternally true to his works, it is conveyed in the themes of divine perfection.[101] Why? It is because God stays the same even in change. Barth claims, "[God] is always the same in every change. . . . He is what He is continually and self-consistently."[102] Although God partakes freely in the alteration of creation, he does so as the sovereign Creator; God's

96. *CD* I/1, 380. In the evolution of his theology, Barth begins with God's sovereignty as foundational in his revision of biblical themes. But as his thought progresses in *CD* II and how his mature theology crystallizes in *CD* IV, it shores up that divine sovereignty is no longer treated exclusively in God. In other words, the early Barth thinks of God in sovereign freedom while the late Barth thinks of God having freedom for humankind. Since Barth is no longer attentive to the traditional God being in and for himself, Barth later on conceives of God as being in and of himself in loving relationship. God is still eternally free in himself, but Barth recasts this statement to emphasize that God's aseity or independence is for the good of humanity.

97. *CD* I/1, 372. Levering, "Christ, the Trinity, and Predestination," 254.

98. See *CD* IV/2, 31–33, 41–44, 62, 65, 74, 86.

99. This is Barth's central argument in *CD* IV/1–2.

100. *CD* IV/1, 157.

101. *CD* II/1, 440, 494.

102. *CD* II/1, 494.

being and essence do not change along with creation.[103] But Barth handles God's unchanging essence in conceiving of Jesus Christ as being the *very God*. This conception brings Barth's reconfigured Christology in contact with his doctrine of the Trinity. Here we can have additional insight on how the God of election is said to be (im)passible.

Because for Barth, the change brought about by the incarnation is not new to God but it is merely a reaffirmation of the same God in eternity, we can deduce that Jesus Christ indeed is the "very God." Christ is the very God because the willingness to be human is a triune decision.[104] The very Godhood of Christ speaks of the consistency in the Godhead vis-à-vis to be for and with humankind. Thus Barth understands God's perfection in the framework of the eternal triunity.[105] We can better critique Barth's thought on this matter by investigating his doctrine of the Trinity.[106]

2.1 The Trinity as Lord in Suffering

Barth interprets the eternal triunity in view of God being the Lord. In fact, he argues that the God who reveals himself as Lord is the "root" of his doctrine of the Trinity.[107] Within the theme of the Trinity as Lord, Barth alludes to the Godhead being the *Yahweh-Kyrios*.[108] The Father, Son, and Spirit are in perfect unity in their "ontic and noetic independence."[109] However, Barth sees the lordship of the Trinity in self-giving.[110] The Trinity, in this case, is inseparable from the "God-manhood of Jesus Christ" (*die Gottmenschheit Jesu Christi*).[111] The God-manhood of Christ, says Barth, does not convey "any declension of God from Himself, any transformation of His divine nature into another or admixture with another."[112] In other words, even if we link the essence of the Trinity to the essence of Christ, the God in and of the election remains eternally in God's self. It

103. *CD* III/3, 8–9.

104. *CD* IV/1, 159.

105. *CD* II/1, 442. For another view about the function of the Trinity; cf. Ayres, *Nicaea and Its Legacy*, 434.

106. §9 of *CD*.

107. *CD* I/1, 353.

108. Lindsay, *Barth, Israel and Jesus*, 58. Soulen, "YHWH the Triune God," 37.

109. *CD* I/1, 352.

110. Price, *Letters of the Divine Word*, 157.

111. Excursus in *CD* II/1, 515. *KD* II/1, 579.

112. Excursus in *CD* II/1, 515.

is in this personal association where the triunity is viewed within the decree.[113] Since Barth articulates the doctrine of God within his over-arching theme that God's being is in God's act, we can further appreciate Barth's treatment of the triune being in God's act of and *in* creation. God's act in creation is not a new theme in Barth since Christology heavily informs his thought in this matter. In other words, the triune being is rightly appropriated in the life of Jesus Christ. Here, the Father, Son, and Spirit act in communion (*Akt des Gemeinsamseins*) or "communityness."[114] It is in such "communityness" that we can speak of the (im)passibility of the Trinity

Barth sees the communityness of the Godhead in terms of the relationship between the three Persons. Hence, what makes the persons of the Godhead to be in the act of communion is key in analyzing Barth's conception of the triune being. He construes:

> The relations in God, in virtue of which He is three-in-one essence, are thus His being Father, in virtue of which God the Father is the Father of the Son, His being Son in virtue of which God the Father is the Father of the Son, His being Son in virtue of which God the Son is the Son of the Father, and His being Spirit, in virtue of which God is the Spirit of the Father and of the Son.[115]

On this account, each divine person is not an autonomous concept. Barth, in a sense, invites his reader to ask: The Father is the father of who?; the Son is the son of who?; the Spirit is the spirit of who? Accordingly, Barth cannot conceive the persons of the Godhead individually. The Trinity has no singularity in a sense that one divine person can be isolated from the other two.[116] Nevertheless Barth's thought on the oneness of God is not simplistic because he holds the "threefold individuality" within the Trinity.[117] This shows that despite the threeness in the Person of God, Barth does not put forward the triessentiality in God.[118] The threeness here exemplifies a single eternal essence in God, not otherwise. Thus in the communityness of the Trinity, there is no such thing as "three departments of activity"; God always acts in triunity.[119]

113. *CD* I/1, 371.

114. *CD* I/1, 534, 537. *KD* I/1, 493.

115. *CD* I/1, 420.

116. *CD* I/1, 407.

117. *CD* I/1, 411.

118. *CD* I/1, 415.

119. *CD* I/1, 415.

The threefold individuality is mere conceptual language to speak of the distinctive characteristics of the three Persons without prejudice to their triunity. This is evident in what Barth calls the "dialectical union and distinction" of the Trinity.[120] But in this concept of the communal act of the Godhead, each divine person strictly participates as one.[121] As regards (im)passibility, in the communal act in Jesus Christ, the Trinity does not receive anything from creation, but rather extends its power to creation to effect the operation of its will. The will of the Trinity, argues Barth, is to reclaim humanity by reconciliation.[122] The Father is with the Son and the Spirit in being the Reconciler.[123] Thus the Trinity's outward act is the "operation of the whole essence of God."[124] With the entirety of God's essence involved in this operation, so the entirety of God is deemed to have been self-moved as the Reconciler. Nevertheless in being moved, the Trinity remains impassible because it is not subjugated by creaturely reality, but rather subdues it by having humanity reconciled. This is the united act of the Father, Son, and Spirit; a sovereign act that can only result to the restitution of its object.[125] In spite of the Trinity's self-movement in the operation of its will, such movement is productively expressed in both the Subject and the object.

Suffering is productively expressed in the Trinity as the Subject because in suffering, the Trinity wins over evil. Suffering has a productive effect on humans as the object because it is in triune suffering that reconciliation is accomplished. In this case, the divine operation is perfected in its Subject and object. In working in and through what is distinct, i.e., creaturely reality, the Trinity remains in its own unique reality. So the triune essence does not dissolve in creation; it is in creation where the three Persons display their oneness in self-giving. This is how the triune essence is said to be perfect.

The triune essence is also conceived to be perfect in power.[126] In being affected, the Trinity is viewed as truly powerful in itself; the power to remain impassible despite being affected.[127] Thus in self-giving, the Trinity is said to

120. *CD* I/1, 369.

121. *CD* I/1, 423–24.

122. *CD* I/1, 419.

123. *CD* I/1, 453.

124. *CD* I/1, 426. *CD* III/1, 16.

125. *CD* I/1, 430.

126. *CD* II/1, 539. For Barth, God's absolute power (*potentia absoluta*) is demonstrated, but not exclusively, as God's ordained power (*potentia ordinata*). *CD* II/1, 541. See Long, *Saving Karl Barth*, 142–44.

127. *CD* IV/2, 360.

have sovereignly suffered, i.e., non-contingent to creation, not in solitariness but in communion. The impassibility of the Trinity is properly appreciated in its three selfless ways because it is in self-giving that Barth locates the divine impassibility. In other words, there is no impassible Trinity if there are no three ways of self-giving. Since anything less triune is no longer a divine communal act, then anything less than triune self-giving does not amount to impassibility. The Trinity's (im)passibility is therefore taken from Barth's understanding of the operation of the divine essence.

Indeed there are no three departments of divine activity as Barth puts it. In the triune will to be a God with and for humanity, the Godhead gives itself *entirely*.[128] This is an "operation of grace" because the Godhead reconciles humanity without reservation, without constraints. Here Barth advances the economic as well as the immanent characteristics of the Trinity.[129] But even though the Godhead is completely active in revealing itself, the conceivability of humans, vis-à-vis the triune act in Jesus Christ, is still limited.[130]

Such limitation echoes Barth's formulation of the veiling and unveiling of God. This is made apparent in his articulation of the suffering of the Father in the humiliation of the Son. It is expressed as the "fatherly fellow-suffering of God"; an idea that is mysterious but true.[131] It is mysterious because of the unreachable depth of the suffering of the Father in sacrificing the Son; but it is true because suffering takes place in human history.[132] However Barth reasons that in this historic suffering, the Godhead does not plunge into something that undoes its true being, but rather exemplifies it. It is in being so that the "true Son of the true Father" is revealed.[133] Suitably, we can also say that the co-Suffering Father is the true Father of the true Son. Hence, there is no God the Father hiding behind or existing above the suffering Son. For Barth, the elected suffering of the Son is also the elected suffering of the Father.

In the agony at Golgotha, Barth continues, "He [the Father] Himself feels it, and taking it wholly and unreservedly to Himself."[134] In other words, the predetermined suffering of the Son is also applicable to the Father. But why is the impassibility of the Godhead maintained in this scenario? Barth sees this predetermined suffering as an act of majesty which coincides with

128. *CD* I/1, 426.
129. *CD* I/1, 382.
130. *CD* I/1, 430.
131. *CD* IV/2, 357.
132. *CD* IV/2, 357.
133. *CD* IV/2, 358.
134. *CD* IV/2, 358.

an act of mercy: "The majestic act of the Son takes place in exact fulfilment of the merciful act of the Father."[135] These two acts however are conceived as "one incontestable living act of God."[136] I posit that in closely examining this formulation, we can see in Barth the impassible suffering of the Trinity.

God's sacrifice is worked out in triunity "inwards and outwards."[137] The two-directional act is not a paradox in view of election. This act, Barth reasons, "does not attest a Yes that may revert to a No. It attests a No which is spoken for the sake of the ensuing Yes."[138] In order to see this argument in light of (im)passibility, we have to deal with the relation *in* God of the following, namely, the merciful and majestic act; the inward and outward act; and the Yes and No. In Barth's framework, these are all conceived as a *single act* of God in God's autonomy and vitality. Thus God's act of mercy is in God's act of majesty, and vice-versa. The Father's merciful act of offering the Son gives way to the majestic act of self-sacrifice. Correspondingly, if God's inward and outward acts are construed, we can say that the merciful act is synonymous with the inward act; likewise, the majestic act is synonymous with the outward act. If this is indeed the case with Barth, we can deduce that in this act, both the Yes and the No are harmoniously applied. It means that God can be said to have been moved in his inward merciful act, while God can also be said to have been unmoved in his outward majestic act. Which is why we can also reply Yes and No to the question whether the Trinity is truly impassible or not in Barth's theology. Therefore, the Trinity is impassible insofar as God's autonomy and majesty are preserved; whereas the Trinity is passible insofar as God's vitality and mercy are affirmed.

The majesty and mercy of the divine act is also true with the Spirit.[139] In the Spirit, says Barth, the "dynamic and teleology" of the connection between the Trinity and Jesus Christ is witnessed.[140] Here, the *perichoresis* of the Godhead is aimed at the existence of Christ. The life of this human is taken in connection with the life of the Godhead. The temporal manifestation of Christ's suffering is the realization of the pre-temporal divine decision. God's ontology is therefore juxtaposed with God's act in human history; the trinitarian (im)passibility is commensurable with the reality of Jesus Christ. It is in this backdrop where the unparadoxicality of the divine sacrifice is clarified despite it being undeniably puzzling. It is the result of Barth's qualification of

135. *CD* IV/2, 358–59.

136. *CD* IV/2, 359.

137. *CD* IV/2, 359.

138. *CD* IV/2, 359.

139. *CD* IV/2, 359–60.

140. *CD* IV/2, 359.

the aim, sequence and fulfillment of God's outworking derived from God's inward act.[141] This is how Barth interprets God's threefold perfection of the suffering Trinity—always in reference to Christ.

2.2 Christological View of the Triune Suffering

After examining the triune perfection in suffering, we now have to investigate how this suffering is also said to be actual. This step is beneficial in seeking the reason for Barth's connection of Christology to the doctrine of the Trinity. Here we have to deal with his christological insight in articulating the Trinity.[142] For Barth, although the suffering of God is in triplicity, however the suffering of the divine persons is properly understood to be *altogether* in Jesus Christ. This threefold theme of suffering does not undermine the personhood of the Godhead. For instance, when Barth says the Holy Spirit is the Spirit of Christ, he does not mean that the Spirit is identical with Christ.[143] But when Christ suffers, the Spirit suffers as a result.

In suffering, therefore, the identity of each Person is preserved. The manner of suffering is unique to each insofar as the Father suffers in sacrificing the Son; the Son suffers in obedience to the Father; and the Spirit suffers in such sacrifice and obedience. Notice that the triune suffering of God does not blur the distinctions between the three Persons. What Barth is highlighting in his christological view of the Trinity is the involvement of each Person in Jesus Christ without detriment to each identity. The identity here does not mean individuality, but rather, the distinguishable self-giving of each Person. In Barth's mind, the self-giving of each Person is distinguished from another Person but with regard to harmony.[144] For example, Barth is specific that the Son is the One crucified on the cross; there is no doubt about the identity of the crucified One. What is remarkable in Barth's articulation is that the Father and Spirit are in harmony with the crucified Son.[145] In other words, Barth cannot see the crucifixion as an individual act of the Son alone; the crucifixion is a communal act.

In this act, the distinction between the three Persons is viewed against the undivided act of self-giving and the integrity of each identity

141. *CD* IV/2, 358–59. See Heppe, *Reformed Dogmatics*, 190.

142. For another perspective regarding the role of the Trinity in divine suffering; cf. von Balthasar, *Theo-Drama*. Volume 5, 57.

143. *CD* I/1, 516–18. Barth here considers Gal 4:6; Rom 8:9; Phil 1:19 and 1 Pet 1:11.

144. *CD* I/1, 437–38.

145. *CD* IV/2, 357.

is appraised in triplicity. The unique self-giving of each Person is considered in view of the perichoretic suffering. In such *perichoresis*, the crucifixion becomes an exhibit of the distinction-in-unity of the Father, Son, and Spirit. In being so, they uniquely participate in the suffering of Jesus Christ. Respectively, the crucifixion is a communal event which displays a communal act. Thus the suffering on Calvary is a participative suffering of the Godhead. The distinction, integrity, and feature in discussion become operative terms in Barth's christological view of the Trinity. These operative terms are comprehended in the united selfless act for humanity. That is why the triple distinctions, integrity and features of the Godhead will remain ambiguous if not appreciated in the life of Jesus Christ.[146] Thus individualistic interpretation of each Person has no place in Barth's doctrine of the Trinity. Even in considering the particular role of each Person in suffering, the idea of individuality is disallowed. Though Barth sees the suffering of the Trinity in three distinct ways, he treats it inseparably.

Any type of trinitarian differentiation without regard to Christology is incompatible with Barth's developed conception of God. Only a conflated uniqueness of each Person at work in Jesus Christ is accommodated in the doctrine of election. If Jesus Christ is indeed the Subject and Object of election, then the Trinity is also understood to be in operation within this formulation.[147] In other words, the Father, Son, and Spirit work together in fulfilling Christ's representation. In being the Subject of election, Christ represents the entirety of the Godhead; while in being the Object of election, Christ represents the entire human race.[148] The subjectivity of election is properly evaluated in its objectivity. The triunity therefore fine tunes, not obscures, the understanding of God's suffering in Christ. In suffering, Christ is the guidepost whereby Barth considers the involvement of the Trinity, also, how humankind gets involved.[149]

In this case, suffering is an element of God's self-disclosure. When Barth says, "God reveals himself through himself," it is a complex statement.[150] God reveals himself *unilaterally* yet still *mysteriously* through himself. T. F. Torrance is right in interpreting Barth along this line in which the Father is self-revealed through the Son and through the Spirit.[151]

146. Jüngel, *God's Being*, 99.

147. *CD* II/2, 157–58. Guretzki, *Explorer's Guide to Karl Barth*, 88–89.

148. Barth, *The Humanity of God*, 46. O'Neil, "Karl Barth's Doctrine of Election," 312–14.

149. See Farlow, *The Dramatizing of Theology*, 47.

150. *CD* I/1, 295.

151. Torrance, *The Christian Doctrine of God*, 90–93.

We can interject that the Father suffers through the Son and through the Spirit; thus the suffering in triunity is adequately interconnected with the suffering of Jesus Christ. This is how God is said to have been perfectly actual in suffering according to Barth.

If God corresponds entirely to himself in revelation, the suffering of Jesus Christ reveals the actual suffering of the Trinity. Suffering, in this regard, does not only point to or mediate God, but rather discloses who God is—a suffering triune deity.[152] We can infer that the perichoretic suffering strengthens Barth's argument for a relational Trinity.[153] In other words, the Trinity is present among human beings in the being of Christ.[154] This thought is deepened in the discussion of God's omnipresence in the triune suffering.[155]

Although God is omnipresent, Barth seeks for the specific indwelling of the Trinity in Jesus Christ. In the world, posits Barth, the "proper presence" of triunity is in Christ.[156] The term "proper presence" carries with it the sense of *strictness* and *directness* of the relation of the Trinity with Christ.[157] Though such notion does not signify an absolutized God due to the divine threeness, yet when Barth considers God's unmistakable presence in Christ, this consideration is pregnant with the view of the Trinity as unreservedly altogether in Christ.[158]

Ontologically speaking, when Barth sees the Trinity in Christ, it is seen in strict and direct sense. It is in a strict sense insofar as the entirety of the triune essence pervades Barth's articulation of divine suffering. It is in a direct sense insofar as there is no gap allowed in-between the Godhead and Jesus Christ. The divine threeness is strictly and directly involved in the suffering of Christ. There is no exemption or immunity of one Person in Christ's pain and misery. If such exemption or immunity is at play in this context, Barth's rigid mindset in conceiving the triunity is compromised. This is not the case when Barth articulates the doctrine of the Trinity in tight connection with the doctrine of election. Any deviation from this framework will result in an improper conception of the Trinity's complete

152. Also see MacDonald, *Karl Barth and the Strange New World within the Bible*, 149.

153. Refer to §8.3 of *CD*.

154. This, in a sense, is Barth's version of the earthly trace of the Trinity (*Vestigium Trinitatis*). *CD* I/1, 399. Lee, *Revelation and the Trinity*, 247–49.

155. See §31.1 of *CD*.

156. *CD* II/1, 484.

157. *CD* II/1, 484.

158. Hunsinger, *Reading Barth*, 140.

presence in Jesus Christ. In this respect, the perfectly actual suffering of the Trinity is intensified.

The formulation of the Trinity's complete presence in Jesus Christ has serious aftereffects for Barth's treatment of the Logos. If the Trinity is unequivocally in Christ, and the Son is apprehended in the eternal union of the Logos and the human Jesus, so the Trinity and the Logos are also inseparable in Barth's thought. If this is so, we have to follow such thought in view of the (im)passible triune God of election.

In Barth's framework, the Logos is somehow synonymously conceived with the Trinity. It means that the role of the Logos corresponds to that of the Trinity in view of Christ's suffering. This is the inevitable result of viewing the Trinity christologically. In the fully developed doctrine of election in *CD* IV/2, the consideration of the Logos is useful in supporting the argument for the (im)passible Trinity.[159] Because God's outworking is revealed in a threefold repetition, and also, the pure actuality of God is repeated and affirmed in the Logos, then the Logos and the Trinity are also historically conceived in recurring unity-in-distinction. This is especially true in advancing Barth's conception of divine suffering because, in considering the relationship between the two, we can better understand God's *majestic humiliation* in which the Crucified is also the Conqueror.[160]

In the one-subject God of election, the Trinity (each Person is in united subjectivity with the other two) is coincident with the Logos (Christ's divinity is in one substance with Christ's humanity). We can therefore infer from Barth's conception here the triune essence being interconnected with the one-substance of Jesus Christ.[161] In addition, despite the incarnation having transpired in the mode of the Son, there is no tenable way of seeing the unlimitedness of the Logos apart from the unlimitedness of the Trinity. We can infer too that when the Son suffers, the Father and Spirit, in essence, also suffer yet distinctively.[162] Nonetheless, each Person, in this case, remains uniquely affected and involved. The three Persons are not mutually affected, but rather *harmoniously* affected in their unity. For instance, Barth takes the incarnation of the Son to be the Father's act of grace and the Spirit's fulfillment of this act.[163] It is to avoid the tendency to de-divinize the persons of the Trinity, (e.g., the Father and Spirit also assume flesh), but also, not to disrupt

159. In this premise, we have to uphold the rigid union-in-distinction of the Logos and Jesus of Nazareth in Barth's reconfigured Christology. *CD* IV/2, 42–49, 352–58.

160. *CD* IV/2, 354.

161. *CD* IV/2, 47.

162. *CD* IV/2, 357.

163. *CD* IV/2, 42–43. Barth nonetheless qualifies, "But it is the Son and not the Holy Spirit who becomes flesh." *CD* IV/2, 43.

the triunity. Yet all talk on the essence of the Trinity finds its true meaning in Barth's subjective articulation of the suffering God in and of election.

2.3 The Subject of Divine Suffering

Barth wishes to articulate God as the absolute Subject (in God's act) as opposed to simply conceiving God in his essence, hence, reducing God to a mere substance.[164] Even though the particularity of the Son is emphasized in considering the topic of divine suffering, for Barth, the *wholeness of God* is the true Subject of this topic. That is why there is no potentiality in the Godhead *per se* in speaking of divine suffering; what is thought to be potential in triunity is already manifested in time. Divine suffering is comprehended to be what the Godhead wills and what it historically realizes in triunity. In this regard, the intra-trinitarian communion progresses into inter-trinitarian relation with creaturely reality.[165] Barth grants that what triunity is in eternity, has been acted out in the world.

Divine suffering is not simplistic, but rather triplistic, because the suffering of Jesus Christ points to the subjective sacrifice of the Godhead. It is in such sacrifice where Barth puts forward the perfect oneness of the Father, Son, and Spirit.[166] Since God's being is upheld in God's act, and this act is in Christ, we can see a decree of suffering which has been applied to the Trinity as well. If this is indeed the case, we can interject that Barth allows to predicate God's sacrificial act in Christ to the Trinity's essential operation. Here we understand more the outward triune act as we seek its inward implication on the Godhead.

For Barth, the suffering of Jesus Christ is God's essential operation. When God decrees himself to be the suffering God in Christ, the Godhead is wholly and truly undivided in its perfection vis-à-vis impeccable self-giving. This perfection is the *worldly* conception of the Trinity because it, Barth urges, exemplifies the triunity *for* humanity.[167] In trinitarian terms, freedom is usually correlated with the immanent Trinity; whereas love is usually affiliated with the economic Trinity. Barth however hints about this notion as essential to God and, in commitment, God truly exercises his freedom (and sovereignty) in a "supreme degree."[168] In this case, God's sympathetic autonomy speaks of God's perfection.

164. Read te Velde, *The Doctrine of God in Reformed Orthodoxy*, 141.

165. Kim, *The Spirit of God and the Christian Life*, 123.

166. *CD* II/1, 476.

167. *CD* I/1, 540; III/3, 87–89.

168. *CD* II/1, 345.

The three Persons are perfectly altogether in the act of suffering. Even if the Father, Son, and Spirit have distinctive self-giving in Jesus Christ's suffering, Barth persists in viewing such roles as repetitive and corroborative. Since the accent is on the oneness (instead of the threeness) of the Godhead even in articulating the *perichoresis*, so divine suffering must be based too on triunity.[169] It can be said here that Christ's suffering demonstrates the perichoretic decision to sacrifice; a sacrifice having triunity as the foreground, and, having *hypostasia* as the background. For Barth, the triunity is the platform for appreciating the relevance of *hypostasia* in explicating the divine suffering.[170] Because the suffering of Jesus Christ is in union with the Logos, and Jesus Christ's suffering is in unity with the Godhead, therefore the former and the latter are not truly distinct from each other (from the standpoint of God's history of suffering). Let us take the cry of dereliction as a test case.[171]

2.4 The Cry of Dereliction and the Trinity

According to Barth, in Jesus's cry of dereliction the Father never *really* leaves the Son.[172] Even if the Father is not the One crucified on the cross, the role of Jesus Christ, in this particular scenario, is seen as a repetition and corroboration of the Father's suffering and also, the Spirit's. Barth asserts:

> With the eternal Son the eternal Father has also to bear what falls on the Son as He gives Himself to identity with the man Jesus of Nazareth. . . . In Jesus Christ God Himself, the God who is the one true God, the Father with the Son in the unity of the Spirit, has suffered what it befell this man to suffer to the bitter end.[173]

It is clear that Barth upholds the unity of the three Persons in the suffering of Jesus Christ "to the bitter end." There is no unequivocal evidence in Barth's writings that the Father and Spirit have abandoned the Son in experiencing cruel hardship, even on the cross. For this reason, the cry of dereliction is a witness to the "fellow-suffering of God Himself" or the "suffering *with*

169. *CD* I/1, 403–4. The debate whether the Trinity is constituted by election or not is potentially a distraction in this book, therefore such line of thought will not be elaborated here.

170. *CD* IV/1, 206–7.

171. See Mk 15:34.

172. *CD* IV/2, 357. See McCormack, "The Passion of God Himself," 169–70.

173. *CD* IV/3, 414.

God Himself" (*Mitleiden Gottes selbst*).[174] This phrase shows that God "has not evaded" the suffering incurred in crucifixion.[175] For Barth therefore, the horror of crucifixion is not something which is incompatible with the Trinity. The triune God truly experiences the violent consequence of being hanged on the cross as Barth alludes to it to be "borne on earth and also in heaven."[176] Here, the seeming partition between transcendence and immanence is quite obscured.[177] The Trinity is seen to have been with Jesus Christ all the time, at every painful moment in this epoch. So the threefold suffering goes beyond the notion of divine compassion; it magnifies God's empathy being a fellow-Sufferer.

True, the Father offers the Son as a sacrifice, but this does not mean that the Son is precisely left on his own at Calvary. Jesus Christ can be viewed as the Godforsaken One in terms of his crying out to the Father, but, this Man can also be viewed as the God-*un*forsaken because he is the true Representative of all human beings.[178] In other words, Christ is God-forsaken being the Reprobate; whereas Christ is the God-unforsaken being the Elect. But because Barth insists that the "Elect of God" must be the "Rejected of God," in this case, Jesus Christ is the God-(un)forsaken.[179] In the interest of the study of divine suffering, let us call this human the *unforsaken Sacrifice*. Jesus Christ is the unforsaken Sacrifice in Barth's doctrines of election and reconciliation because of two reasons: first, being the universal Identifier of humankind; the Son of God (in divine reality) cannot be seen to have been abandoned, otherwise this would implicate the abandonment of humankind by the Father—an idea hardly accommodated in Barth;[180] second, the subject of isolation is the Servant—Jesus Christ, but this is also the Lord.[181] These explain why Barth calls the cry of dereliction as "supremely" experiencing the cross.[182]

174. *CD* IV/3, 414. *KD* IV/3, 478.

175. *CD* IV/3, 414.

176. *CD* IV/3, 414.

177. For another insight about this matter; cf. Rahner, *The Trinity*, 22.

178. Bauckham, "God's Self-Identification with the Godforsaken in the Gospel of Mark," 264.

179. *CD* IV/3, 413.

180. *CD* II/1, 422; IV/1, 158–59. Barth reasons, "It is at once the death-cry of the man who dies in Him [Christ] and the birth-cry of the man who comes to life in Him." IV/3, 413. Here Jesus's cry has soteriological tone. II/1, 414.

181. Excursus in *CD* IV/2, 168.

182. *CD* IV/2, 612. Moreover, Barth sees this cry as both "death-cry" and "birth-cry." IV/3, 413.

The concept of the unforsaken Sacrifice is beneficial in understanding Barth in this context. With this concept, Barth's theme of God's self-disclosure in hiddenness is sustained due to the following: (1) Despite the Son's suffering in the flesh, the Father and Spirit clearly do not suffer as such. (2) Although the Son is said to have been rejected (to some extent) by the Father, the Spirit is left unattended in this occasion, i.e., rejected the Son too, or rejected *with* the Son. (3) Even if the idea of abandonment of the Son by the Father is inferred, it remains unsettled whether such abandonment is literal or symbolic. So the tension inherent in the manifestation of the threefold suffering on Calvary is left hanging. In other words, this topic still stands puzzling in Barth's engagement with divine suffering. Respectively, Jürgen Moltmann gives more insight especially on expositing the empathetic suffering of God.

For Moltmann, God suffers alongside humanity; an act primarily for the God-self.[183] This act makes evident the Father's faithfulness to the Son *before* it can be taken as a witness to God's faithfulness to humanity.[184] The Father's faithfulness does not stand in the way to accommodate the notion of the abandonment of the Son. This is so because Moltmann's interpretation of Jesus's cry is indeed Markan-shaped. Moltmann claims, "Jesus died with the signs and expressions of a profound abandonment by God."[185] The historical reality of the agony of Jesus Christ on Calvary is pivotal in arguing for the suffering of the Trinity.

The cry of dereliction, argues Moltmann, is not according to Christ's humanity, but "in the relationship between Father and Son."[186] It means the cry does not only signify the Son's agony but also the Father's. Here the Father is deprived of a son, as the Son is deprived of a father.[187] In this mutual experience, the idea of suffering is interjected in the negation of identities: the Father suffers "Sonlessness" while the Son suffers "Fatherlessness."[188] Remarkably however, Moltmann also alludes that the abandonment occurred at Calvary is but a "brief moment" so that in experiencing abandonment, Jesus Christ might represent humankind's forsakenness.[189] Concerning the Holy Spirit, Moltmann says that we can appreciate the Spirit's participation

183. Lauber, *Barth on the Descent*, 151.

184. Moltmann, *Crucified God*, 124, 239.

185. Moltmann, *Crucified God*, 147.

186. Moltmann, *Crucified God*, 241.

187. Moltmann, *Crucified God*, 249.

188. Moltmann, *Crucified God*, 192, 243.

189. Moltmann, *The Way of Jesus Christ*, 180. Coombe, "Reading Scripture with Moltmann," 134–35.

in this context as being the force behind the Father's abandonment, and, the Son's self-surrender.[190] The Spirit is the power behind the will of the Father and Son to undergo suffering in their own unique ways.[191]

Having explicated how the three Persons suffer in Jesus's cry, Moltmann points out the significance of the cross in speaking of divine reality. His theology of the cross makes the weight of the triune reality fall on created time.[192] Moltmann posits, "So a truly Christian theology has to make Jesus's experience of God on the cross the centre of all our ideas about God: that is its foundation."[193] Thus in Moltmann's view, the cross is foundational in his doctrine of God; it is true as well in his doctrine of the Trinity. The "knowledge of the cross" is the basis to properly conceive the triune God.[194]

In such proposition, Jesus's cry is what constitutes the knowledge about divine suffering. Since the cross is central to the outworking of the three Persons, love through self-sacrifice is the heart of *perichoresis*.[195] The cross therefore is taken in a trinitarian way as "an event concerned with a relationship between persons in which these persons constitute themselves in their relationship with each other."[196] Thus the accent here, according to Moltmann, should be on the historical constitution of the immanent Trinity. The specific actualization of the Trinity *on the cross* is at odds with Barth's theology.[197] In Barth's reasoning, the Godhead is already self-constituted and self-actualized long before the cross event.[198] Even though the Trinity is revealed in human history, the triunity itself coincides with the decree. The triune God has given itself in eternity.

On the one hand, for Barth, an indescribable fellow suffering in the dying cry of Jesus Christ matches the eternal bond between the Father and Son. On the other hand, for Moltmann, such bond is matched by

190. Moltmann, *Crucified God*, 244.

191. Moltmann, *Crucified God*, 247.

192. Moltmann, *Crucified God*, 265. This position is in contrast to Robert Jenson's view that God's true reality is derived from pre-temporality. Jenson, *Alpha and Omega*, 92. See Jenson's view on "The Primal Decision to Suffer."

193. Moltmann, *Crucified God*, x.

194. Moltmann, *Crucified God*, 241.

195. Moltmann, *Crucified God*, 245.

196. Moltmann, *Crucified God*, 245.

197. Moltmann states, "The form of the crucified Christ is the Trinity." Moltmann, *Crucified God*, 246. Whereas Barth asserts that the Trinity is the "ground" of all creaturely actualizations, which of course includes the crucified Christ. *CD* IV/2, 113. In this, the non-contingent triune nature is upheld.

198. *CD* IV/2, 113.

unparalleled mutual loss in the said incident.[199] Although both theologians reject a strict Patripassian interpretation of Jesus Christ's death, Barth does not account the cry of dereliction to signal the Father's absence.[200] Contrary to Moltmann's view, the Father has never been a non-Father to the Son.[201] This is due to Barth's vicarious conception of the empathetic God.[202] The agony on Calvary, Barth postulates, is not primarily for God, but rather, it is principally a representative act in light of election. It is also in such proxy act that the suggestion of abandonment (even in a brief moment) is accommodated with caution. And more importantly, Barth's doctrines of God and the Trinity are not grounded in the theology of the cross. Despite the cross being vital in conceiving the divine suffering, it is not the center, but only part of the contemporaneity of the events enclosed in the history of suffering.

The mutual suffering in the form of abandonment suggests a "separation in community"; an idea incompatible with Barth's conception of triunity.[203] Here the lordship of the Godhead is not utilized, perhaps due to Moltmann's avoidance of a divine domineering image.[204] For Barth, the element of lordship in speaking of the triune suffering is indispensable. The Godhead suffers as Lord—a dominant theme in God without God being domineering because this lordship is demonstrated in the freedom of self-giving. Barth and Moltmann do concur that triunity is dynamic (thus it should not be viewed in static fashion), albeit the latter does not see God's suffering in trinitarian terms, and, paradoxically too.[205] Also unlike Barth, Moltmann never portrays the Spirit's role at Calvary in any way analogous to that of the Father's or the Son's. Thus the Spirit's personhood is not as pronounced in Jesus's cry as in Barth's articulation. Significantly, for Moltmann, the Godhead's pathos in history is inhospitable to any suggestion of impassibility; an assertion that Barth contends.[206]

199. Coombe, "Reading Scripture with Moltmann," 133.
200. *CD* IV/2, 357–58. Moltmann, *Crucified God*, 244.
201. *CD* I/1, 470. Moltmann, *Crucified God*, 244.
202. Tseng, *Karl Barth's Infralapsarian Theology*, 255.
203. Moltmann, *Crucified God*, 244.
204. Neal, *Theology as Hope*, 108, 113.
205. *CD* I/1, 369–70. Moltmann, *Crucified God*, 244, 255.
206. Moltmann, *Crucified God*, 270–72. *The Trinity and the Kingdom*, 25–26.

2.5 The Triadic Actuality of Divine Suffering

Barth sees the triune (im)passibility in divine constancy and actuality.[207] God's actuality is conveyed as something consistently continuous, hence the term "eternal actuality."[208] In this context, the ontological underpinnings of God's being imply an actuality of suffering on the Trinity itself. Barth's concept of actualism is within his understanding of God's history of suffering. The actuality of God's assumption of flesh is an act of divine perfection because the humanity which Jesus Christ takes does not discount the unchanging change in God. By being human, God exercises his selfless lordship over change in sacrifice.

This conception is, I think, to some extent within the Lutheran tradition.[209] What is untraditional with Barth's notion of actualism is the ontological bearing of the incarnation. Correspondingly, the suffering of Jesus Christ underlines the threefold determination of God. Divine actualization refers to God's act in the history of suffering which speaks of the very nature of the Godhead. So Barth's concept of divine actualism is always in line with his christological view of the Trinity.[210]

God, posits Barth, can be said to have been in constant and actual perfection in the election of Jesus Christ.[211] To that end, the Godhead is in "perfect being" in its threefold sacrifice.[212] The Godhead remains true to itself even in the paradox of suffering because it remains preeminent in all things at all times. That is why Barth attests, "the Godhead of the true God is not a prison whose walls have first to be broken through if He is to elect and do what He has elected and done in becoming man."[213] Since God's decree makes suffering essential to God's being, i.e., self-giving, so including suffering in the divine life does not entail an alteration in God. It is only in human perspective where suffering *appears* to be new to God; hence epistemologically perceived as a change in God. This is the complexity of Barth's notion of reiteration-in-change as he ontologically hints about the divine suffering in view of God's constancy.

207. *CD* I/1, 457.

208. *CD* I/1, 494.

209. Luther, *Luther's Works*, 25:151, 31:56.

210. Hunsinger, *Reading Barth*, 122. Also see Holmes, *The Quest for the Trinity*, 24.

211. *CD* I/1, 491. Jones, *The Humanity of Christ*, 148.

212. *CD* IV/1, 187.

213. *CD* IV/2, 84.

To better understand Barth, George Hunsinger supposes that impassibility is perhaps the test case for exploring God's constancy.[214] Hunsinger views a perfect God (even in change) insofar as perfection is seen in light of the divine selfless act. God is perfect precisely in its negative effect, vis-à-vis electing humanity in himself. Appropriately, the change in God ought to be taken in the context of God's perfection in humility. Hunsinger's supposition should be conducted in view of God's *eternal actuality* in suffering. So I would argue that in Barth's view, divine (im)passibility underscores the eternal selflessness of God reiterated in threefold suffering.

The threefold suffering of God raises the difficult and unavoidable question as to what suffering might mean for God, and about the ways that divine suffering may *not* be analogous to that of the creature. Donald MacKinnon hints that suffering itself is God's "acceptance of the ultimate triviality and failure of human existence."[215] Though suffering does not have the final say on creaturely reality, God nevertheless meets suffering head-on in Jesus Christ. In Christ, MacKinnon entertains the idea of tragic failure as shown at Calvary.[216] Even if God gives suffering a new sense in reconciliation, Christ still truly becomes an outcast and derelict.[217] In considering the "logic of the Gospel," for MacKinnon, Christ's suffering suggests defeat, whereas for Barth, it suggests providence, hence not defeat.[218] Barth grants that providence denotes God's superiority over creation; thus the notion of defeat in divine self-giving is denied.[219] Barth is consistent in arguing for the triumph of God in suffering; there is neither a sense of tragic failure, let alone defeat, in Christ's agony and death. Notwithstanding Barth's acknowledgment of the horror of what Christ has to undergo, such horror however has turned Christ into a Victor.[220]

For Barth, therefore, victory and not defeat is what suffering might mean for God. Thus divine suffering is not analogous to that of the creature

214. Hunsinger, *Reading Barth*, 167. Hunsinger interprets Barth's notion of actualism as a motif and not as a system. Hunsinger, *Reading Barth*, 167. Actualism as a motif, Hunsinger continues, has appropriation of orthodoxy as influenced by Anselm of Canterbury and G. W. F. Hegel. With Anselm, Barth acknowledges many of the divine attributes associated with trinitarian orthodoxy, i.e., immutability and impassibility in particular. With Hegel, Barth underlines God's inner being as truly alive and not latent. The result, Hunsinger infers, was a "cross between the two." Hunsinger, *Reading Barth*, 128.

215. MacKinnon, "Philosophy and Christology," 81.

216. MacKinnon, *Themes in Theology*, 152–53.

217. MacKinnon, "Philosophy and Christology," 81.

218. This is in view of the role of Judas Iscariot. Cane, *The Place of Judas Iscariot in Christology*, 87.

219. *CD* III/3, 3, 9.

220. Bloesch, *Jesus is Victor!*, 105.

as long as its process and outcome are well considered. In the process of suffering, the three Persons are actively involved in the world *without* being entrapped by creaturely reality. In this involvement, suffering itself is overcome instead of the Godhead being overcome. Suffering can never and will never cause tragic failure against the supreme power and lordship of God. This is the core of divine victory, in Barth's mindset, which results from the selfless suffering of God.

For this reason, Barth writes: "God the Father raised Him [Jesus Christ] from the dead, and in so doing recognized and gave effect to His death and passion as a satisfaction made for us."[221] The idea of failure in God is not viable here simply because death is treated in conjunction with resurrection. Even though death is the climax of Jesus Christ's suffering, yet it also heralds the overcoming of suffering, and especially, of death itself. This is the reason why Barth sees this series of happenings as *the Christ-event*. In this event, death and resurrection are conjoined; there is no death without resurrection, so there is no death without the triumph over death.

It is apparent that in God's triumph, the Father is the One who raised Jesus Christ from death. This poses a serious question on Barth's conception of the triune suffering: Who becomes vulnerable to creaturely reality—is it only the Son?; or is it the Trinity? If it is only the Son who dies (because it is only the Son who assumes the flesh), vulnerability to creaturely reality solely applies to the Son. If this is so, it might be argued that it is not the *fullness* of God who suffers; fullness in the sense that there is neither reservation nor constraint in self-giving. There is no doubt that Barth's God suffers in election, but the Father's and Spirit's suffering are not unto death. Although this is in line with the distinctive suffering of the Godhead, this formulation nevertheless signals a sort of restriction in the triune suffering.

However, since the fullness of God is revealed in Jesus Christ according to Barth, so it is the fullness of God who becomes vulnerable. It is here where the concepts of fullness and subjection must be critically analyzed. It seems that for Barth, even though the Father and Spirit do not undergo death *per se*, yet the two experience death through the Son. Despite their transcendence over death, the Father and Spirit still relate with the death the Son subjects himself to. Again, this notion is congruent with Barth's transcendent-yet-relational deity of election. Because Christ is the "very God" who is subjected to the terrible conditions in the far country, therefore the term *very God* means that there is no restriction in the being of God insofar as suffering is concerned. In addition, Barth consistently argues for the unity of the Godhead in going into the far country: where

221. *CD* IV/1, 157.

the Son journeys into, in essence, is also where the Father *is* and the Spirit *is*. Hence, the Trinity is not collapsed in this journey because this selfless endeavor is truly a joint decision-in-act of God.

But still, the question on the entirety of God in relation to vulnerability remains. Though Barth conceives of divine suffering in threeness, yet he somehow fails to unpack the one-in-threeness and the threeness-in-one conceptions of God in the death of Jesus Christ. Granting that it is only the Son who died, this begs the question of the eternal unity within the Godhead. What happened to the Father and Spirit upon the death of the Son? Also, what holds Barth in speaking of the death of all three Persons on the cross? Despite Barth's coherent argument on the eternal homogeneity and indivisibility in and of the Trinity, he steps back from building a case for the death of the *entirety* of God (even though death in this regard means victory over death itself). Of course Barth's line of thinking regarding the fullness of God is revealed in Jesus Christ, therefore, it is fair to say that the death of Christ represents the death of God himself. But I am not satisfied with the thought that the Father has truly given his *all*, and the Spirit has given his *all*, if this "all" does not include death. I am aware that the death of the Father and Spirit is not a requirement for election, or reconciliation, or even redemption; however the insusceptibility from death of these two Persons creates a rift in conceiving the totally selfless God of election.[222]

2.6 God's Vulnerability to Suffering

In Jesus Christ, Barth can say that the fullness of God suffers without being compelled to say that the entirety of God dies. Also, in Jesus Christ, Barth can argue for the vulnerability of God to creaturely reality without having to argue in favor of the unqualified insusceptibility of the Trinity. Here we can put to the test Barth's ideas of capacity and capability as it refer to God being affected. Is the concept of divine vulnerability synonymous with the concept of divine potentiality in Barth's schema? Can we infer that in Barth, the entirety of Godhead is not vulnerable to creaturely reality, yet it has the potential for suffering?

For Barth, since the Son of God truly becomes vulnerable to creaturely reality, it can be inferred that vulnerability, in this sense, is not foreign to the Trinity. In this case, Barth is in agreement with Hans Urs von Balthasar. Balthasar asserts, "If it is possible for one Person in God

222. I am aware of Barth's non-usage of the words "fullness" and "entirety" but this does not hinder me from using these words because of his formulation: Jesus Christ is the full revelation of God.

to accept suffering . . . then evidently it is not something foreign to God, something that does not affect him. It must be something profoundly appropriate to his divine Person."[223] The assertion for vulnerability in God (in the Son) without directly stating that the triune God has the potential for suffering (being wholly vulnerable) is the point of contention in how Barth renders the divine suffering. In allowing for the notion of vulnerability to the triune life, Barth risks the transcendence of God over creation; nonetheless, in disallowing the experience of suffering, Barth also risks the relational God of election. So Barth refrains from attributing vulnerability to the Trinity but he does not refrain from attributing the experience of suffering to the Trinity as well.

In other words, although the potentiality to be affected by outside factors is only ascribed to the Son of God, Barth however supports the idea that the Trinity is not immune to be acted upon from without. The Godhead's internal impassibility or the inherent incapacity for direct suffering does not outweigh the three Persons's perichoretic association with the suffering of Jesus Christ. So God is capable of being acted upon from without provided that the triune decision-in-act to suffer fits Barth's formulation of non-contingency. In this manner, the idea of God merely allowing himself to be affected becomes plausible insofar as vulnerability is referred to the Son only, but inconclusive insofar as the willingness to be affected is referred to the Father, Son, and Spirit.

Jesus Christ's suffering therefore is not something incoherent with the non-vulnerability of the Godhead. As Barth puts it, "It is not at all the case that God has no part in the suffering of Jesus Christ even in His mode of being as the Father."[224] Although this statement does not in any way advance the doctrine of Patripassianism, Barth however puts forward the Father's (and Spirit's) assumption of the "alien suffering" of humanity.[225] That is why this alien suffering is said to be not foreign to the Godhead. The fellow-suffering of the Father, despite its mysterious character, is somehow given light here, especially in its relation to creation. Barth adds:

> God is free to be wholly inward to the creature and at the same time as Himself wholly outward. . . . This is how He meets us in Jesus Christ. His revelation in Jesus Christ embraces all these apparently so diverse and contradictory possibilities. They are all His possibilities.[226]

223. Balthasar, *Theo-Drama*. Volume 3, 226.

224. *CD* IV/2, 357.

225. *CD* IV/2, 357.

226. Excursus in *CD* II/1, 315. Also see Hunsinger "*Mysterium Trinitatis*," 168–69.

The "wholly inwardness" pertains to the distance between the Creator and creature; but in Jesus Christ, the "wholly outwardness" of God becomes real as the Creator enters into covenant with the creature. In conceiving the Trinity in this regard, we can say that the Father, Son, and Spirit are said to be wholly inward by being wholly outward; as such is made possible in Jesus Christ. In being wholly outward, the Godhead does not undo its wholly inwardness in view of the humiliation-exaltation paradigm. In the severe degradation of the Creator, the creature is highly esteemed. With this, we can see why the Trinity's internal life is coincident with its external life. For Barth, the triunity is undeniably a being for and in creation. This is how the Trinity embraces both impassibility and passibility; notwithstanding the subtle differences in understanding vulnerability and capacity to be affected concerning divine suffering. The Trinity is impassible because of its non-vulnerability in itself while the Trinity is passible too because it is affected in Jesus Christ. The issues at hand are better appreciated in Barth's conception of divine immanence.

The true meaning of divine immanence, Barth construes, is in God being supremely temporal in the world, i.e., in the world but not *of the world*.[227] God can be in the world without being entangled with creaturely reality in being transcendent-yet-relational. It is in this argumentation that the pantheistic and panentheistic inadequacies are exposed.[228] Nonetheless God indeed is limited in the world because God is said to have been limited in time according to Barth. The caveat in this formulation is in the subject and object of limitation. As long as God is the One who limits himself then God's submission (not subjugation) to creaturely reality is properly dealt with.

Since for Barth, God creates time and he chooses not to live without it, thus God's non-contingency to time does not hinder him from existing in it. This is so in order for God's eternity to cover time, and, to manifest the history of suffering. When Barth says that God is revealed as Christ, God is said to have been truly affected. God's choice to be vulnerable is possible in the divine operation in and through time. Since everything under time is subject to change, therefore God is also seen to have been changed in God's choice to be in time. But Barth is careful in his argumentation; he rather says that God is in time without being suppressed by it. In this way, change is thought to be something limitedly applied to the Trinity.

In considering the allowance for the change in God in Barth's thought, the notion of potentiality is also given light. There is no outside event and action that can affect God simply because these have no potentiality to cause

227. *CD* III/2, 437.

228. Excursus in *CD* II/1, 315.

him to change. It is also true, however, that the Son can never be properly conceived in his eternality without being associated with his human essence. Barth's argument for God's pre-temporal assumption of the human essence has to be qualified. The formulation of the Son of God as always the Son of Man must not be taken in strict conjunction with the Trinity.

If it is only the Son who is vulnerable to creaturely reality, it is logical to conclude that with Barth, it is only the Son who undergoes change in the divine outworking. But again, if he (Son of God and Son of Man) does change, it also begs the question: Why is it that the Father and Spirit do not change with the Son? Because there is no categorical answer in Barth's doctrine of the Trinity, one might think that the reason for this lies with the distinction among the divine persons. Thus such distinction implies the Trinity's capability to resist change due to the triune decision to choose the Son for the incarnation. Also, the fact that the Godhead did choose incarnation for the Son rules out (at least in principle) the idea of divine incapacity and highlight God's freedom to choose for and in God's self. In addition to the unchangeableness of the triune free love, the Father and Spirit are conceived to be unchangeable against creaturely change, hence immutable as taught in the Western tradition. The logical incompatibility between capability and incapacity in speaking of the change in God is made compatible in Barth's discourse on (im)passibility as it relates to God's decree.

What should be clarified is the insusceptibility of the Father and Spirit in the being of Jesus Christ. If this extrapolation is correct, the Son of God (if the *oneness* of the Trinity is to be insisted) in a sense cannot be truly viewed to be always in Jesus Christ. Here, the Son of God is partially the Son of Man because as God, the Son of God is indivisibly conceived with God the Father and God the Holy Spirit. Such line of thought eventually leads to a quasi-Monarchian, quasi-Nestorian view of God. Because of this logical direction, Barth's conception of the Logos must be revisited too.

If the Father and Spirit remain insusceptible from creaturely reality (even in Jesus Christ), then what about the Logos? If we say that the Logos *becomes* susceptible to what befalls Jesus due to Barth's one-subject Christ, so the Logos and the Trinity cannot be viewed to be strictly congruent vis-à-vis vulnerability. The Logos is perfect in its union with the humanity of Christ, yet, the Trinity, in a way, is perfect in its partial connection with Christ. It is partial in a sense because Jesus Christ can bleed and die, but, not the Trinity. Therefore the notion of divine suffering being constitutive of God's essentiality must be taken with caution. Suffering, in this context, is not unequivocally unto death. We can infer that with Barth, death is only predicated to Jesus Christ, not even to the Son of God. If this is indeed the trajectory of Barth's thought, it could suggest tritheism due to the

Son's subjection to death in view of the Father's and Spirit's non-subjection to death. However, if death is to be predicated to the Son of God as well, then any suspicion of tritheism is avoided. Unfortunately, Barth is quite unclear on this matter.

What is clear in Barth, however, is the notion of the indivisibility of the Trinity's outworking. Though the Father and Spirit do not have to die in order to demonstrate their self-giving, their sacrifice is still *real* and *actual* in the life of Jesus Christ. Perhaps this thought, one might think, suffices in contemplating what Barth means by this: Jesus Christ who is elected to suffer and die *is* definitely the revealed God. In consideration of Barth's God, suffering and selflessness are deemed reciprocal. Since God is selfless, suffering does not impugn God's very nature. God wills to suffer and does suffer because he has nothing in himself to protect or to sustain. God is God irrespective of what happens to him, even in suffering. In fact, in suffering, God has shown he is indeed the Lord God since suffering does not undermine himself. Suffering rather reveals that God is truly selfless in his trinitarian lordship.

Moreover, God's election and selflessness are also not contradictory in Barth. Since God is selfless, self-election to stand in the position of selfish humanity does not contradict God's very being. Here, the Electing and the Elected Subject in the triplicity of the (im)passible God is underpinned. Thus with Barth, the eternal decree does not contradict the divine selflessness. Since God is selfless, God's decree does not counter God's very being. God wills to be this God and does relate himself as such because he has nothing in himself to protect or to sustain in fulfilling the decree. God is God without regard to what happens to him according to the decree. In fact, by decreeing to be this God in relation to humankind, God shows he is indeed God since the decree does not undermine himself but rather the opposite. In other words, in triplistic selflessness, God remains perfectly and undividedly in himself. The decree rather reveals God as the Lord in the decree; it is demonstrated in triunity. This concept of selflessness however has stirred strong theo-sociological reactions.

Feminist reactions to divine suffering, especially as it relates to the Trinity, speak negatively about Barth's understanding of God. The self-determined vulnerability of God can be hi-jacked to put forward the agenda of dependency with gender associations. For instance, Sarah Coakley criticizes Barth's subordinate view of women by stating: "to incorporate 'vulnerability' into the trinitarian understanding of God evades the feminist issues."[229] For her, the divine ontological self-abasement indeed has cultural and sexual

229. Coakley, *Powers and Submission*, xix–xx. Coakley cites *CD* III/2, §45.

repercussions, e.g., the subordination of women and the low estimation of women's functional worth in the post-War society.[230] Catherine LaCugna similarly points out that Barth's gendered notion of sacrifice wherein the divine will to be vulnerable somewhat legitimates women's submission to men. She stresses that in speaking of the Trinity "a relational ontology understands both God and creature to exist and meet as persons in communion."[231] The harmonious interrelationship between women and men is exemplified because of God's association with humanity. In this regard, LaCugna is critical of how Barth's explanation of the intimate communion between the Persons of the Trinity can support yoking or free submission between opposite sex, though often at the expense of the female.[232]

Barth however has no intention of legitimizing subjugation or exploitation of any human being, but rather he wishes to highlight the concept of community (not inferiority) which originates from the triune freedom to love.[233] When Barth discusses the idea of "vulnerability," he uses it strictly in terms of how immense God is willing to lower himself in order to lift fallen humanity up from its destitute state of self-destruction. In other words, the subjugation or exploitation of women is outside of Barth's agenda, explicitly or implicitly. The humiliation of the incarnate God neither invokes nor supports the humiliation of any person by another person because "humility is not at all resignation"; it is not something which leads one to despair.[234]

Furthermore, Barth firmly speaks of God upholding his glory (even in self-sacrifice) instead of abrogating it. In Barth's thought, the threefold selflessness of God is not about self-denial. God does not have to deny himself in order to be selfless, but rather God remains in himself by being selfless in trinitarian perspective. There is nothing in the Godhead which hinders itself from being selfless—God *is* self-giving in and of himself. The non-negotiable threefold selflessness, for Barth, undeniably supports a suffering yet consistent Trinity.

Having examined the triune selflessness in suffering, we will attend to the reason why Barth conceives of it as eternal.

230. Coakley, *God, Sexuality and the Self*, 266–67.

231. LaCugna, *God for Us*, 250.

232. LaCugna, *God*, 252–54, 272–73. Here LaCugna reads *CD* III/4, 119–20.

233. See Sonderegger's reading of Barth on this matter in "Barth and Feminism," in *The Cambridge Companion to Karl Barth*, 258–73.

234. *CD* II/1, 213–14.

3. The Eternality of Divine Suffering

God is selfless in offering himself. Barth construes this in trinitarian terms focusing on "the eternal Son of the eternal Father."[235] The Father's selflessness is demonstrated in the offering of the Son, and the Son's selflessness is seen in the obedience to the Father.[236] It is in this context where the suffering of the Godhead is advanced. Likewise, it is here where Barth says that God is truly constant in himself. Thus the eternality of the triune suffering is still within Barth's conception of God's constancy and actuality. God's constancy is revealed in his actuality and God's actuality is derived from God's constancy. If God is actual in himself, God is also constant in himself.[237] Here God is said to have been constant in his actuality, hence, God is eternal. So when Barth thinks of the eternality of divine suffering, he is referring to God being affected in both pre-temporality and temporality.[238] We have tackled Barth's conception of the affected God in chapter 2. We will now look at the question of affectivity in conjunction with (im)passibility, namely, from Barth's perspective of God's constant selflessness. When does he see God to have been *actually selfless*?

When we dealt with the foreground of the affected God vis-a-vis creation, we did not investigate specifically the eternality of divine suffering. Since Barth holds to the idea of God being affected in the decree, we have to closely inspect it with God being affected in time. The decision to suffer in Jesus Christ covers the eternality of God. Although it is only in the created time where divine suffering can be said to be an actual event, it does not do away with Barth's formulation of the decree as "real" risk and threat against God in eternity.[239] In this case, God's sacrifice therefore has begun in God's primal decision to be for humanity.

God's primal decision is elucidated in Barth's Christology, specifically in the Son's willingness to obey the Father prior to creation.[240] God is conceived to have humbled himself by the decree to assume humanity. God decides to make humanity part of the Godhead by determining the Son of God to also be the Son of Man. For Barth, the Godhead is being inclusive in this regard; God does not mind to be *discomforted* in God's inner life. What God does mind is the welfare of human beings by securing their future. God does this

235. *CD* IV/1, 157.

236. *CD* IV/1, 157.

237. *CD* II/1, 341–42. Hunsinger, "Truth as Self-Involving," 41.

238. For Barth, God being affected in election means God has willed unto himself a being antagonistic of himself.

239. This is an overcome reality according to Barth. *CD* IV/2, 161.

240. McCormack, "Divine Impassibility," 159, 162.

by taking to himself creaturely insecurity and hopelessness, hence God is said to have essentially suffered as a result.

3.1 The Primal Decision to Suffer

Barth claims that God's sorrow preceded that of humankind in the primal decision.[241] Human contradiction is brought into the fullness of the Godhead, i.e., in God's own being. However, Barth qualifies that sorrow is bundled with rejoicing, like death is bundled with life in God's reality. In taking such antithesis into himself, God eternally participates in suffering.[242] What Barth avoids here is the ambiguity of a generalized triune nature wherein the Trinity is viewed apart from humanity.[243] We can interject therefore that what is decreed in the life of Jesus Christ is the reality of the Trinity. Triunity is rightly conceived in conjunction with Jesus Christ in Barth's doctrine of election.[244] For this reason, God's pre-temporal suffering is inseparable from God's suffering in time. God, in a sense, extends to time in the outworking of his condescension; it is in the world where God reveals the eternality of his self-giving. It is in this orientation wherein Barth advances the constant suffering deity. God's primal decision to suffer and its actualization in time *is* what Barth conceives of as the history of divine suffering. This history is not the history of the Son of God alone, but rather the history of the Trinity.

What is actual in God, Barth observes, does not conform to what is actual in humans. God's actuality can also be in and of himself; being unconditioned *ad extra*. Barth's idea of the actuality of the decree is "prior to all external events"; the triune decision to suffer is indeed true but not without its actual historical occurrence in Jesus Christ.[245] So when the notion of the affected God is underlined, God is said to have been (im)passibly actual.[246] In other words, Barth sees God to have been selfless in including humanity in God's being. The eternality of divine suffering speaks of the *already but not yet* in God. For instance, the Son's anticipated

241. *CD* III/1, 380.

242. *CD* III/1, 380–81. Barth writes, "He [God] has taken the creature to Himself even before it was, namely, in His own Son, who willed to live and die as a man for all men, as a creature for all creatures. He thus took it to Himself even in its very contradiction." *CD* III/1, 380–81. Also see II/2, 157, 172; IV/1, 66, 70, 145, 158.

243. *CD* II/1, 348–49.

244. *CD* IV/2, 336–37.

245. *CD* II/2, 175; IV/2, 113.

246. *CD* IV/2, 155.

human essence can be deemed as reality in the Godhead.[247] This explains God's history of suffering as one concurrent event which Barth calls "movement" (*der Bewegung*)—a *single moment* of decision to act; an act in accordance with God's undisturbed and uninterrupted will.[248]

We can take a single movement *kenosis* in Barth's theopaschite thinking: the incarnation as already real *in essence* before the created time in the *Logos incarnandus*. Jesus Christ cannot be isolated to being in time only. Christ can also be said to be timeless insofar as the singularity of the essence and event of the Son of God and the human Jesus are considered. Thus Barth cannot conceive of the *Logos incarnandus* apart from the Word incarnate; likewise he cannot conceive of the Son of God apart from Jesus Christ. In fact, Barth has no interest in engaging with the notion of *Logos asarkos* because it does not serve his concept of God being constantly continuous in eternity. In this particular reading of Barth, I side with Robert Jenson's objection to the *Logos asarkos* over Paul Molnar's insistence of it.[249]

It is clear in Barth that God pre-temporally decides to be in the person of Jesus Christ; but this decision cannot be said to be demarcating a foreground and background in the triune nature. Noticeably, Jenson reformulates this notion by noting that in God's decided nature the "content of this decision" is the "free relatedness" of the Trinity to humankind.[250] In other words, whenever Jenson reads Barth's rendition of the triune God, he sees God's movement into time.[251] Yet intriguingly, Jenson reads Barth to propose that "everything that happened in Jesus Christ's history on earth happened in eternity, and in God's pretemporal eternity."[252] Thus the Christ-event in time is treated as "sign and mirror of the eternal decree."[253] This seems to suggest that "the weight of reality falls on pretemporal eternity."[254]

247. Pertaining to the eternity of the triune God, Barth claims, "We are speaking about the God who is also eternally the Son, who is begotten of the Father and yet of the same essence with Him, . . . we are speaking about the God who is also eternally the Spirit, who proceeds from the Father and the Son but is of the same essence as both." *CD* II/1, 615.

248. *KD* II/1, 693, 719–20; *CD* II/1, 615, 638–39.

249. Jenson, *Systematic Theology*. Volume 1, 140. Jenson thinks that in Barth, the *Logos asarkos* is implausible. *The Triune Identity*, 140. In contrast, Paul Molnar argues that the *Logos asarkos* in Barth's theology is crucial in recognizing God's ultimate freedom. Molnar, *Divine Freedom and the Doctrine of the Immanent Trinity*, 58–59.

250. Jenson, *God after God*, 127.

251. Jenson, *God*, 128.

252. Jenson, *Alpha and Omega*, 78–79. Here Jenson cites *CD* II/2, 7, 8.

253. Jenson, *Alpha*, 92.

254. Lee, *Trinitarian Ontology*, 23. Lee adds that Jenson explains further that "the pretemporal Jesus and his events become a center of gravity and absorb the ontological

The *mirror* imagery appears quite hazy, thus questionable. The element of contemporaneity in speaking of the divine reality is somehow screened due to the disruption of the critical balance between eternity and time. This, I think, is the weakness of Jenson's reading against Barth's formulation of the contingent contemporaneity of the history of suffering.

The mirror imagery, however, should not be entirely discarded since Barth's articulation of this matter conveys what might, to some extent, dovetail with Jenson's view. Barth elucidates that "the name and person of Jesus Christ was *in the beginning* with God."[255] But while Barth reflects on God's determination in the Son, this retrospective manner of argument does not necessarily support the weight of reality Jenson has in mind.[256] For Barth, the triune being is "weighed and measured" by eternity.[257] In other words, the concurrency of the dual histories prevents any impartial perception of divine reality.

To be consistent with Barth's articulation of the will and reference behind the decree, the divine and human histories should be treated in balance, i.e., in contingent contemporaneity. This method is convenient in presenting a sustained picture of God's reality.[258] Though there is a slight coherence between Barth and Jenson in terms of the eternal reality of God, Jenson's emphasis on the pre-temporal against the temporal marred Barth's idea of God's eternality. Nonetheless, Jenson's proposal in this regard is not "wrong-headed" but merely inordinate in terms of forcing his argument into Barth's thought.

The strength of Jenson's reading against Barth's view of the history of suffering, however, is in the purpose of the created time. In it, God is revealed instead of being abstracted from it. God's movement in time can be said to be constitutive of the divine being. This means that God *is* in how God manifests himself in and through creation, i.e., in Jesus Christ. We both concur that with Barth, the triune reality is the "one revealed in Christ"; the being of the Trinity is in "living self-repetition" in the being of Jesus Christ.[259] But since Jenson reads Barth to have viewed the being of the Trinity not as fixed, but rather as an ongoing being in time, then the

weight of the temporal Jesus and the temporal history into the pretemporality." Lee, *Trinitarian Ontology*, 23.

255. *CD* II/2, 175. Italics mine.

256. *CD* II/2, 175–76.

257. Excursus in *CD* II/1, 610.

258. See Hunsinger, *Reading Barth*, 120–21.

259. Jenson, *God*, 124–25.

idea of pre-temporality is abandoned. Here I part ways with Jenson.[260] He reassesses the triune being to be completed in "succession when God takes the form of creation to be the form of God's eternity."[261]

Jenson asserts that Barth has a concept of a "pre-existent Jesus."[262] If the Son obeys the Father in the being of Jesus, and the Son is always obedient to the Father, therefore the Son of God is always Jesus Christ. Thus "Jesus *is* the eternity of God."[263] This is what I repudiate from Jenson's interpretation: Jesus is always the Son, "there is no time [God's time] before the reality of the Incarnation."[264] Jenson believes that Barth has voided the timeless God by locating Jesus Christ's experience in what "formerly occupied by timelessness."[265] It is the result of a strict statement that "God *lives* his being."[266] Though I also see the concept of a pre-existent Jesus in Barth, but this Jesus is only in Platonic sense, i.e., only in essence, not in its physical reality. In other words, the pre-existent Jesus in the Trinity is the *Logos incarnandus*. God has reality before incarnation, but this reality is inseparable from incarnation. Barth eschews the idea of completion in succession in explaining the essentiality of the Trinity. But Barth indeed has a concept of "succession" in speaking of the Trinity; he applies it to the fellowship initiated by the Trinity with creatures, not to the being of the Trinity.[267] This is evident in his articulation of the inward-outward triune act; deemed as a single act which promotes the one and *complete* God. For Barth, God in this case has incontestably one nature—the divine nature inclusive of human essence.

The idea of completion in succession applies strictly to the Son of God; not to the Trinity. Under Barth's ontological schema, the Son's pre-temporal essence, in a sense, is yet to be completed in the incarnation (fully God but not fully human). The Son of God has only become fully human in Jesus Christ. In this, the Son of God has not always been, in totality, the Son of Man; unless Barth accommodates the Son of Man to be totally human in the *Logos incarnandus*. Barth insists, and consistent in this insistence, that the Son of God is *always* the Son of Man in Jesus Christ. The word "always" however is conceived in the already-but-not-yet paradigm, especially in

260. Jenson, *God*, 128.
261. Jenson, *God*, 128.
262. Jenson, *God*, 129.
263. Jenson, *God*, 130.
264. Jenson, *God*, 132.
265. Jenson, *God*, 132.
266. Jenson, *God*, 134.
267. *CD* II/1, 615–16.

Barth's notion of a completed *event*.[268] Thus whenever "always" is replaced by the word "becomes" (or its derivative), it is employed analogically, not ontologically, to provide footing for the transformation of human beings (from being rejected to being elected).[269]

By extrapolation, the Trinity can be deemed to be always passible (because of God's decision to suffer), hence, the impassibility of God is true but it never becomes real because God *is* according to his will. It shows that in being God, humanity is within the divine life through Jesus Christ. This, in my analysis, is who God eternally is because he determines it to be. Although it implies the eternal and harmonious suffering of the three Persons, yet it holds to that which had never been: an impassible triune God. In other words, in divine existence, God is already a *changed* God. Here we deal with the Father, Son, and Spirit, united in an eternal decision and an eternal expectation of the incarnated God. Because, for Barth, God never willed not to be without Jesus Christ, it means that the essence of this human is presumed to be *within* the Trinity.

What is apparent in my reading is that Barth sees God as altogether one in each and every aspect of the triune being. Since the essence of the Son is already actual and complete in itself prior to the incarnation; this statement is also true of the Godhead.[270] Jenson postulates that Barth somewhat eliminates the idea of God's timelessness by merging the pre-temporal and temporal eternity.[271] Though this merging is valid in Barth's conception of divine suffering, it nevertheless means that pre-temporality has no use in this context. "Pre-temporality" is not a useless word in Barth, if it is used in speaking of God's history of suffering. Of course, the pre-temporal suffering (decision to include humanity in the triune being) is attached to the temporal suffering (the triune being in Jesus Christ), but God's suffering in time cannot be understood properly without going back to the primal decision. It is therefore required to examine the foundation of divine suffering before Christ's suffering can be viewed in trinitarian terms; otherwise, suffering cannot be associated with the Godhead.

I also argue that the foundation of triune suffering is derived pre-temporally. Barth elucidates that in Jesus Christ "eternity became time"; God "takes time to Himself" and makes it "the form of His eternity."[272] In such

268. Haley, *The Humanity of Christ*, 127–29.

269. See *CD* IV/2, 102–3, 271, 514.

270. *CD* IV/2, 113. Molnar, "Incarnation," 114.

271. Jenson, *God*, 68–69, 155.

272. *CD* II/1, 616.

foreordination, the three Persons mutually share in essence.[273] Barth deploys the term "now of eternity" (*nunc aeternitatis*) to explicate how God's eternality orders temporal reality.[274] It is in this context where Barth posits God's simultaneity and everlasting duration in speaking of the triune being.[275] We can tackle here the issue revolving the suffering of the Godhead. When did the Godhead suffer? Barth understands it to be both outside and inside all relations of time, i.e., the pre-temporal decision to suffer in Jesus Christ and its temporal actualization.[276] In the Now of eternity, this decision-actualization is regarded as onto-relational perichoretic movement of the Father, Son, and Spirit (in order and succession) "without destroying their special relationships with each other, without arbitrariness in this relationship" (*ohne Zerstörung ihrer besonderen Verhältnisse untereinander, ohne Willkür in diesem Verhältnis*).[277] The movement however in the triune suffering "does not signify the passing away of anything, a succession which in itself is also beginning and end."[278] Thus Barth's formulation of the Now of eternity precludes any notion of naked eternity. God is timeless insofar as it relates to the "defects of our time"; God is also temporal insofar as it considers the primal decision.[279] Thus the impassible triune suffering is said to be timeless and also in time; or simply stated, it is understood to be eternal.

In the "unsurpassable reality" of the Godhead, says Barth, we have to deal with the concepts of "pre-temporality, supra-temporality and post-temporality."[280] God is pre-temporal according to Barth: "Always and everywhere and in every way God exists as the eternal One in the sense of this pre-temporality."[281] In this notion, we can better appreciate Barth's basis for the triune suffering:

> We cannot understand Him [God] without this pre-existence in His divinity. . . . For this pre-time is the pure time of the Father and the Son in the fellowship of the Holy Spirit. And in this pure divine time there took place the appointment of the eternal Son for the temporal world, there occurred the readiness of the Son

273. *CD* II/1, 615.

274. *CD* II/1, 615.

275. *CD* II/1, 608.

276. *CD* II/1, 608. For a different view of the meaning of divine eternality; cf. Augustine's "ever-present eternity." Excursus in *CD* III/1, 70.

277. My own translation of *KD* II/1, 693. Cf. *CD* II/1, 615.

278. *CD* II/1, 614.

279. *CD* II/1, 617–18.

280. *CD* II/1, 620–21.

281. *CD* II/1, 621.

> to do the will of the eternal Father, and there ruled the peace of the eternal Spirit—the very thing later revealed at the heart of created time in Jesus Christ.[282]

This shows the importance of referring to pre-temporality in understanding the perichoretic act in the created time. The usage of the terms "pre-time" and "pre-creation" is important in conceiving the divine selflessness, and, what truly is at stake in the obedience of the Son to the Father. In what Barth calls the Son's "appointment" for what is temporal, the idea of self-sacrifice is implied. When Barth says God is pre-temporal, it goes with the idea that God, who is not obliged to have fellowship with humans, or, even to create them, decides to do these willingly.[283] That is why the view of a pre-time deity "bears the name of Jesus Christ."[284] Here the concept of pre-existent Jesus is helpful in seeing eternity as coincident with time without nullifying the fact that "eternity is *also* before time."[285] Additionally, the pre-existent Jesus underscores God as supra-temporal whereby eternity is taken to "embrace time on all sides."[286] The election of Jesus Christ therefore is Barth's platform in arguing for the suffering of the Trinity.

The incontestable one nature of the Trinity is fortified in Barth's comprehension of the eternality of suffering.[287] This stresses the unbreakable interconnection of the pre-temporal and temporal suffering of God in election. But is it possible to view, at least to some degree, the triune suffering apart from its temporal characteristic? The answer is yes as laid out in this work. Mark Lindsay however differs.

Lindsay reads Barth to argue, "[I]t is impossible to conceive of the Son's suffering if we distance the experience of that suffering from Jesus's essential Jewishness."[288] Lindsay adds that *in the fullness of his divinity*, Christ "bears the suffering of the Cross deep into the Godhead."[289] As the temporal suffering of God looks back into the triune decision to suffer, the latter also looks forward into the former. We cannot separate the two in

282. Excursus in *CD* II/1, 622. The "rule of peace" in this text is indeed the essential condition of God in pre-temporal eternity despite the anticipation of the incarnation because the self-determined suffering and death are means to exalt God, not undermine God's sovereignty.

283. *CD* II/1, 622.

284. *CD* II/1, 622. Barth cites John 8:58 and Eph 1:4.

285. Excursus in *CD* II/1, 623. Italics mine.

286. *CD* II/1, 623.

287. Lee, *Trinitarian Ontology*, 23.

288. Lindsay, *Reading Auschwitz*, 160–61.

289. Lindsay, *Auschwitz*, 160–61.

Barth's perspective of God's history of suffering. But such noetic challenge *is not* insurmountable in Barth's theopaschite view.[290] The Son's suffering (in essence) is derived from the pre-temporal willingness of the Son to obey the Father. In deciding to make humanity part of himself (prior to incarnation), God, in this postulation, is said to have *compromised* himself. The decision to become incarnate *is* the decision to suffer.[291]

Nevertheless, Barth explicates, the dimension of the history of suffering is appreciated in the created time:

> The history of the royal man crowned in His death on Golgotha, Jesus, by being its meaning and content, has this dimension of the eternity of the will of God, which has happened in Him on earth, in time.[292]

This passage speaks of Jesus Christ as the "meaning and content" (*Jesus hat, indem das ihr Sinn und Inhalt ist*) of God's history of suffering. Though we can hardly appreciate the pre-temporal suffering of God, albeit Barth makes it poignant that Jesus Christ gives dimension to what God has eternally willed in himself. It is possible to conceive God's pre-temporal sacrifice, yet deficient without God's temporal sacrifice since the divine self-giving is made concrete in worldly time. The dimension therefore of God's history of suffering is measured in the incarnation, passion, death, resurrection, and glorification of Christ. The temporal manifestation of Christ's suffering is the realization of the pre-temporal divine suffering.

Thus for Barth, God is said to have suffered *not only* as a result of the incarnation, i.e., in the passion and crucifixion, but God's suffering is said to have been *real* (by way of anticipation) in the primal decision. What I think Barth conveys is the appropriation of the affected being of God in God's inclusive act.[293] With Barth, accurately speaking, God suffers in eternity: "And as election by Him it is indirectly identical with that beginning willed and posited by the condescension and self-suffering of God."[294] It implies a pre-creation decision to suffer actualized in the incarnation. Despite the

290. Considering the inseparability of the dual moments in divine suffering as discussed in the previous chapter.

291. In human actuality, God *is yet* to suffer in the world.

292. My own translation of *KD* IV/2, 586: "*Die Geschichte des in seinem Tod auf Golgatha gekrönten königlichen Menschen Jesus hat, indem das ihr Sinn und Inhalt ist, diese Dimension von der Ewigkeit des Willens Gottes her, der in ihm auf Erden, in der Zeit, geschehen ist.*" The ET does not accurately capture what Barth has in mind in formulating God's history of suffering. Cf. *CD* IV/2, 518.

293. *CD* IV/2, 187–88.

294. *CD* II/2, 122.

complexity of Barth's articulation here, we can still say that *the pre-incarnate Christ within the Trinity* is an argument for the possibility of conceiving the triune suffering apart from the suffering of Jesus Christ.

Bruce McCormack is right in thinking that in Barth the "self-positing God" (the Father) is the same as the "self-posited God" (the Son).[295] So if the Son of God anticipates being in Jesus Christ, then the Father is with the Son in this anticipation. In this scenario, the triune God (in pre-incarnation) can never be ontologically conceived aside from the affected God. But contrary to McCormack's assertion, even in light of a historicized interpretation of the Trinity, Barth does not explicitly dispense the notion of impassibility.[296]

3.2 The Affected God and Impassibility

What Barth clearly exclaims is a God who is (im)passible in including humanity in the triune being. But he never, especially in *CD* IV/1–2, implies that impassibility has anything to do with God's un-involvement or extrication with creation, much less with the experience of Jesus Christ. As I argued in chapter 3, what Barth amplifies is a constantly continuous suffering deity. With the atonement as its core, the *kenosis* becomes strictly a matter of divine decision; it is properly viewed in the concurrent event of eternity. In other words, Barth understands the divine suffering as within the theme of the affected God paired with impassibility.[297] He sees the triune God to have embraced both impassibility and passibility as the One who is eternally inclusive; having inclusive freedom (only God possesses) in a continuous selfless love (only God can give).

In conceiving God as faithful, perfect, and selfless in Jesus Christ, Barth interjects (im)passibility right at the heart of the Trinity.[298] George Hunsinger frames the issue of connecting Christ's suffering with the Godhead in three main elements: first, "eternal constituents" wherein God is constituted as triune in essence and will through God's "primordial act";[299] second, "essential predications" in which the Godhead in and of itself is already constituted as having divine attributes, i.e., eternality, simplicity, immutability, impassibility, et al.;[300] third, "material determinations" in which the election and incarnation are contingent upon divine properties

295. McCormack, "Divine Impassibility," 171.

296. *CD* II/1, 370–71; II/2, 79.

297. *CD* IV/1, 164–68.

298. McCormack, "The Passion," 168.

299. Hunsinger, *Reading Barth*, 140.

300. Hunsinger, *Reading Barth*, 140.

whereby God remains altogether God even without these properties, e.g., divine suffering.[301] For Hunsinger, these elements in and of God are key in properly conceiving the Godhead with creation, hence to say that it is *clear* in Barth that God's inner life is affected in the election of Jesus Christ is an overstatement.[302]

Barth attends to the first element only in conjunction with the third because he views God to be eternally constituted in God's determination to be human. Accordingly, the triune God's life is eternally and voluntarily bound with time and with the world.[303] There is no Trinity before or beyond the desire to include humanity within the God-self. What I think is true in Barth's position is that God is the Subject without any rigid "trinitarian differentiation."[304] This is why the essentiality of the Godhead is always *with* Jesus Christ, whether in essence or in flesh. Therefore Jesus Christ's lived reality speaks of the ontological being of God as perfectly and faithfully selfless. This standpoint is a milestone in Barth's quest to speak of the Trinity in election.

What is not an overstatement is McCormack's point that the Barthian conception of Christ's self-emptying has its root in the eternal submission of the Son. It is grounded in the relationship between the Son and the Father as affirmed by the Spirit. This makes the *kenosis* as an ontological reality of the Trinity.[305] In such a premise, McCormack is convinced of the affected Godhead (yet only in part) in the suffering and death of the Son.[306] But still, the passion of Jesus Christ, says McCormack, "is the passion of God Himself."[307] The uncompromising christological view of the Trinity in rendering the divine suffering is somehow missing here. As a result, McCormack, to a degree, has ended up collapsing the Trinity at Calvary, unlike Jürgen Moltmann who has managed to keep the Godhead intact even in discussing who is truly forsaken on the cross.[308] Evidently, for Barth, the trinitarian view of divine suffering is indispensable in his doctrine of God.

301. Hunsinger, *Reading Barth*, 141.

302. Hunsinger, "Election and the Trinity," 195. This supposition is somewhat akin to Peter Kline's assertion that any creaturely reality is ascribed only to Christ's "lived reality" and not to the ontological being of God. Kline, "You Wonder Where the Spirit Went," 96. Also see Marshall, "The Dereliction of Christ and the Impassibility of God," 298.

303. *CD* I/1, 384. Lee, *Revelation and Trinity*, 248.

304. Braaten, "A Trinitarian Theology of the Cross," 117.

305. *CD* IV/1, 238–40. McCormack, "The Doctrine of the Trinity," 104.

306. McCormack, "The Passion," 165.

307. McCormack, "The Passion," 164–65. Cf. *CD* IV/1, 246–47. Also see Webster, *Karl Barth*, 10, 91 and *The Domain of the Word*, 117.

308. McCormack, "The Passion," 168. Moltmann, *Crucified God*, 241–44.

3.3 The Ground for God's Suffering in Eternity

In Barth's talk of divine suffering, the Godhead is "the ultimate ground" for interpreting the suffering of Jesus Christ; not otherwise.[309] The perichoretic act *ad extra* speaks of the outward-looking nature of God. The outward-looking triunity therefore eternally interests itself in what is not God, or even, against God. This is why I think Paul Molnar, with George Hunsinger, argue that there is no inconsistency in Barth's treatment of the Trinity.[310] What Barth conveys, Molnar observes, is a God who exists as eternally triune even without creation.[311] Election only follows the existence of the Trinity and this could not be "logically reversed" except if the incarnation and crucifixion are conceived as essential to God.[312] Yet, I would argue, Barth cannot conceive of the Trinity without election, especially in considering impassibility.

(Im)passibility is not something disadvantageous to Barth's discussion of the Trinity. In fact, the conceptions of the personal Logos and the Godmanhood of Christ are thought to be aesthetically proper to God:

> This is not to qualify what we have already said about the beauty of the being of God as such and of the Trinity in particular. But how do we know God's being and the Trinity except by revelation and therefore from the existence of the Son of God in His union with humanity? We must even say that the Son or Logos of God already displays the beauty of God in a special way in His eternal existence and therefore within the Trinity, as the perfect image of the Father.[313]

The inclusion of the Logos and Jesus Christ, Barth asserts, does not diminish, but rather enhances the understanding of the Trinity in light of election. Therefore the *homoousion*, or "unity of substance of the three distinctive divine persons" is reconceived in Barth's theology.[314] The union of the Logos and Jesus Christ reflects the eternal triunity. This is the beauty of the "once-for-allness" of God; a beauty amplified in glorious perfection as well as in personal association.[315] The eternity of the personal Logos is not at all differ-

309. *CD* III/2, 192–93.

310. Molnar, *Divine Freedom*, 62. Hunsinger, "Election and the Trinity," 112.

311. Molnar, *Divine Freedom*, 63. For Molnar, Barth's doctrine of the Trinity is controlled by his ontological understanding of God. Molnar, "Understanding the Trinity," 38.

312. Molnar, "Understanding the Trinity," 38.

313. Excursus in *CD* II/1, 661.

314. Excursus in *CD* II/2, 96.

315. Excursus in *CD* II/2, 96. *CD* II/1, 615. This aesthetic theology differs from

ent from the eternity of the Trinity.[316] The Trinity, in this sense, is personal within the rubric of God's history of suffering.

I support my argument with the manner by which Barth treats eternity with the Trinity. He attests:

> The whole being and life of God is an activity, both in eternity and in worldly time, both in Himself as Father, Son and Holy Spirit, and in His relation to man and all creation. But what God does in Himself as the Creator and Governor of man is all aimed at the particular act in which it has its centre and meaning. And everything that He wills has its ground and origin in what is revealed as His will in this one act.[317]

On this account, the "ground and origin" of divine suffering is placed in the triune decision-and-act. Barth views this as one divine concurrent history with humankind. The triune governing of creation cannot be taken apart from the triune suffering. The Trinity therefore is synonymous with the triune orientation to humanity; an act of generous commitment.[318] Even at the dawn of Barth's revisit of the Trinity, he already shows interest in the indissoluble triune selflessness. He does this by underscoring the threefold relationship of God's act in the history of suffering.[319] As a result, (im)passibility would be historicized in Barth's thought. How? By referring to his reconfiguration of divine aseity within God's primal decision.[320] Hence Jeff McSwain calls it as "Christo-realism" because it is only in Jesus Christ where we can hint of this vibrant perichoretic act.[321] Though the Trinity exists inclusive of humanity, Barth does not explicitly or implicitly describe such existence to strictly correspond to aseity, i.e., the Godhead's immunity from suffering.

The relational Trinity is foremost in advancing the self-giving of God in election. It is however unclear if Barth argues for the priority of the Trinity over election, or vice-versa, simply because he never fixed his attention, at least in his later theology, on the exclusive God.[322] This is so especially

---

the classic "appearance model" of Hans Urs von Balthasar. See Bychkov and Fodor, *Theological Aesthetics after von Balthasar*, xvi.

316. Excursus in *CD* II/2, 110.

317. *CD* IV/1, 7.

318. *CD* IV/1, 7.

319. *CD* I/1, 340, 382. See §§8–9 of *CD*.

320. *CD* IV/2, 453.

321. McSwain, *Movement of Grace*, 144.

322. McCormack asserts, "No election, no Trinity" as opposed to Hunsinger's position of "No Trinity, no election." Hunsinger, *Reading Barth*, xi.

in terms of analyzing God with God, i.e., existence *per se* and decision to exist. What is obvious here is that the being or existence of the triune God is properly understood in the history of suffering vis-à-vis "eternity-become-time."[323] In other words, the theological themes of ontology, actualization, historicization or even election itself are taken to highlight (not undermine) the triune altruistic act in Jesus Christ.

Evaluation

Since Barth begins his proper theology with Jesus Christ, it is reasonable to consider his doctrine of the Trinity with his Christology. The (im)passible Trinity is supported in view of the Logos for a number of reasons. (1) The triune essence is reflected in the Logos because the Logos fully partakes of the divine essence. It means that the Logos has no independent essence from the Trinity. (2) Since the Trinity and the Logos are parallel in their reality (in Jesus Christ) outside the series of created reality, their reality cannot be different from one another. In fact, the reality of the Trinity coincides with the reality of the Logos. (3) The constancy of the Trinity cannot be handled uniquely from the constancy of the Logos cognizant of the decree. It means that the eternality of the Logos is seen in the eternality of the Trinity. (4) The inclusion of the human essence (Jesus Christ) within the triunity cannot be considered apart from the anticipated flesh of the Logos. There is a place in the Godhead specifically designated for the *Logos incarnandus*. (5) The Trinity and the Logos are both conceived in a single-event in divine history. This means that the two are situated in one eternal continuum of God's reality. (6) The Holy Spirit is not distinctly perceived from the transcendent Spirit of the Logos. In principle, the two are conjoined in the treatment of divine omnipresence. (7) The triune decision to suffer cannot be taken apart from the involvement of the Logos in the crucifixion of Jesus Christ. In Barth's conception, therefore, whatever is ascribed to the Godhead cannot be taken separately from the Logos, and, vice-versa. This is the outcome of Barth's innovative definition of *an-enhypostasis*.[324]

Here, the personal Logos is interconnected with the relational Trinity. It is in this interconnection where Jesus Christ is said to be eternally *within* the Trinity. This is the humanity God has rendered unto himself. If Jesus Christ is the true humanity, so this is the humanity God has assumed in eternity past.[325] In this sense, God has given his humanity to human beings;

323. Cassidy, *Karl Barth on Time*, 89.

324. Haley, *The Humanity of Christ*, 7.

325. Barth suggests a pre-existent human Jesus *with* the Logos. *CD* II/2, 95–99.

not the other way around. More importantly, if this were so, one could argue that there was no pre-temporal divine suffering. But I do not think Barth builds his logic of the eternal suffering of God on the trueness of Christ's humanity, but rather, in the essence of humanity God has determined for himself. This might seem a semi-Kantian approach to the conflicting issues on impassibility because of the eternal nature of such self-determination. God is the absolute objective in accessing the condition of possibility of divine suffering.[326] Hence, we can neither affirm nor deny the projected expectation of God's sacrificial act because of its own domain, i.e., the primal decision. What we can do is to analyze what Barth has in mind in discussing vulnerability in relation to God's decree.

Humanness, in Barth's thought, means vulnerability since only God is aseitic. So God has made himself vulnerable *ad extra* in the decision to include humanity within the Godhead; yet in his vulnerability, God maintains his lordship.[327] The self-determined vulnerability in the Trinity (specifically in the God-manhood of Jesus Christ) also addresses the issue of whether the incarnation itself is God's history of suffering; or the incarnation is only part of that history? Based on my assessment, Barth's trinitarian vista of vulnerability defines God's history of suffering as constantly continuous, vis-à-vis eternity. Barth avoids here the Hegelian collapse of divinity, or in this case the triunity, into history because the reality of the Trinity orders creaturely reality; it can never be the opposite. The events in the economy (in human history) however are crucial in Barth's conception of the triune being. For this reason, the threefold suffering in the incarnated God is said to be fundamental in understanding the being-in-act of the Godhead; its decision to be vulnerable is never independent from the cross-event. Thus Hegel's historical call does not sway Barth's rethinking of the divine personhood. However, Barth's conception of the "antithesis" in view of God contra what is not God, to quite a degree, is a borrowed language from Hegel.[328] In addition, the "apotheosis" of humanity in reaction to God's negation of negation appears to be Hegelian.[329]

The triune act is Barth's antidote against tritheism or the simplistic modalistic Monarchianism. The trajectory of his argumentation on (im)passibility heads in a dialectic direction: the vulnerability of the relational

---

Cortez, *Embodied Souls, Ensouled Bodies*, 23. Also see McSwain, *Simul Sanctification*, 22.

326. Leigh, *Freedom and Flourishing*, 149. La Montagne, *Barth and Rationality*, 216.

327. See Kettler, "The Problem with 'Preferential Love,'" 157–58.

328. Hegel, *Lectures on the Philosophy of Religion*, 71.

329. Goroncy, *Hallowed Be Thy Name*, 234, 238.

Trinity does not nullify the immunity of the immanent Trinity.[330] This, however, does not suggest a Trinity behind the Trinity because the eternal triune God is properly viewed in Jesus Christ. In effect, what I think Barth fails to satisfactorily address are the following: first, the extent to which Christology informs the doctrine of the Trinity; second, the ambiguity of the triune being apart from the being of Jesus Christ; and lastly, the pre-temporal change in the Trinity. What Barth does not fail to do, in this regard, is to *cautiously* tread the road between novelty and conventionality.

The semantic dispute over the use of (im)passibility in relation to the Trinity and election cuts right to the heart of Barth's doctrine of God. The consideration of suffering in view of God's consistent faithfulness, perfection and selflessness is the locus in rightly appropriating the eternality of divine sacrifice. The ontological comprehension of divine suffering, in Barth's mind, can be regarded as a particular epistemological posture due to his over-arching formulation: God's being is in God's act.[331] The things about God (being), and, the way we know the things of God (understanding) are both accessed solely from God's self-revelation. On both counts, God is always triune because God always acts in triunity. We know God always acts as such because the Scriptures tell it so. This is the foundation of Barth's conception of the triune suffering.

Barth gives justice to the conception of God's triadic self-giving when he postulates constancy with actuality. In God's history of suffering, the three Persons are inevitably actualized and historicized. Because for Barth, God is in what God does, then ontology is inseparable from history—whether in divine history or human history. God's history of suffering however is seen in the combined history; the triune inward-outward act is conceived in contingent contemporaneity. This is where the foreordination of God's sacrifice is highlighted. The revelation of triunity is in a pure duration because eternity and time are treated in the being of the Godhead. Thus impassibility and passibility are also merged in conceiving election.[332]

330. Thus we have no knowledge of the invulnerable Trinity since Barth does not dwell on this area.

331. Barth's conception of God as heavily informed by his Christology has fundamental continuity throughout *Church Dogmatics*. Referring to Barth's theological thinking, Klaas Runia puts it, "True, the emphases shift, but that never means a complete rejection of the old emphases. It only means that new accents and aspects are added, and that the old one, with their original function, are now integrated into a more balanced whole." Runia, *Karl Barth's Doctrine of Holy Scripture*, 209.

332. Nathan Barczi comments, "In obedience to this determination, the impassible suffers - in the flesh and as man, but for Barth God *is* this man and so there need be no qualification placed on the statement: the impassible suffers." Barczi, "Support Me in the 'Whelming Flood,'" 18.

It is evident in Barth's later theology that election is constitutive of the trinitarian relations such that there is no immanent trinity as traditionally understood. The argument that God is (im)passible in God's self, and, in union with Jesus Christ on account of his suffering stands plausible. This does not mean however that God is triune only on account of election and thereby inescapably united to the economies of creation and salvation. Barth's God still remains unconstrained in himself even in election. Barth, therefore, always carries the threeness in God in his late doctrine of election, but within the divine unity as it relates to impassibility. The divine sacrificial act *pro nobis* will further the investigation of the inclusive nature of the Godhead.[333] It is invaluable to keep in mind not to sway Barth in directions that would take his theopaschite theology for granted.[334] It would be better if Barth scholars would arrive at a consensus to allow the tensions in reconsidering the suffering of God, namely, the hiddenness of the participation of the Father and Spirit in the Son's agony at Calvary. After all, Barth's theology, as coined by David Hart, reflects "the heterodox schools of thought" because it is largely traditional in letter, yet untraditional in spirit.[335] This description depicts the Barthian treatment of the triune suffering, and also, brings humanity face-to-face with the enigmatic God of election.

And lastly, the fact that the idea of the Son's pre-temporal assumption of human essence is advanced here, it already implies the suffering of God because, for Barth, what is accounted as human undeniably opposes what is divine. When he consistently argues that the Son of God is forever the Son of Man, it means that the being of Jesus Christ itself is one of *eternal self-sacrifice*.[336]

333. Reed, "[Review] Reading Barth with Charity," para. 28.

334. Thus Michael Reeves comments that "all the 'Barth-speak' can feel like razor wire designed to keep out the uninitiated." *Theologians You Should Know*, 310.

335. Hart, "No Shadow of Turning," 186. Also see Nimmo, *Karl Barth: A Guide for the Perplexed*, 201.

336. The conception of the divine and human becoming one yet standing over against each other is encapsulated in Barth's phrase: "God is God, man is man." Anderson and McCormack, *Karl Barth and the Making of Evangelical Theology*, 26.

Conclusion

In seeking to understand how Barth addresses the question of divine (im)passibility, I began with the question of how his doctrine of election changes over time. Throughout the course of this enterprise, I have argued for the increasing role of the Son of God very early on in Barth's doctrine of election. I have shown that in Barth's proposition, God is sovereign in orientating the Son towards humankind. Such a proposition is the product of Barth's yearning to bear witness to the God who is the hope for the world. Here, the disconnect between God and human beings—that was, arguably, emphasized too strongly in the *Römerbrief* period—is reappraised in consideration of the connecting link that is the self-giving of Jesus Christ as Son of God. Divine sovereignty, determination, and representation have emerged as reliable predictors of Barth's initial step in examining the suffering in and of God. This sovereignty carries with it the Western canonical notions of immutability and impassibility.

The first chapter explored the christological revision of the doctrine of election from the *Göttingen Dogmatics* to the *Church Dogmatics*. I argued that Barth has no doctrine of immutability whereby God is said to be immovable or unchangeable in time. This is due to the conviction of God being not invariable because God is eternally sovereign in his will. To press further the issue of God's variability, I placed Barth's assertion on God's being in juxtaposition with Jesus Christ's two natures. If Jesus Christ, the Son of God in the flesh is also the electing God, it prefigures not merely the unity, but also, the oneness of essence of divinity and humanity.

In the period between his lectures on John Calvin and the writing of *Church Dogmatics*, Barth did not discuss divine suffering, immutability, or impassibility because his thought on election was simply not yet developed to the point where he could accommodate these terms. What is apparent is that Barth was trying to find solutions to the classic dispute over the negativity implied in the hidden God, and, God's seemingly unsympathetic attitude towards the reprobate. Also, Barth struggles to couple together God's sovereignty and love with the idea of the Son's *kenosis*. Such struggle is amplified by his lack of extensive exposition of the relation of eternity to worldly time and vice-versa.

This study has indicated that, at this period in Barth's career, Jesus Christ's role in election was still underdeveloped to put forward a truly relational God in and of the election. This could have been remedied if Barth had already formalized his thoughts on the actualization of God's suffering by grounding it in the historicization of the Godhood in Jesus Christ. It has been observed that the historicization of the Logos is absent in this period. A historicized Logos is not a way forward in Barth's desire to speak of God's sovereignty over creation. Nonetheless, Barth's progressive understanding of this actualization gives him a framework to work on expounding its theological repercussions. I argued that his actualistic yet dialectical method of rendering divine transcendence and immanence is effective in explaining the actuality of God in Jesus Christ.

The second chapter took the developed role of Jesus Christ in election into critical consideration. In Barth's exegesis in *CD* II/1–2, God is said to have willed to be affected in being the Substitute. I have identified that it is with this divine freedom that God elects Christ to be the Reprobate on behalf of humanity. Consequently, the election of Christ is considered the election of suffering. In Christ being the Reprobate, it is clear in Barth that though God suffers, God's essentialities are unstifled.

This work has demonstrated that Barth begins to tackle divine suffering in the context of Jesus Christ being the perfect sacrifice. The eternal decree reveals a God who has determined himself to be a suffering God by being in Christ. It is against this backdrop where Barth's reworked doctrine of election impacts his treatment of divine suffering. To that end, the Logos is seen to be closely knitted with Jesus Christ where the two can no longer be regarded separately.

Barth elaborates his engagement on impassibility in the succeeding chapter of this study as God is conceived in Jesus of Nazareth. Such engagement is to the extent where election can no longer be considered apart from divine sacrifice. With his initial engagement with impassibility, Barth finds ways wherein the incarnation speaks directly of the God-self, without any form of guise so as to underscore the true essence of God's self-revelation. Jesus Christ's two natures, therefore, are couched in the sense that the attention is not on the distinction between the two, but rather on the union. I argued that Barth's more cohesive treatment of divinity and humanity becomes the basis of formulating a doctrine of divine constancy. In this constancy, Barth breaks away from the canonical conception of immutability in order to make the best out of what it means to say that God is alive—alive in himself and alive especially in unity with human beings. Such liveliness is integral in considering the election itself.

In Barth's theological reconstruction, constancy in affection, as well as the variableness in sovereignty, are foremost in conceiving the electing God. This is where the notion of divine suffering is seen to have originated, so much so that Barth is ready to say that God does not mind to be inconvenienced *ad extra*. What is inconvenient, in ontological terms, is to include the human essence in the divine life. With this in mind, we cannot consider God to be rigidly in and *for* himself; God wills to be affected because he wills to be this God. But even here, it remains unclear whether Barth sustains the canonical concept of impassibility. What is made clear is that in the election in Jesus Christ, passibility can be viably accommodated. This is part of the known-unknown paradigm in Barth's understanding of God. God is conceived to have himself compromised, but God remained true to his decree. It is in this context that I argued that Barth rethinks the divine freedom to be fully integrated in divine love. This is the crux of what is entailed in God becoming human.

This work has provided a progression from election to reconciliation in *CD* IV/1–2 in view of Christ's role in the works of God. In Barth's reformulation, God volunteers to suffer; yet it is God's choice to suffer that makes God victorious. In being so, God is said to have embraced the *opposites* of the Western orthodox view of divine being, i.e., impassibility and passibility. This provides traction for Barth's engagement with impassibility.

It has been confirmed that although God suffers, he nevertheless overcomes suffering itself. God does this, according to Barth, by having to suffer what befits humans in order to put an end to their suffering. Here, the inevitability of human suffering is viewed against the unnecessary suffering of God. In Jesus Christ, we have witnessed how these dissonant adjectives of suffering meet. This, so it seems, is the bittersweet experience that arises out of combining divine and creaturely realities. It has been argued that divine reality is not suffocated with creaturely reality. In fact, the latter testifies to the vitality of the former.

I cannot find any more fitting approach to divine suffering other than to look at it through the lens of God's concrete decision. It would seem reductionistic to posit in this way, but such a decision, in Barth's schema, is the focal point where we can make sense of how it is possible to associate God with suffering. Thus, this study has recurrently used terms that reflect such an idea; namely, "will," "choice," and "voluntary act," because Barth does not shy away from conceiving God's pain and sorrow as a *self-determination*.

So, is Barth's God impassible in his doctrine of election? Barth's God is (im)passible in election. I had to qualify this by reviewing God's impassibility as Barth conveys it. Since God is perfect *in se* then God is indeed that which is self-determined. Ultimately, I have established that God is not incapable of suffering so God is not incapable of change. When Barth says that God is the Lord who serves, he implies that God is changed in suffering but not at the demise of the God-self. In a sense, Barth's God is therefore both impassible and passible; any penchant for either impassibility or passibility is moderated.

This project has demonstrated that Barth's rendition of divine suffering implies the following: First, God becomes human because of God's unchangeable will. Secondly, God suffers because of his immovable concern for humanity. Thirdly, God voluntarily bears the liabilities of humans because of God's active decision. Fourthly, God assumes reprobation because of God's self-election. Finally, God is humiliated as the Servant as God is exalted as the Lord.

I have also argued that the suffering deity is not a by-product of pantheism or panentheism because Barth maintains the diastasis between Creator and creature. Despite such diastasis, God is seen to have conceded to difficulty and distress in assuming flesh. Barth's articulation of the union of the two natures is fine-tuned to a point wherein suffering is no longer confined to Jesus Christ but includes the Logos. This is the key to Barth's conception of the eternality of divine suffering. I have shown that the inseparable being of the Logos and Jesus Christ is pivotal in Barth's rethinking of the God of election. The (im)passibility of God is derived from the being-in-union of the enfleshed Word.

The most obvious finding to emerge from this study is that divine suffering is not contingent upon what is external of God. The suffering God is not held hostage by the covenant. Rather, the suffering involved is God's initiative and only God has the sole authority to consummate it. I have argued that, in Barth's conception, God exhibits his constancy with himself by suffering since suffering is central to the decree. It is likewise in suffering that God displays his glory because the real essence of divine glory is in sacrifice out of pure love. The results of this investigation show that in explicating God as impassible yet simultaneously passible, Barth is not forced to detract wholesale from the Reformed and Lutheran traditions. This is important in considering how Barth has managed to sustain God's free activity in the incarnation.

In the final exploration of Barth's late Christology, I have witnessed a steady pro-human soteriology. To this end, Barth manages to keep the redemptive assurance in Jesus Christ from the confusion caused by religious relativism. That God's absolute freedom finds its substance and consummation in unexhausted love means that God completely reconciles all humanity to himself in God's self-giving. Here the subjective sense of Christ's representation follows after the objective sense; i.e., Jesus is the meaning and content of God's history of suffering.

God's suffering in the *Logos incarnandus* suggests that the reconciliation of all is also eternal. I have indicated that it is so because human essence is eternally in God by virtue of the decree. It is implied in Barth's reshaped theology that divine suffering is constitutive of the being of God, and it is upon this basis that complete and total reconciliation is also constitutive of being human. Divine freedom, therefore, cannot serve as a Trojan horse against divine grace in Barth's doctrine of election. Indeed, for Barth, God's freedom and God's love are better appreciated if the two are welded together inseparably. Since God in and of himself freely chooses to suffer, this implies that God likewise is a self-sacrificing God.

So what is non-negotiable with Barth's God? Perhaps some would say it is sovereignty, or is immutability, or is constancy. Yet, so far, I have come to conclude that with Barth, all these attributes find their meaning in God's zealous solidarity with humanity; a divine choice, sacrificial decision and act. God's active decision to love freely is the lynchpin in conceiving election within the doctrine of God. Barth's thought in this regard, I have argued, cannot be in any way nuanced; it is a kind of commitment paired with non-contingency. This is why I deem Barth to be Reformed in a controversial fashion; though radical in thought, he upholds a christocentric confession of faith. I have suggested that the central theme of the *Church Dogmatics* is God being the One who loves in freedom. It denotes divine suffering, with a balanced view that God is impassible yet passible—far from being an oxymoron, but as realistically constitutive of God in reconciliation and redemption. However, it can be conceded that the inherent enigma in Barth's conception of God's dialectic attributes is best left open.

The concluding chapter has traced the impact of Barth's recasting of divine suffering on his doctrine of the Trinity. It has become obvious that there is no sustained interest in Barth in the dichotomy between Christology and the doctrine of the Trinity. Since I have established that it is clear in Barth's formulation that the election of Christ is eternal, so Christ's election is also seen as the election of the Godhead. The ontological bearing of triunity on the formulation of *an-enhypostasia* becomes evident here. The suffering of the Trinity in eternity, therefore, can be taken to be constitutive of the suffering of the God-manhood of Jesus Christ; not otherwise. The Trinity is said to have suffered in God being faithful and perfect in selflessness. In this regard, what I think Barth says of Jesus Christ is what he says of the triune God; yet it cannot be the other way around because it could lead to dyophysitism—something which Barth avoids.

In sum, Barth's views on impassibility and the suffering of God changed between 1924 and the early 1940s, and then again in the mid-1950s, because of the reconfiguration of his Christology. This evolution made Barth's doctrine of election truly christocentric—Jesus Christ becomes the Subject and Object of election. In further application, Barth's understanding of the doctrine of impassibility as a critique of Chalcedonian Christology can be taken paradoxically. He agrees with Chalcedon because God in Jesus Christ is seen to have been impassible in suffering; he also disagrees with Chalcedon because the union-in-distinction of Christ's two natures fosters a passible God. The (im)passible deity in and of election implies a reconciled-redeemed humankind since in Christ, all people find their eschatological identity.

The findings from this study make several contributions to the current literature. First, there is no need to conceive God as solely impassible, or solely passible, because God can be truly and actually understood as both in the history of suffering. Second, the God of Barth is said to be constant yet mutable in the way it is perceived dialectically in suffering (Barth's God is not of two minds). Finally, this work has affirmed that the renewed role of the Logos in the one-subject Christ, and, the covenantal theme of election are vital components of Barth's accommodation of a suffering God. These findings aid our understanding of the suffering of God and provide a basis for further research.

The *locus in quo* of divine suffering, I have argued, is in the self-determination of God for humankind. Barth's pursuit of a free God who is also eternally committed to human beings is indeed impressive. This might have sated Barth's desire for solid hope after going through devastating experiences; something he could not find from what humans could offer. Also, this project has affirmed that the semantic disputes between impassibility and passibility, constancy and mutability, distinctiveness and universality are splendidly treated in unison in Barth's mature theology. But it does not hide the fact that Barth, as a dogmatician, continually sends shockwaves in each revision he makes in conceiving God. This, I think, catapults Barth to prominence in a dualistic fashion; i.e., positively and negatively—he becomes the subject of intellectual admiration for some, the object of theological criticism for others.

Returning to the question posed at the beginning of this study, I can now say that Barth's God is indeed a suffering God. God elects himself in eternity to be with us at the cost of *disturbing* the divine inner life. If we take Barth at his word, the misery, agony, and death of Jesus Christ are merely the results of God's self-election. Yet, the death in mind is not at the demise of the sovereign. In the election of suffering, that which is sovereign remains. Barth's God therefore is impassible in his eternal being, but suffers in Jesus Christ; hence God is both passible and impassible in a strictly defined and limited way.

Indeed, it is in the sovereign action of God that the elected suffering is beyond our description. In willing to be moved, God does not merely sympathize with uncounted abused people across the globe—like the Filipino woman recalled at the outset of this project—but, more valuably, God has already shared his glory with them.

Bibliography

Allen, Michael. *Karl Barth's Church Dogmatic: An Introduction and Reader*. London: T. & T. Clark, 2012.

Anderson, Clifford B., and Bruce L. McCormack, eds. *Karl Barth and the Making of Evangelical Theology*. Grand Rapids: Eerdmans, 2015.

Althoff, Dale R. "Freedom and Love in the Thought of Karl Barth." PhD diss., Princeton University, 1976.

Anderson, Cynthia Peters. *Reclaiming Participation: Christ as God's Life for All*. Minneapolis: Fortress, 2014.

Anselm. *Basic Writings*. 2nd ed. Translated by S. N. Deane. La Salle, IL: Open Court, 1962.

Aquinas, Thomas. *Summa Theologiae*. 60 vols. Translated by the Fathers of the English Dominican Province. Charlottesville, VA: InteLex, 1993.

Asbill, Brian D. *The Freedom of God for Us: Karl Barth's Doctrine of Divine Aseity*. London: T. & T. Clark, 2015.

Augustine. *Confessions*. Translated by Henry Chadwick. Oxford: Oxford University Press, 1991.

Aulén, Gustaf. *The Faith of the Christian Church*. Translated by Eric H. Wahlstrom. Reprint, Eugene, OR: Wipf & Stock, 2002.

Ayres, Lewis. *Nicaea and Its Legacy: An Approach to Fourth-Century Trinitarian Theology*. Oxford: Oxford University Press, 2006.

Balthasar, Hans Urs von. *Theo-Drama: Theological Dramatic Theory, Volume V: The Last Act*. San Francisco: Ignatius, 2003.

Barnett, Victoria. *For the Soul of the People: Protestant Protest against Hitler*. 1st ed. Oxford: Oxford University Press, 1998.

Barczi, Nathan A. "Support Me in the 'Whelming Flood': Karl Barth and His Interpreters on Christ, Chalcedon, and the Suffering of the Impassible God." *Academia* (March 2011), 1–22, accessed August 29, 2019. https://www.academia.edu/1971933/Support_Me_in_the_ Whelming_Flood_Karl_Barth_and_His_Interpreters_on_Christ_Chalcedon_and_the_ Suffering_of_the_Impassible God?email_work_card=title.

Barth, Karl. *Anselm, Fides Quarens Intellectum (Faith in Search of Understanding)*. Translated by Ian W. Robertson. New York: The World, 1960.

———. *Christ and Adam: Man and Humanity in Romans 5*. Translated by T. A. Smail. New York: Collier, 1962.

———. *Church Dogmatics*. Vols. I–IV. Translated by G. T. Thomson, Johnston H. Knight, Geoffrey W. Bromiley, Thomas F. Torrance and R. J. Ehrlich, edited by Geoffrey W. Bromiley and Thomas F. Torrance. Edinburgh: T. & T. Clark, 1936, etc.

———. *Church Dogmatics*. Vols. I–IV. Translated by Geoffrey W. Bromiley and Thomas F. Torrance. Edinburgh: T. & T. Clark, 2009.

———. *Deliverance to the Captives*. Translated by M. Wieser. London: SCM, 1961.

———. *Dogmatics in Outline*. Translated by G. T. Thompson. London: SCM, 1966.

———. *The Epistle to the Ephesians*. Edited by R. D. Nelson. Translated by R. M. Wright. Grand Rapids: Baker Academic, 2017.

———. *The Epistle to the Romans*. 2nd ed. Translated by Edward C. Hoskyns. Oxford: Oxford University Press, 1968.

———. *Evangelical Theology: An Introduction*. Translated by Grover Foley. New York: Holt, Rinehart and Winston, 1963.

———. "Fate and Idea in Theology." In *The Way of Theology in Karl Barth: Essays and Comments*, translated by George Hunsinger, edited by H. M. Rumscheidt, 25–61. Allison Park, PA: Pickwick, 1986.

———. "God, Grace and Gospel: Evangelical Theology in the Nineteenth Century." *Scottish Journal of Theology Occasional Papers*, no. 8, (1959) 53–74.

———. *God in Action: Theological Addresses*. Translated by E. G. Homrighausen and Karl J. Ernst. Eugene, OR: Wipf & Stock, 2005.

———. *Gottes Gnadenwahl*. Munich: Kaiser, 1936.

———. *The Göttingen Dogmatics* I, edited by Hannelotte Reiffen. Translated by Geoffrey W. Bromiley. Grand Rapids: Eerdmans, 1991.

———. *The Great Promise*. Eugene, OR: Wipf & Stock, 2004.

———. *The Humanity of God*. Translated by John Newton Thomas and T. Weiser. Louisville, KY: Westminster John Knox, 1996.

———. *Die Kirchliche Dogmatik*. Vol. I–IV. Zürich: Evangelischer Verlag AG. Zollikon, 1959.

———. *The Knowledge of God and the Service of God according to the Teaching of the Reformation: Recalling the Scottish Confession of 1560* (Gifford Lectures 1937 & 1938). Translated by J. L. M. Haire and Ian Henderson. Eugene, OR: Wipf & Stock, 2005.

———. "Letter to Rade, 19.6.1915." In *C. Schwöbel*, edited by Karl Barth and Martin Rade, 132–40. Gütersloh: Mohn, 1981.

———. *On Religion: The Revelation of God as the Sublimation of Religion*. Translated by Garrett Green. London: T. & T. Clark, 2006.

———. "The Paradoxical Nature of the 'Positive Paradox': Answers and Questions to Paul Tillich." In *The Beginnings of Dialectic Theology*, edited by James M. Robinson, 287–96. Richmond, VA: John Knox, 1968.

———. *Pierre Maury: Nous qui pouvons encore parler . . . : Correspondence 1928–1956*. Edited by Bernard Raymond. Lausanne: L'Age d'Homme, 1985.

———. *Prayer and Preaching*. Translated by Sara F. Terrien and B. E. Hooke. London: SCM, 1964.

———. *Protestant Theology in the Nineteenth Century*. Grand Rapids: Eerdmans, 2002.

———. *Revolutionary Theology in the Making: Barth-Thurneysen Correspondence, 1914–1925*. Translated by James D. Smart. Richmond, VA: John Knox, 1964.

———. *Der Römerbrief*. 20th ed. Zürich: TVZ Theologischer Verlag, 1999.

———. *The Teaching of the Church Regarding Baptism*. Translated by Ernest A. Payne. London: SCM, 1948.

———. "A Thank You and a Bow: Kierkegaard's Reveille," *Canadian Journal of Theology* XI (1965) 3–7.

———. *Theology and Church: Shorter Writings 1920–1928*. Translated by Louise P. Smith. Eugene, OR: Wipf & Stock, 2015.

———. *The Theology of John Calvin*. Translated by Geoffrey W. Bromiley. Grand Rapids: Eerdmans, 1995.

———. *The Theology of the Reformed Confessions*. Translated by D. L. Guder and J. J. Guder, Columbia Series in Reformed Theology. Louisville, KY: Westminster John Knox, 2002.

———. *Witness to the Word: A Commentary to John 1*. Lectures at Münster in 1925 and Bonn in 1933, edited by W. Fürst; translated by Geoffrey W. Bromiley. Reprint, Eugene, OR: Wipf & Stock, 2003.

———. *The Word of God and the Word of Man*. Translated by D. Horton. New York: Harper & Row, 1957.

Bauckham, Richard. *God Crucified: Monotheism and Christology in the New Testament*. Didsbury Lectures. Carlisle, UK: Paternoster, 1998.

———. "God's Self-Identification with the Godforsaken in the Gospel of Mark." In *Jesus and the God of Israel: God Crucified and Other Studies on the New Testament's Christology of Divine Identity*, 254–68. Milton Keynes, UK: Paternoster, 2009.

Bender, Kimlyn. *God's Time for Us: Barth on the Reconciliation of Eternity and Time in Jesus Christ*. Bellingham, WA: Lexham, 2016.

———. *Karl Barth's Christological Ecclesiology*. London: Routledge, 2016.

Berkhof, Hendrikus. *Christian Faith: An Introduction to the Study of the Faith*. Reprint, Grand Rapids: Eerdmans, 1990.

Bettenson, Henry. *Documents of the Christian Church*. Oxford: Oxford University Press, 1947.

Billings, Todd. "Scripture." In *The Cambridge Companion to Reformed Theology*, edited by Paul T. Nimmo and David A. Fergusson, 11–27. Cambridge: Cambridge University Press, 2016.

Bloesch, Donald G. *Jesus is Victor! Karl Barth's Doctrine of Salvation*. Eugene, OR: Wipf & Stock, 2001.

Bonhoeffer, Dietrich. *Letters and Papers from Prison*. London: SCM, 1967.

Braaten, Carl E. "A Trinitarian Theology of the Cross." *Journal of Religion* 56, no. 1 (1976) 113–21.

Bradbury, Rosalene. *Cross Theology: The Classical Theologia Crucis and Karl Barth's Modern Theology of the Cross*. Eugene, OR: Pickwick, 2011.

Brian, Rustin E. *Covering Up Luther: How Barth's Christology Challenged the Deus Absconditus That Haunts Modernity*. Veritas. Eugene, OR: Cascade, 2013.

Bromiley, Geoffrey W. *Introduction to the Theology of Karl Barth*. Edinburgh: T. & T. Clark, 2000.

Brouwer, Rinse H. Reeling. *Karl Barth and the Post-Reformation Orthodoxy*. London: Routledge, 2016.

Brunner, Emil. *The Christian Doctrine of God, Dogmatics*. Vol. I. London: Lutterworth, 1949.

Bulgakov, Sergius. *Lamb of God*. Translated by Boris Jakim. Grand Rapids: Eerdmans, 2008.

Burgess, Andrew. *The Ascension in Karl Barth*. London: Routledge, 2017.

Burnett, Richard E., ed. *The Westminster Handbook to Karl Barth*. Louisville, KY: Westminster John Knox, 2013.

Busch, Eberhard. *Barth in Conversation: Vol. 1, 1959–1962*. Louisville, KY: Westminster John Knox, 2017.

———. *The Great Passion: An Introduction to Karl Barth's Theology*. Translated by Geoffrey W. Bromiley, edited by D. L. Guder and J. J. Guder. Grand Rapids: Eerdmans, 2004.

———. *Karl Barth: His Life from Letters and Autobiographical Texts*. International ed. London: SCM, 2012.

Bychkov, Oleg, and James Fodor, eds. *Theological Aesthetics after von Balthasar*. London: Routledge, 2008.

Calvin, John. *Institutes of the Christian Religion*, Vols. I–II. Translated by Henry Beveridge. Peabody, MA: Hendrickson, 2007.

Cane, Anthony. *The Place of Judas Iscariot in Christology*. London: Routledge, 2017.

Capper, John Mark. "Karl Barth's Theology of Joy." PhD thesis, University of Cambridge, 1998.

Carbine, Rosemary P., and Hilda P. Koster, eds. *The Gift of Theology: The Contribution of Kathryn Tanner*. Minneapolis: Fortress, 2015.

Carson, D. A. *Divine Sovereignty and Human Responsibility: Biblical Perspectives in Tension*. London: Marshall, Morgan & Scott, 1981.

Cassidy, James J. *Karl Barth on Time, Eternity, and Jesus Christ*. Bellingham, WA: Lexham, 2016.

Castelo, Daniel. *The Apathetic God: Exploring the Contemporary Relevance of Divine Impassibility*. Paternoster Theological Monographs. Eugene, OR: Wipf & Stock, 2009.

Chadwick, Henry. *Henry Chadwick: Selected Writings*. Grand Rapids: Eerdmans, 2017.

Chételat, Pierre. "Hegel's Philosophy of World History as Theodicy: On Evil and Freedom." In *Hegel and History*, edited by W. Dudley, 215–30. Albany, NY: State University of New York Press, 2009.

Coombe, Cameron. "Reading Scripture with Moltmann: The Cry of Dereliction and the Trinity." *Colloquium* 48, no. 2 (2016) 130–45.

Chung, Paul S. *Karl Barth: God's Word in Action*. Eugene, OR: Cascade, 2008.

Chung, Sung Wook, ed. *Karl Barth and Evangelical Theology*. Milton Keynes, UK: Paternoster, 2006.

———. "Seeds of Ambivalence Sown: Barth's Use of Calvin in Der Römerbrief II (1922)." *Evangelical Quarterly* 73, no. 1 (2001) 37–58.

Clark, R. S., ed. *Covenant, Justification and Pastoral Ministry: Essays by the Faculty of Westminster Seminary California*. Phillipsburg: P & R, 2007.

Clough, David. *Ethics in Crisis: Interpreting Barth's Ethics*. Abingdon, UK: Routledge, 2016.

Coakley, Sarah. *God, Sexuality and the Self: An Essay 'On the Trinity'*. Cambridge: Cambridge University Press, 2013.

———. *Powers and Submission: Spirituality, Philosophy and Gender*. Oxford: Blackwell, 2002.

Cocksworth, Ashley. *Karl Barth on Prayer*. London: Bloomsbury T. & T. Clark, 2015.

Collins, Paul M. *Trinitarian Theology West and East: Karl Barth, the Cappadocians, and John Zizioulas*. Oxford: Oxford University Press, 2001.

Colwell, John. *Actuality and Provisionality: Eternity and Election in the Theology of Karl Barth.* Eugene, OR: Wipf & Stock, 2011.

Cortez, Marc. *Embodied Souls, Ensouled Bodies: An Exercise in Christological Anthropology and Its Significance for the Mind/Body Debate*, 16–39. London: Bloomsbury T. & T. Clark, 2008.

Crisp, Oliver D. *Deviant Calvinism: Broadening Reformed Theology.* Minneapolis: Fortress, 2014.

Cross, Terry L. *Dialectic in Karl Barth's Doctrine of God.* New York: Lang, 2001.

Daley, Brian E. *God Visible: Patristic Christology Reconsidered.* Oxford: Oxford University Press, 2018.

Davies, Brian, and G. R. Evans, eds. *Anselm of Canterbury: The Major Works.* Oxford: University of Oxford, 1998.

Dawson, R. Dale *The Resurrection in Karl Barth.* Reprint, London: Routledge, 2017.

Deddo, Gary. *Karl Barth's Theology of Relations*, Vol. 1. Eugene, OR: Wipf & Stock, 2015.

Dempsey, Michael T., ed. *Trinity and Election in Contemporary Theology.* Grand Rapids: Eerdmans, 2011.

de Vera, Nixon. "The Controversy of a Calvinist Theology on Election." Research essay, University of Divinity, 2015.

———. "The Crack in the Rock: Seeing God through the Darkest Times." *Adventist World* 5, no. 3 (2009) 12–13.

Diller, Kevin. "Karl Barth and the Relationship between Philosophy and Theology." *Heythrop Journal* 60 (2010) 1035–52.

Dolamo, Ramathate. "Karl Barth's Contribution to the German Church Struggle against National Socialism." *Studia Historiae Ecclesiasticae* 36 (2010) 233–50.

Dolezal, James E. *God without Parts. Divine Simplicity and the Metaphysics of God's Absoluteness.* Eugene, OR: Pickwick, 2011.

Dreyer, Wim A. "Barth on Election and the Canons of Dort." *In die Skriflig* 52, no. 2 (2018) 1–9.

Drury, John L. *The Resurrected God: Karl Barth's Trinitarian Theology of Easter.* Minneapolis: Fortress, 2014.

Eckman, James P. *Exploring Church History: A Guide to History, World Religions, and Ethics.* Wheaton, IL: Crossway, 2008.

Elgendy, Rick. "Hope, Cynicism, and Complicity: Worldly Resistance in Reinhold Nieburh's Criticism of Karl Barth." *Journal of Political Theology* 17, no. 2 (2016) 182–98.

Emery, Gilles. "The Immutability of the God of Love and the Problem of Language Concerning the 'Suffering of God.'" In *Divine Impassibility and the Mystery of Human Suffering*, edited by James F. Keating and Thomas Joseph White, 27–76. Grand Rapids: Eerdmans, 2009.

Esminger, Sven. *Karl Barth's Theology as a Resource for a Christian Theology of Religions.* London: Bloomsbury T. & T. Clark, 2014.

Fairbairn, Donald. *Grace and Christology in the Early Church.* Oxford: Oxford University Press, 2003.

———. "Patristic Exegesis and Theology: The Cart and the Horse." *Westminster Theological Journal* 69, no. 1 (2007) 1–19.

Farlow, Matthew. *The Dramatizing of Theology: Humanity's Participation in God's Drama.* Eugene, OR: Pickwick, 2017.

Farrow, Douglas. *Ascension and Ecclesia: On the Significance of the Doctrine of the Ascension for Ecclesiology and Christian Cosmology*. Grand Rapids: Eerdmans, 1999.

Fesko, John V. *Beyond Calvin: Union with Christ and Justification in Early Modern Reformed Theology (1517–1700)*. Göttingen: Vandenhoeck & Ruprecht, 2012.

Fiddes, Paul S. *The Creative Suffering of God*. Oxford: Clarendon, 1992.

Gallaher, Brandon. *Freedom and Necessity in Modern Trinitarian Theology*. Oxford: Oxford University Press, 2016.

Galli, Mark. *Karl Barth: An Introductory Biography for Evangelicals*. Grand Rapids: Eerdmans, 2017.

Garr, John D. *Christian Fruit—Jewish Root: Theology of Hebraic Restoration*. Atlanta: Golden Key, 2015.

Gavrilyuk, Paul L. "God's Impassible Suffering in the Flesh." In *Divine Impassibility and the Mystery of Human Suffering*, edited by James F. Keating and Thomas Joseph White, 127–49. Grand Rapids: Eerdmans, 2009.

———. "The Kenotic Theology of Sergius Bulgakov." *Scottish Journal of Theology* 58, no. 3 (2005) 251–69.

———. *The Suffering of the Impassible God: Dialectics of Patristic Thought*. Oxford: Oxford University Press, 2006.

Giberson, Karl W., ed. *Abraham's Dice: Chance and Providence in the Monotheistic Traditions*. Oxford: Oxford University Press, 2016.

Gibson, David. *Reading the Decree: Exegesis, Election and Christology in Calvin and Barth*. London: T. & T. Clark, 2009.

Gockel, Matthias. *Barth and Schleiermacher on the Doctrine of Election: A Systematic-Theological Comparison*. Oxford: Oxford University Press, 2006.

———. "Harmony without Identity: A Comparison of the Theology of Election in Pierre Maury and Karl Barth." In *Election, Barth, and the French Connection: How Pierre Maury Gave a "Decisive Impetus" to Karl Barth's Doctrine of Election*, edited by Simon Hattrell, 129–50. Eugene, OR: Pickwick, 2016.

———. "How to Read Karl Barth with Charity: A Critical Reply to George Hunsinger." *Modern Theology* 32, no. 2 (2016) 259–67.

Godsey, John D. *Karl Barth: How I Changed My Mind*. Richmond, VA: John Knox, 1966.

Goetz, Ronald G. "The Karl Barth Centennial: An Appreciative Critique." *Christian Century*, May 7, 1986, 458–63.

———. "The Suffering God: The Rise of a New Orthodoxy." *Christian Century* 103 (1986) 385–89.

Goroncy, Jason. *Hallowed Be Thy Name: The Sanctification of All in the Soteriology of P. T. Forsyth*. London: T. & T. Clark, 2013.

———. "Sanctification." In *The Wiley Blackwell Companion to Karl Barth*, edited by George Hunsinger and Keith L. Johnson, 303–16. Chichester, UK: Wiley Blackwell, 2019.

———. "'That God May Have Mercy upon All': A Review-Essay of Matthias Gockel's *Barth and Schleiermacher on the Doctrine of Election*." *Journal of Reformed Theology* 2, no. 2 (2008) 113–30.

Gorringe, Timothy J. *Karl Barth: Against Hegemony*. 1st ed. Oxford: Clarendon, 1999.

Graham, J. Michele. *Representation and Substitution in the Atonement Theologies of Dorothee Sölle, John Macquarrie, and Karl Barth*. New York: Lang, 2005.

Grant, Robert. *The Early Christian Doctrine of God*. Reprint, Charlottesville, VA: University of Virginia Press, 2015.

Grillmeier, Aloys. *Christ in the Christian Tradition: From the Apostolic Age to Chalcedon (451)*. Vol. 1. 2nd rev. ed. Louisville, KY: Westminster John Knox, 1988.

Griswold, Daniel M. *Triune Eternality: God's Relationship to Time in the Theology of Karl Barth*. Minneapolis: Fortress, 2015.

Grudem, Wayne. *Systematic Theology: An Introduction to Biblical Doctrine*. Grand Rapids: Zondervan, 1994.

Gunton, Colin E. *Act and Being: Towards a Theology of the Divine Attributes*. Grand Rapids: Eerdmans, 2003.

———. *The Christian Faith: An Introduction to Christian Doctrine*. Oxford: Blackwell, 2002.

———. "The Doctrine of God: Karl Barth's Doctrine of Election as Part of his Doctrine of God." *The Journal of Theological Studies* 25, no. 2 (1974) 381–92.

———. *Theology through the Theologians: Selected Essays 1972–1975*. Edinburgh: T. & T. Clark, 1996.

Guretzki, David. *Explorer's Guide to Karl Barth*. Downers Grove, IL: IVP Academic, 2016.

Habets, Myk, ed. *Third Article Theology: A Pneumatological Dogmatics*. Minneapolis: Fortress, 2016.

Haley, James P. *The Humanity of Christ: The Significance of the Anhypostasis and Enhypostasis in Karl Barth's Christology*. Eugene, OR: Pickwick, 2017.

Hall, Stuart G. "The Christology of Melito." *Studia Patristica* 13 (1963) 154–68.

———, ed. *Melito of Sardis*. 1st ed. Oxford: Clarendon, 1979.

Harasta, Eva, and Brian Brock. *Evoking Lament: A Theological Discussion*. Edinburgh: T. & T. Clark, 2009.

Härle, Wilfried. "Der Aufruf der 93 Intellektuellen und Karl Barths Bruch mit der liberalen Theologie." *Zeitschrift für Theologie und Kirche* 72 (1975) 207–24.

Harnack, Adolf von. *History of Dogma*, Vol. 3. 3rd ed. Kensington, UK: CreateSpace Independent, 2015.

Harrison, Victoria S., ed. *The History of Evil in the Early Twentieth Century: 1900–1950 CE*. Vol. 5. London: Routledge, 2018.

Hart, David Bentley. "No Shadow of Turning: On Divine Impassibility." *Pro Ecclesia* 11, no. 2 (2002) 184–206.

Hartwell, Herbert. *The Theology of Barth: An Introduction*. London: Duckworth, 1964.

Hauerwas, Stanley. *With the Grain of the Universe: The Church's Witness and Natural Theology*. Reprint, Grand Rapids: Baker Academic, 2013.

Hector, Kevin W. "God's Triunity and Self Determination and Self-Determination: A Conversation with Karl Barth, Bruce McCormack and Paul Molnar." *International Journal of Systematic Theology* 7 (2005) 246–61.

Hegel, G. W. F. *Lectures on the Philosophy of Religion*. Edited by P. C. Hodgson. 1st ed. Oxford: Oxford University Press, 2006.

Helm, Paul. *John Calvin's Ideas*. Oxford: Oxford University Press, 2004.

Henry, Carl F. H. *God Who Stands and Stays, Volume VI: God Who Stands and Stays, Part Two*. Wheaton, IL: Crossway, 1999.

Heppe, Heinrich. *Reformed Dogmatics*. Reprint, edited by E. Bizer. Translated by G. T. Thomson. Reprint, Eugene, OR: Wipf & Stock, 2008.

Heron, Alaisdair I. C. "Karl Barth: A Personal Engagement." In *The Cambridge Companion to Karl Barth*, edited by John B. Webster, 296–306. Cambridge: Cambridge University Press, 2006.

Higton, Mike. *Christ, Providence, and History: Hans W. Frei's Public Theology*. London: T. & T. Clark, 2004.

Hitchcock, Nathan. *Karl Barth and the Resurrection of the Flesh: The Loss of the Body in Participatory Eschatology*. Cambridge: James Clarke, 2013.

Hocking, Jeffrey S. *Freedom Unlimited: Liberty, Autonomy, and Response-ability in the Open Theism of Clark Pinnock*. Eugene, OR: Wipf & Stock, 2010.

Holmes, Christopher R. J. *Revisiting the Doctrine of the Divine Attributes: In Dialogue with Karl Barth, Eberhard Jüngel, and Wolf Krötke*. Bern: Lang, 2007.

Holmes, Stephen R. *The Quest for the Trinity: The Doctrine of God in Scripture, History and Modernity*. Downers Grove, IL: InterVarsity, 2012.

Hoogsteen, Ted. "Vere Deus, Vere Homo: A Comparative Study between Calvin and Barth on the Basis of the extra Calvinisticum and the communication idiomatum." PhD diss., Theologische Hogeschool te Kampen, 1983.

Hunsinger, George. *Disruptive Grace: Studies in the Theology of Karl Barth*. Grand Rapids: Eerdmans, 2002.

———. "Election and the Trinity: Twenty-five Theses on the Theology of Karl Barth." In *Trinity and Election in Contemporary Theology*, edited by M. T. Dempsey, 91–114. Grand Rapids: Eerdmans, 2011.

———. *Evangelical, Catholic and Reformed: Essays on Barth and Related Themes*. Grand Rapids: Eerdmans, 2015.

———. "*Mysterium Trinitatis*: Barth's Conception of Eternity." In *For the Sake of the World: Karl Barth and the Future of Ecclesial Theology*, edited by George Hunsinger, 165–90. Grand Rapids: Eerdmans, 2004.

———. *How to Read Karl Barth: The Shape of His Theology*. Oxford: Oxford University Press, 1993.

———. *Karl Barth and Radical Politics*. 2nd ed. Eugene, OR: Wipf & Stock, 2017.

———. *Reading Barth with Charity: A Hermeneutical Proposal*. Grand Rapids: Baker Academic, 2015.

———. "Truth as Self-Involving: Barth and Lindbeck on the Cognitive and Performative Aspects of Truth in Theological Discourse." *Journal of the American Academy of Religion* 61, no. 1 (1993) 41–56.

Jenson, Robert W. *Alpha and Omega: A Study in the Theology of Karl Barth*. Eugene, OR: Wipf & Stock, 2002.

———. "Cur Deus Homo? The Election of Jesus Christ in the Theology of Karl Barth." PhD diss., Heidelberg University, 1959.

———. *God after God: The God of the Past and the God of the Future, Seen in the Work of Karl Barth*. Minneapolis: Fortress, 2010.

———. "Ipse Pater Non Est Impassibilis." In *Divine Impassibility and the Mystery of Human Suffering*, edited by James F. Keating and Thomas Joseph White, 117–26. Grand Rapids: Eerdmans, 2009.

———. "Karl Barth." In *The Modern Theologians: An Introduction to Christian Theology in the Twentieth Century*, 2nd ed., edited by David F. Ford, 21–35. Oxford: Blackwell, 1977.

———. *Systematic Theology*. Vol. I. Oxford: Oxford University Press, 2001.

———. *The Triune Identity: God according to the Gospel.* Reprint, Eugene, OR: Wipf & Stock, 2002.

Johnson, Adam J. *God's Being in Reconciliation: The Theological Basis of the Unity and Diversity of the Atonement in the Theology of Karl Barth.* London: T. & T. Clark, 2014.

———, ed. *T. & T. Clark Companion to Atonement.* London: Bloomsbury T. & T. Clark, 2017.

Johnson, Keith L. *Karl Barth and the Analogia Entis.* London: T. & T. Clark, 2010.

Johnson, W. Stacy. *The Mystery of God: Karl Barth and the Postmodern Foundations of Theology.* Louisville, KY: Westminster John Knox, 1997.

Jones, Paul Dafydd. *The Humanity of Christ: Christology in Karl Barth's Church Dogmatics.* London: T. & T. Clark, 2008.

———. "The Riddle of Gethsemane: Barth on Jesus's Agony in the Garden." In *Reading the Gospels with Karl Barth*, edited by Daniel L. Migliore, 124–54. Grand Rapids: Eerdmans, 2017.

Jüngel, Eberhard. *God as the Mystery of the World: On the Foundation of the Theology of the Crucified One in the Dispute between Theism and Atheism.* Translated by Darrell L. Guder. Grand Rapids: Eerdmans, 2014.

———. *God's Being Is in Becoming: The Trinitarian Being of God in the Theology of Karl Barth.* London: T. & T. Clark, 2004.

———. *Karl Barth, A Theological Legacy.* Translated by G. E. Paul. Louisville, KY: Westminster John Knox, 1986.

Kaltwasser, Cambria. "Karl Barth on What Makes Us Human." *The Thread* (November 2017). https://thethread.ptsem.edu/articles-1/barth-on-what-makes-us-human.

Kärkkäinen, Veli-Matti. *Christ and Reconciliation: A Constructive Christian Theology for the Pluralistic World.* Grand Rapids: Eerdmans, 2013.

Keating, James F., and Thomas Joseph White, eds. *Divine Impassibility and the Mystery of Human Suffering* Grand Rapids: Eerdmans, 2009.

Kelly, J. N. D. *Early Christian Doctrines.* Rev. ed. New York: Harper & Row, 1978.

Kettler, Christian D. *The Breadth and Depth of the Atonement: The Vicarious Humanity of Christ in Church, the World, and the Self.* Eugene, OR: Pickwick, 2017.

———. "The Problem with 'Preferential Love': *Should Love Depend upon My Initiative?* A Challenge for Reformed Theology—An Answer from the Vicarious Humanity of Christ." In *Evangelical Calvinism: Volume 2: Dogmatics and Devotion*, edited by Myk Habets and Bobby Grow, 152–83. Eugene, OR: Pickwick, 2017.

Kim, Jinhyok. *The Spirit of God and the Christian Life: Reconstructing Karl Barth's Pneumatology.* Minneapolis: Fortress, 2014.

Kirkland, Scott A. *Into the Far Country: Karl Barth and the Modern Subject.* Minneapolis: Fortress, 2016.

Kitamori, Kazoh. *Theology of the Pain of God: The First Original Theology from Japan.* Eugene, OR: Wipf & Stock, 2005.

Klempa, William. "Barth as a Scholar and Interpreter of Calvin." *Seventh Colloquium on Calvin Studies* (1994) 31–49.

———. *A Unique Time of God: Karl Barth's WWI Sermons.* Louisville, KY: Westminster John Knox, 2016.

Kline, Peter. "You Wonder Where the Spirit Went." In *Karl Barth in Conversation*, edited by W. Travis Mcmaken and David W. Congdon, 91–108. Eugene, OR: Pickwick, 2014.

Klooster, Fred H. *The Significance of Barth's Theology: An Appraisal: With Special Reference to Election and Reconciliation*. Eugene, OR: Wipf & Stock, 2006.

Kojiro, Masami. "God's Eternal Election in the Theology of Karl Barth." PhD diss., University of Aberdeen, 1996.

Komline, Han-luen Kantzer. "Friendship and Being: Election and Trinitarian Freedom in Moltmann and Barth." *Modern Theology* 29, no. 1 (2013) 1–17.

Küng, Hans. *Justification: The Doctrine of Karl Barth and a Catholic Reflection*. Louisville, KY: Westminster John Knox, 2004.

LaCugna, Catherine Mowry. *God for Us: The Trinity and Christian Life*. San Francisco: HarperSanFrancisco, 1991.

La Montagne, D. Paul. *Barth and Rationality: Critical Realism in Theology*. Eugene, OR: Cascade, 2012.

Langdon, Adrian. *God the Eternal Contemporary: Trinity, Eternity, and Time in Karl Barth*. Eugene, OR: Wipf & Stock, 2012.

Lauber, David. *Barth on the Descent into Hell: God, Atonement and the Christian Life*. London: Routledge, 2017.

Lawrenz, Mel. *The Christology of John Chrysostom*. Lewiston, NY: Mellen, 1997.

Lee, Daniel D. *Double Particularity: Karl Barth, Contextuality, and Asian American Theology*. Minneapolis: Fortress, 2017.

Lee, Jung Young. *God Suffers For Us: A Systematic Inquiry into a Concept of Divine Passibility*. Leiden: Nijhoff, 1974.

Lee, Sang Hoon. *Trinitarian Ontology and Israel in Robert W. Jenson's Theology*. Eugene, OR: Pickwick, 2016.

Lee, Sang-Hwan. *Revelation and Trinity: The Formative Influence of the Revelation of the Triune God in Calvin's 1559 Institutes and Barth's Church Dogmatics*. Bloomington, IN: iUniverse, 2011.

Leftow, Brian. "God's Impassibility, Immutability, and Eternality." In *The Oxford Handbook of Aquinas*, edited by B. Davies and E. Stump, 173–86. Oxford: Oxford University Press, 2017.

———. "Immutability." *Stanford Encyclopedia of Philosophy* (05 August 2014). http://www.plato. stanford.edu/entries/immutability/#3.

Leigh, Robert. *Freedom and Flourishing: Being, Act, and Knowledge in Karl Barth's Church Dogmatics*. Eugene, OR: Cascade, 2017.

Leith, John H. *John Calvin's Doctrine of the Christian Life*. Eugene, OR: Wipf & Stock, 1989.

Levering, Matthew. "Augustine and Aquinas on the Good Shepherd: The Value of an Exegetical Tradition." In *Aquinas the Augustinian*, edited by M. Dauphinais, B. David and M. Levering, 205–42. Washington, DC: Catholic University of America Press, 2007.

———. "Christ, the Trinity, and Predestination: McCormack and Aquinas." In *Trinity and Election in Contemporary Theology*, edited by M. T. Dempsey, 244–76. Grand Rapids: Eerdmans, 2011.

Lewis, Alan E. *Between Cross and Resurrection: A Theology of Holy Saturday*. Grand Rapids: Eerdmans, 2003.

Lindsay, Mark R. "Barth, Berkovits, Birkenau: On Whether It Is Possible to Understand Karl Barth as a Post-Holocaust Theologian." In *Karl Barth: Post-Holocaust Theologian?* edited by George Hunsinger, 1–13. London: Bloomsbury T. & T. Clark, 2018.

———. *Barth, Israel, and Jesus: Karl Barth's Theology of Israel*. Farnham, UK: Ashgate, 2007.

———. *The Covenanted Solidarity: The Theological Basis of Karl Barth's Opposition to Nazi Antisemitism and the Holocaust*. New York: Lang, 2001.

———. "Ecclesiology and Election in the Early Fathers." *Colloquium* 49, no. 1 (2017) 74–88.

———. "Pierre Maury, Karl Barth, and the Evolution of Election." In *Election, Barth, and the French Connection: How Pierre Maury Gave a "Decisive Impetus" to Karl Barth's Doctrine of Election*, edited by Simon Hattrell, 107–28. Eugene, OR: Pickwick, 2016.

———. *Reading Auschwitz with Barth: The Holocaust as Problem and Promise for Barthian Theology*. Eugene, OR: Wipf & Stock, 2014.

Livingstone, E. A., ed. *The Oxford Dictionary of the Christian Church*. 3rd ed. Oxford: Oxford University Press, 1997.

Loewe, William P. "Two Theologians of the Cross: Karl Barth and Jürgen Moltmann." *The Thomist* 41, no. 4 (1977) 510–39.

Lohse, Bernhard. *A Short History of Christian Doctrine*. Minneapolis: Fortress, 1985.

Long, D. Stephen. *Saving Karl Barth: Hans Urs von Balthasar's Preoccupation*. Minneapolis: Fortress, 2014.

Loon, Hans van. *The Dyophysite Christology of Cyril of Alexandria*. Leiden: Brill, 2009.

Luther, Martin. *Luther's Works*, 55 vols. Edited by J. J. Pelikan and H. T. Lehmann. Philadelphia: Fortress, 1986.

MacDonald, Neil B. *Karl Barth and the Strange New World within the Bible: Barth, Wittgenstein, and the Metadilemmas of the Enlightenment*. Carlisle, UK: Paternoster, 2001.

MacKinnon, Donald. "Philosophy and Christology." In *Borderlands of Theology: And Other Essays*, 55–81. Eugene, OR: Wipf & Stock, 2011.

———. *Themes in Theology: The Threefold Cord, Essays in Philosophy, Politics and Theology*. London: Bloomsbury T. & T. Clark, 1987.

Marga, Amy. *Karl Barth's Dialogue with Catholicism in Göttingen and Münster: Its Significance for His Doctrine of God*. Tübingen: Mohr Siebeck, 2010.

Marshall, Bruce D. "The Dereliction of Christ and the Impassibility of God." In *Divine Impassibility and the Mystery of Human Suffering*, edited by James F. Keating and Thomas Joseph White, 246–98. Grand Rapids: Eerdmans, 2009.

Maury, Pierre. *Election, Barth, and the French Connection: How Pierre Maury Gave a "Decisive Impetus" to Karl Barth's Doctrine of Election*. Edited by Simon Hattrell. Eugene, OR: Pickwick, 2016.

———. "Election et Foi." *Foi et Vie* 27 (1936) 203–23. German translation: *Erwählung und Glaube*. Zollikon-Zurich: Theologischer, 1940.

———. *Predestination and Other Papers*. Translated by E. Hudson. London: SCM, 1960.

McCormack, Bruce L. "Divine Impassibility or Simply Divine Constancy? Implications of Karl Barth's Later Christology for Debates over Impassibility." In *Divine Impassibility and the Mystery of Human Suffering*, edited by James F. Keating and Thomas Joseph White, 150–86. Grand Rapids: Eerdmans, 2009.

———. "The Doctrine of the Trinity: An Attempt to Reconstruct Barth's Doctrine in the Light of His Later Christology." In *Trinitarian Theology After Barth*, edited by Myk Habets and Phillip Tolliday, 87–118. Eugene, OR: Wipf & Stock, 2011.

———. *Engaging the Doctrine of God: Contemporary Protestant Perspectives*. Grand Rapids: Baker, 2008.

———. *Karl Barth's Critically Realistically Dialectical Theology*. Oxford: Oxford University Press, 1997.

———. "Karl Barth's Christology as a Resource for a Reformed Version of Kenoticism." *International Journal of Systematic Theology* 8, no. 3 (2006) 243–51.

———. "Longing for a New World: On Socialism, Eschatology and Apocalyptic in Barth's Early Dialectical Theology." In *Theologie im Umbruch der Moderne: Karl Barths frühe Dialektische Theologie*, edited by Georg Pfleiderer and Harald Matern, 135–49. Zürich: Theologischer Verlaine, 2014.

———. *Orthodox and Modern: Studies in the Theology of Karl Barth*. Grand Rapids: Baker Academic, 2008.

———. "Participation in God, Yes, Deification, No: Two Modern Protestant Responses to an Ancient Question." In *Denkwürdiges Geheimnis. Beiträge zur Gotteslehre. Festschrift für Eberhard Jüngel zum 70. Geburtstag*, edited by I. U. Dalferth, J. Fischer and H. P. Grosshans, 347–74. Tübingen: Mohr Siebeck, 2006.

———. "The Passion of God Himself: Barth on Jesus's Cry of Dereliction." In *Reading the Gospels with Karl Barth*, edited by Daniel L. Migliore, 155–72. Grand Rapids: Eerdmans, 2017.

McCormack, Bruce L., and Clifford B. Anderson, eds. *Karl Barth and American Evangelism*. Grand Rapids: Eerdmans, 2011.

McDonald, Suzanne. *Re-Imaging Election: Divine Election as Representing God to Others and Others to God*. Grand Rapids: Eerdmans, 2010.

McDowell, John C. "Afterword." In *Election, Barth, and the French Connection: How Pierre Maury Gave a "Decisive Impetus" to Karl Barth's Doctrine of Election*, edited by Simon Hattrell, 155–73. Eugene, OR: Pickwick, 2016.

———. *Hope in Barth's Eschatology: Interrogations and Transformations beyond Tragedy*. Farnham, UK: Ashgate, 2001.

———. "Learning Where to Place One's Hope: The Eschatological Significance of Election in Barth." *Scottish Journal of Theology* 53 (2000) 316–38.

———. "Much Ado about Nothing: Karl Barth's Being Unable to Do Nothing about Nothingness." *International Journal of Systematic Theology* 4, no. 3 (2002) 319–35.

McDowell, John C., and Mike Higton. *Conversing with Barth*. Aldershot, UK: Ashgate, 2004.

McFarland, Ian. "Challenges in Christology." *St John's Timeline* (April 2017). https://m.youtube. com/watch?v=mqkxHLBjoeQ.

———. "Spirit and Incarnation: Toward a Pneumatic Chalcedonianism." *International Journal of Systematic Theology* 16 (2014) 143–58.

McGinnis, Andrew M. *The Son of God beyond the Flesh: A Historical and Theological Study of the Extra Calvinisticum*. London: T. & T. Clark, 2016.

McGrath, Alister E. *The Christian Theology Reader*. Oxford: Wiley Blackwell, 2017.

———. *The Making of Modern German Christology, 1750–1990*. 2nd ed. Reprint, Eugene, OR: Wipf & Stock, 2005.

McGuckin, John A. *St. Cyril of Alexandria: The Christological Controversy: Its History, Theology, and Texts*. Reprint, Crestwood, NY: St Vladimir's Seminary Press, 2010.

McKenny, Gerald. "'Freed by God for God': Divine Action and Human Action in Karl Barth's *Evangelical Theology* and Other Late Works." In *Karl Barth and the Making of Evangelical Theology*, edited by Clifford B. Anderson and Bruce L. McCormack, 119–38. Grand Rapids: Eerdmans, 2015.

McKim, Donald K. *Theological Turning Points: Major Issues in Christian Thought.* Louisville, KY: Westminster John Knox, 1989.

McMaken, W. Travis, and David W. Congdon, eds. *Karl Barth in Conversation.* Eugene, OR: Wipf & Stock, 2014.

McSwain, Jeff. *Movement of Grace: The Dynamic Christo-realism of Barth, Bonhoeffer, and the Torrances.* Eugene, OR: Wipf & Stock, 2010.

———. *Simul Sanctification: Barth's Hidden Vision for Human Transformation.* Eugene, OR: Pickwick, 2018.

Meredith, Anthony. *Christian Philosophy in the Early Church.* London: T. & T. Clark, 2012.

Meyendorff, John. "Chalcedonians and Monophysites after Chalcedon." *The Greek Orthodox Theological Review* 10, no. 2 (1964–65) 16–30.

Migliore, Daniel L. "The Journey of God's Son: Barth and Balthasar on the Parable of the Lost Son." In *Reading the Gospels with Karl Barth*, edited by Daniel L. Migliore, 80–105. Grand Rapids: Eerdmans, 2017.

Mikkelsen, Hans Vium. *Reconciled Humanity: Karl Barth in Dialogue.* Grand Rapids: Eerdmans, 2010.

Milbank, John, et al., eds. *Radical Orthodoxy: A New Theology.* London: Routledge, 1999.

Molnar, Paul D. "Can the Electing God be God without Us? Some Implications of Bruce McCormack's Understanding of Barth's Doctrine of Election for the Doctrine of the Trinity." *Neue Zeitschrift für Systematiche Theologie und Religionsphilosophie* 49, no. 2 (2007) 199–222.

———. *Divine Freedom and the Doctrine of the Immanent Trinity: In Dialogue with Karl Barth and Contemporary Theology.* 2nd ed. London: Bloomsbury T. & T. Clark, 2017.

———. "Incarnation." In *The Westminster Handbook to Karl Barth*, edited by Richard E. Burnett, 111–14. Louisville, KY: Westminster John Knox, 2013.

———. "Understanding the Trinity: Occasion for Unity or Division." *Colloquium* 49, no. 2 (2017) 36–54.

Moltmann, Jürgen. *The Crucified God.* Anniversary ed. Translated by R. A. Wilson and J. Bowden. Minneapolis: Fortress, 2015.

———. "The Election of Grace: Barth on the Doctrine of Predestination." In *Reading the Gospels with Karl Barth*, edited by Daniel L. Migliore, 1–15. Grand Rapids: Eerdmans, 2017.

———. *The Living God and the Fullness of Life.* Louisville, KY: Westminster John Knox, 2015.

———. "Predestination: Karl Barth's Doctrine of the Election of Grace." https://jasongoroncy.com/2015/06/22/jurgen-moltmann-on-predestination-karl-barths-doctrine-of-the-election-of-grace/

———. *The Trinity and the Kingdom of God.* Reprint. Minneapolis: Fortress, 1993.

———. *The Way of Jesus Christ.* Minneapolis: Fortress, 1995.

Morrison, Stephen D. *Karl Barth in Plain English.* Pickerington, OH: Beloved, 2017.

———. "Karl Barth on God's Self-humiliation and Political Preference for the Poor." *Theology Corner* (March 2018). https://www.theologycorner.net/2018-blog-conference/2018/3/4/day-3-karl-barth-on-gods-self-humiliation-and-political-preference-for-the-poor.

Moseley, Carys. *Nations and Nationalism in the Theology of Karl Barth*. Oxford: Oxford University Press, 2013.

Mozley, J. K. *The Impassibility of God: A Survey of Christian Thought*. Reissue ed. Cambridge: Cambridge University Press, 2014.

Naudé, Piet. *Pathways in Theology: Ecumenical, African and Reformed*. Edited by H. van der Westhuizen. Stellenbosch: SUN, 2015.

Neder, Adam. "History in Harmony: Karl Barth on Hypostatic Union." In *Karl Barth and American Evangelism*, edited by Bruce L. McCormack and Clifford B. Anderson, 148–76. Grand Rapids: Eerdmans, 2011.

———. *Participation in Christ: An Entry Into Karl Barth's Church Dogmatics*. Louisville, KY: Westminster John Knox, 2009.

Neal, Ryan A. *Theology as Hope: On the Ground and Implications of Jürgen Moltmann's Doctrine of Hope*. Eugene, OR: Pickwick, 2008.

Nimmo, Paul T. "The Compassion of Jesus Christ: Barth on Matthew 9:36." In *Reading the Gospels with Karl Barth*, edited by Daniel L. Migliore, 67–79. Grand Rapids: Eerdmans, 2017.

———. *Karl Barth: A Guide for the Perplexed*. London: Bloomsbury T. & T. Clark, 2017.

———. "Karl Barth and the concursus Dei—A Chalcedonianism Too Far?" *International Journal of Systematic Theology* 9 (2007) 58–72.

Nolan, Kirk J. *Reformed Virtue after Barth: Developing Moral Virtue Ethics in the Reformed Tradition*. Louisville, KY: Westminster John Knox, 2014.

Ogletree, Thomas W. *Christian Faith and History: A Critical Comparison of Ernst Troeltsch and Karl Barth*. Louisville, KY: Westminster John Knox, 2003.

Oh, Peter S. *Karl Barth's Trinitarian Theology: A Study of Karl Barth's Analogical Use of the Trinitarian Relation*. London: T. & T. Clark, 2006.

Olson, Roger E. "Was Karl Barth a Universalist? Another Look at an Old Question." *Patheos* (March 2013). http://www.patheos.com/blogs/rogereolson/2013/03/was-karl-barth-a-universalist-a-new-look-at-an-old-question.

O'Neil, Michael. "Karl Barth's Doctrine of Election." *Evangelical Quarterly* 76, no. 4 (2004) 311–26.

Palma, Robert J. *Karl Barth's Theology of Culture: The Freedom of Culture for the Praise of God*. Eugene, OR: Pickwick, 1983.

Pannenberg, Wolfhart. *Jesus—God and Man*. 2nd ed. Translated by L. L. Wilkins and D. A. Priebe. Philadelphia: Westminster, 1977.

———. *Systematic Theology*. Vol. 1. Reprint. Grand Rapids: Eerdmans, 2010.

Parry, Ken. *The Blackwell Companion to Eastern Christianity*. Oxford: Blackwell, 2010.

Peckham, John C. *The Love of God: A Canonical Model*. Downers Grove, IL: InterVarsity, 2015.

Pelikan, Jaroslav. *The Emergence of the Catholic Tradition (100–600), Vol. 1: A History of the Development of Doctrine*. Chicago: University of Chicago Press, 1975.

Peterson, Paul Silas. *The Early Karl Barth: Historical Contexts and Intellectual Formation 1905–1935*. Tübingen: Mohr Siebeck, 2018.

Pinnock, Clark H. *Most Moved Mover: A Theology of God's Openness*. Carlisle, UK: Paternoster, 2001.

Pokrifka, Todd. *Redescribing God: The Roles of Scripture, Tradition, and Reason in Karl Barth's Doctrines of Divine Unity, Constancy, and Eternity*. Eugene, OR: Pickwick, 2010.

Price, Richard, and Michael Gaddis, trans. *The Acts of the Council of Chalcedon*. Vol. 1. Liverpool: Liverpool University Press, 2007.

Price, Robert B. *Letters of the Divine Word: The Perfections of God in Karl Barth's Church Dogmatics*. London: T. & T. Clark, 2011.

Puffer, Matthew. "Dietrich Bonhoeffer in the Theology of Karl Barth." In *Karl Barth in Conversation*, edited by David W. Congdon and W. Travis McMaken, 46–61. Eugene, OR: Pickwick, 2014.

Quasten, Johannes. *Patrology, Vol. 3: The Golden Age of Greek Patristic Literature, from the Council of Nicaea to the Council of Chalcedon*. South Bend, IN: Ave Maria, 2005.

Qu, Li. *Concrete Time and Concrete Eternity: Karl Barth's Doctrine of Time and Eternity and Its Trinitarian Background*. Carlisle, UK: Langham Monographs, 2014.

Rahner, Karl. *Foundations of Christian Faith: An Introduction to the Idea of Christianity*. Translated by William V. Dych. New York: Seabury, 1978.

Reed, Austin. "[Review] Reading Barth with Charity: A Hermeneutic Proposal by George Hunsinger." *Reformed Forum* (May 2015). https://reformedforum.org/review-reading-barth-charity-hermeneutic-proposal-george-hunsinger.

Reeves, Michael. "An Evangelical Assessment of Barth." (October 2015). https://m.youtube.com/ watch?v=urMRd4QMzgo.

———. *Theologians You Should Know: An Introduction: From the Apostolic Fathers to the 21st Century*. Wheaton, IL: Crossway, 2016.

Reeves, Ryan M. "Disputes on Christ: Nestorian and Cyril." (February 2015). https://m.youtube. com/watch?v=804j5xrlJLM.

Roberts, Richard H. *A Theology on its Way? Essays on Karl Barth*. Edinburgh: T. & T. Clark, 1991.

Rumscheidt, H. Martin, ed. *The Way of Theology in Karl Barth*. Eugene, OR: Wipf & Stock, 1986.

Runia, Klaas. *Karl Barth's Doctrine of Holy Scripture*. Eugene, OR: Wipf & Stock, 2018.

Rutledge, Fleming. *The Crucifixion: Understanding the Death of Jesus Christ*. Grand Rapids: Eerdmans, 2017.

Schwöbel, Christoph. *Karl Barth—Martin Rade: Ein Briefwechsel*. Gütersloh: Guetersloher Verlagshaus, 1985.

———. "Theology." In *The Cambridge Companion to Karl Barth*, edited by John B. Webster, 17–36. Cambridge: Cambridge University Press, 2006.

Scrutton, Anastasia Philippa. *Thinking through Feeling: God, Emotion and Passibility*. New York: Continuum, 2011.

Shedd, W. G. T. *Dogmatic Theology*, Vol. II. 2nd ed. Nashville: HarperCollins, 1980.

Shippey, R. C. "The Suffering of God in Karl Barth's Doctrines of Election and Reconciliation." PhD diss., Southern Baptist Theological Seminary, 1991.

Shults, F. L. "Dubious Christological Formula: From Leontius of Byzantium to Karl Barth." *Theological Investigations* 57 (1996) 431–46.

Sirvent, Roberto. *Embracing Vulnerability: Human and Divine*. Eugene, OR: Wipf & Stock, 2014.

Smith, Mark D. J. "Testimony to Revelation: Karl Barth's Strategy of Bible Interpretation in *Die Kirchliche Dogmatik*." PhD thesis, University of Sheffield, 1997.

Smythe, Shannon Nicole. *Forensic Apocalyptic Theology: Karl Barth and the Doctrine of Justification*. Minneapolis: Fortress, 2016.

Sonderegger, Katherine. "Barth and Feminism." In *The Cambridge Companion to Karl Barth*, edited by John B. Webster, 258–73. Cambridge: Cambridge University Press, 2006.

Soulen, R. Kendall. "YHWH the Triune God." *Modern Theology* 15, no. 1 (1999) 25–54.

Stratis, Justin. *God's Being towards Fellowship: Schleiermacher, Barth and the Meaning of "God is Love."* London: T. & T. Clark, 2019.

Sumner, Darren O. *Karl Barth and the Incarnation: Christology and the Humility of God.* London: T. & T. Clark, 2014.

Swann, Christopher C. "Discipleship on the Level of Thought: The Case of Karl Barth's Critique of the Religion of Revelation." In *Revelation and Reason in Christian Theology*, 160–74. Bellingham, WA: Lexham, 2018.

Swinburne, Richard. "The Coherence of the Chalcedonian Definition of the Incarnation." In *The Metaphysics of the Incarnation*, edited by A. Marmodoro and J. Hill, 153–67. Oxford: Oxford University Press, 2011.

te Velde, Dolf. *The Doctrine of God, Examined in Reformed Orthodoxy, Karl Barth, and the Utrecht School.* Leiden: Brill, 2013.

———. *Paths Beyond Tracing Out: The Connection of Method and Content in the Doctrine of God, Examined in Reformed Orthodoxy, Karl Barth, and the Utrecht School.* Delft, Netherlands: Eburon, 2010.

Thompson, John. *Christ in Perspective: Christological Perspectives in the Theology of Karl Barth.* Norwich, UK: Hymns Ancient & Modern, 2012.

Ticciati, Susannah. *Job and the Disruption of Identity: Reading beyond Barth.* London: Bloomsbury T. & T. Clark, 2005.

Torrance, Thomas F. *The Christian Doctrine of God: One Being Three Persons.* Edinburgh: T. & T. Clark, 2001.

———. *Karl Barth: An Introduction to His Early Theology, 1910–1931.* London: SCM, 1962.

———. *Incarnation: Person and Life of Christ.* Edited by R. T. Walker. Milton Keynes, UK: Paternoster, 2015.

———. *The Trinitarian Faith: The Evangelical Theology of the Ancient Catholic Church.* Edinburgh: T. & T. Clark, 1988.

Tseng, Shao Kai. *Karl Barth's Infralapsarian Theology: Origins and Development, 1920–1953.* Downers Grove, IL: IVP Academic, 2016.

Van Kuiken, E. Jerome. *Christ's Humanity in Current and Ancient Controversy: Fallen or Not?* London: Bloomsbury T. & T. Clark, 2017.

Wai-yiu Wan, Milton. "Authentic Humanity in the Theology of Paul Tillich and Karl Barth." PhD thesis, University of Oxford, 1984.

Ward, Graham. *Barth, Derrida and the Language of Theology.* Cambridge: Cambridge University Press, 1995.

———. "Barth, Hegel, and the Possibility for Christian Apologetics." In *Conversing with Barth*, edited by John McDowell and Mike Higton, 53–67. Aldershot, UK: Ashgate, 2004.

———. "Barth, Modernity, and Postmodernity." In *Cambridge Companion to Karl Barth*, edited by John B. Webster, 274–95. Cambridge: Cambridge University Press, 2006.

Ward, Keith. *Rational Theology and the Creativity of God.* Oxford: Blackwell, 1982.

Webb, Stephen H. *Jesus Christ, Eternal God: Heavenly Flesh and the Metaphysics of Matter.* Oxford: Oxford University Press, 2012.

Webster, John B. *Barth's Earlier Theology: Scripture, Confession and Church*. London: T. & T. Clark, 2005.

———. *The Domain of the Word: Scripture and Theological Reason*. London: T. & T. Clark, 2012.

———. *Karl Barth*. 2nd ed. London: Continuum, 2004.

———. *Word and Church: Essays in Christian Dogmatics*. Edinburgh: T. & T. Clark, 2001.

Weinandy, Thomas G. "Cyril and the Mystery of the Incarnation." In *The Theology of St. Cyril of Alexandria: A Critical Appreciation*, edited by T. G. Weinandy and D. A. Keating. London: T. & T. Clark, 2003.

———. *Does God Change?* Still River, MA: St. Bede, 1985.

———. *Does God Suffer?* South Bend, IN: University of Notre Dame Press, 2000.

Wen, Clement Yung. "Maximum the Confessor and the Problem of Participation." *The Heythrop Journal* 58, no. 1 (2017) 3–16.

Williams, Stephen N. *The Election of Grace: A Riddle without a Resolution?* Grand Rapids: Eerdmans, 2015.

Winn, Christian T. Collins. *"Jesus is Victor!" The Significance of the Blumhardts for the Theology of Karl Barth*. Eugene, OR: Pickwick, 2009.

Wu, Kuo-An. *The Concept of History in the Theology of Karl Barth*. Edinburgh: University of Edinburgh Press, 2011.

Wynne, Jeremy J. *Wrath among the Perfections of God's Life*. London: T. & T. Clark, 2010.

Yewangoe, Andreas A. *Theologia Crucis in Asia: Asian Christian Views on Suffering in the Face of Overwhelming Poverty and Multifaceted Religiosity in Asia*. Amsterdam: Brill Rodopi, 1987.

Yocum, John. *Ecclesial Mediation in Karl Barth*. London: Routledge, 2004.

Yuen, Alfred H. *Barth's Theological Ontological of Holy Scripture*. Eugene, OR: Pickwick, 2014.

Zellweger, Barbara. "Karl Barth." *Biography / Center for Barth Studies* (November 2017). http://barth.ptsem.edu/karl-barth/Biography.

www.ingramcontent.com/pod-product-compliance
Lightning Source LLC
LaVergne TN
LVHW010935100826
845153LV00001B/44

* 9 7 8 1 7 2 5 2 6 4 1 6 8 *